Histories of Infamy

Histories of Infamy

Francisco López de Gómara and the Ethics of Spanish Imperialism

Cristián A. Roa-de-la-Carrera
Translated by Scott Sessions

UNIVERSITY PRESS OF COLORADO

Published by the University Press of Colorado
5589 Arapahoe Avenue, Suite 206C
Boulder, Colorado 80303

 The University Press of Colorado is a proud member of
the Association of American University Presses.

The University Press of Colorado is a cooperative publishing enterprise supported, in part, by Adams State College, Colorado State University, Fort Lewis College, Mesa State College, Metropolitan State College of Denver, University of Colorado, University of Northern Colorado, and Western State College of Colorado.

∞ The paper used in this publication meets the minimum requirements of the American National Standard for Information Sciences — Permanence of Paper for Printed Library Materials. ANSI Z39.48-1992

Library of Congress Cataloging-in-Publication Data

Roa-de-la Carrera, Cristián Andrés, 1969–
 Histories of infamy : Francisco López de Gómara and the ethics of Spanish imperialism / Cristián A. Roa de la Carrera ; translated by Scott Sessions.
   p. cm.
 Includes bibliographical references and index.
  ISBN 0-87081-813-9 (hardcover : alk. paper) 1. López de Gómara, Francisco, 1511–1564. Historia general de las Indias. 2. America — Early accounts to 1600 — History and criticism. 3. America — Discovery and exploration — Spanish — Early works to 1800 — History and criticism. 4. Indians, Treatment of — Historiography. 5. Spain — Colonies — America — Historiography. 6. Imperialism — History — 16th century — Historiography. 7. Mexico — History — Conquest, 1519–1540 — Historiography. I. Title.
  E141.G637 2005
  970.01'6 — dc22

                                                                    2005022809

Design by Daniel Pratt

14   13   12   11   10   09   08   07   06   05   10   9   8   7   6   5   4   3   2   1

To Gabriela and Andrés

⤜ Contents ⤛

Contents

⟳ Foreword ⟲

FRANCISCO LÓPEZ DE GÓMARA AND
THE LITERARY DYNAMICS OF INFAMY

Some years ago, *Life* magazine did an issue on the twenty-five most significant events in world history. Near the top of the list was the Spanish conquest of Mexico and the fall of the Aztec empire and its capital city of Tenochtitlan. The article made its case with a quote from the Spanish historian Francisco López de Gómara, who claimed that after the creation of the world by God and the coming of Jesus Christ on earth, the Spanish colonization of Mexico was the third most significant event in the history of mankind. Gómara's cosmological design of history gave enormous prestige to Spanish culture, Christianity, and imperialism, and claimed that the conquest offered a kind of redemption for the "savage" Indians of Mexico. A hidden purpose of Gómara's claim was to place his magnum opus, the *Historia general de las Indias y Conquista de México*, at the end point in a sacred literary tradition that began with the book of Genesis, peaked in the Christian Gospels, and became incarnated in the imperial policies of Spain in the New World.

As a young scholar working on the role of the mythology of Quetzal-coatl's return in the apparent abdication of Motecuhzoma to Cortés, I was thrilled to see Mexico, Tenochtitlan, and the formation of New Spain identified by *Life* as a major part of world history. My enthusiasm was driven in part by my distress about the overall neglect of Mesoamerican and especially Mexican history and religion in the education of U.S. citizens about World Religions. In the official version of Religious Studies curricula, great attention was given to Hinduism (that other "Indies"), Buddhism, Christianity, and Judaism, but American Indian religions, and especially the religious and cultural forms that developed out of the encounters between Europeans and Amerindians, were and still are downplayed. And here was a widely read U.S. magazine locating the political creation of Mexico and the New World near the center of history in the religious tones of a Spaniard.

As Cristián A. Roa-de-la-Carrera notes in his highly valuable and innovative *Histories of Infamy: Francisco Lopez de Gómara and the Ethics of Spanish Imperialism*, Gómara's book "became the most comprehensive and frequently cited treatment of the history of the American territories colonized by Spain" (p. 1). We are also surprised to learn that this popularity and influence was undermined by the fact that "Gómara was one of the most despised apologists of Spanish imperialism in the sixteenth century." This literary duality creates a conundrum for the contemporary reader of the conquest chronicles. How could a book that was so widely influential be deeply detested at the same time? Did literate Spaniards have a taste for books they found politically embarrassing? Or does this seeming contradiction point to a richer literary and rhetorical environment in which Spaniards wrote, read, and imagined their own history in the New World? Roa-de-la-Carrera explores this and many other dimensions of Gómara's prestige and infamy by illuminating the rhetorical environment in which he wrote as well as his spectacular failure in producing an "ethically persuasive argument in favor of Spanish imperialism" (p. 2). What Gómara and many of his compatriots faced in telling the story of the Spaniards in Mexico was the profound contradiction between their insatiable expansionist desires that transformed the economy and theology of Europe and parts of the Americas and the slow-moving but relentless hurricane of Spanish violence that came to haunt many reports that arrived in Spain from the Indies. As Roa-de-la-Carrera shows us, the discourse of wonder had an evil twin — the discourse of infamy — and this twinship could not, regardless of how hard some writers tried, be concealed. What the author of this fine book does is illuminate the rhetorical complexity of this twinship, a complexity that historian of religions Charles H. Long calls "the dynamics of concealment." In his classic study of American religions, Long insists on giving critical attention to the marriage of the philosophical advances of the Enlightenment with the vicious political practices of colonialism in the Americas. What has been left out of our critical relationship with the intellectual achievements of the Enlightenment are the sophisticated ways these achievements contributed to the dynamics of concealment of imperialism's infamies. What the present book reveals are the tortuous rhetorical difficulties the Spaniards faced, as well as the stylistic brilliance and ethical extremes to which Gómara went in concealing and diminishing the record-setting human costs and destruction of Spanish imperialism. Gómara developed a high-minded literary style and sophisticated historical design to show just how wonderful the "ends" of Spanish imperialism were in the face of overwhelming evidence that the imperial "means" were insults to both God and the Spanish crown. Or, in the author's words, Gómara strove to find a way to show the "good that could be attained by means such as conquest, settlement, and the subjugation of indigenous peoples" (p. 2).

In this rich and readable portrayal of the Spanish rhetorical platform, following to some extent the writings and insights of Rolena Adorno, Roa-de-la-Carrera is especially adept at revealing the intimate relationship between historical writing and imperialism. For this author, historiography is both a literary art and a prodigious form of political action with surprising social consequences. Roa examines this vital relationship between "action," "ethics," and historical writing in fresh and provocative ways. One of the thrilling dimensions of the book is the author's fascination with the powerful role that historical writing played in not only framing the cultural debate concerning the history of the Indies but also in reflecting and influencing the activities of colonization. While Gómara did not win the debates of his day, he lived and wrote in a time when these books and voices came to have a material and political power in how Spanish colonization was practiced and understood. It is not that these "historical" books were determinative of imperial practice, but the production of this knowledge not only supported maritime expansion and communication, it also played roles in the mapping of New Spain, the shaping of the character of imperialism, and the construction of the image of the exemplary Spanish male warrior and ruler.

We find a section entitled "History as Influence" showing how Gómara's *Historia* not only summarized but also socially nurtured the shared influence between the Spanish emperor and the prestige of Cortés. This is followed by a section on "Historiography and Empire Building" that illustrates the potent resource that Gómara's book became for the construction and work of the royal bureaucracy and colonial administrators. Because of Spain's voracious commitment to the conquest and settlement of New Spain, the numerous "Histories" that were written became discursive combatants among themselves and also contributed to the creation of a dynamic "discursive landscape" in which intense debates about many aspects of Spanish imperialism erupted. We read about "Sacred History" and its hidden role in defining and controlling territories — writing imbued with religious claims functioned to aid in the acquisition of new lands. Roa-de-la-Carrera shows us how Gómara in particular wrote his history to aid in the political and cultural mapping of the new acquisitions of specific lands as an aid to justify the conquest. Central to the purposes of histories is the way that Spaniards both for and against the violence of the Conquest were caught up in the collective construction of what the Spanish writers and politicians were most concerned about: not the definition and making of "power," as manly scholars today insist on, but "authority" — divine, social, and political authority. Gómara, seen through this author's eyes, is seeking to achieve an "Authority of Discourse" — namely *his* discourse, his *Historia*, in order to construct a multi-dimensional ethical rationale for what he knew was not only the creation of a New World but also the "destruction of the Indies." What this ethics of Spanish imperialism needed most of all, and what upset the other now famous writer of the Conquest, Bernal Díaz del Castillo, was a sophisticated story with an exemplary hero whose achievements were rooted in social, sacred, and even cosmological authority, prestige, and legitimacy. Gómara chose to illustrate his ethical history as a triumphal march led by the human exemplum, namely Fernando Cortés. As Roa-de-la-Carrera shows, in Gómara's vision, the conquest was achieved and resulted, in part, in a "World of Fernando Cortés." History as Hero and Heroic World.

During the last twenty years a scholarly assault has been made on the dangerous naiveté of the "conquest" metaphor, language, and mythology. The worldwide celebrations and critiques, stimulated by the 500th anniversary of 1492, resulted in an unsuccessful attempt to replace the word/trope/metaphor "conquest" with "encounter" to symbolize what historically took place in the settlement and exchanges of the New World by Europeans. Powerful interpretive works by Charles Gibson, Anthony Padgen, Stephan Greenblatt, William Taylor, Rolena Adorno, and many others have uncovered the exchanges, transculturations, shared histories, contact zones, and rhetorical prose projects that informed and were concealed in the writings of Fernando Cortés, Bartolomé de las Casas, Álvar Núñez Cabeza de Vaca, Bernal Díaz del Castillo, and others. And while Gómara has been the subject of some critiques and useful interpretations, no one has turned their interpretive method as creatively toward Gómara's literary infamy in the way that Roa-de-la-Carrera has in this book. Gómara comes to us not simply as a sophisticated villain, but as vividly situated and ethically challenged within the rhetorical battles, Christian theology, and economic ends he confronted in the immediate decades after the conquest. He had unique access to the memories and claims of Cortés and other conquerors, but he had to reshape them according to a literary/political world of anger, hyper-masculine arrogance, imperial despotism, desperate claims and counter claims about the story, the production of wealth, the definition of territory, sacred authority, and God. He was the most elegant of the writers and his intellectual production, so ingeniously analyzed by Roa's social vision and understanding, was both tantalizing and disgusting to readers.

Most interesting perhaps is the insight Roa gives us into the Spanish literati and their readers in the sixteenth century. While it might be thought they would thirst after stories glorifying Spain's superiority, in fact numerous Spaniards reacted with intense skepticism, repulsion, and doubt about Gómara-like claims. Roa gets us into this dynamic atmosphere of Spanish readers by addressing the question, "What discursive conditions made it possible for sixteenth-century readers to react critically to apologetic representations of the Spanish conquest such as Gómara's?" (p. 5). We must follow Roa-de-la-Carrera's argument about complexity here and avoid thinking of critics like Las Casas as solely on one side of this contradiction and Gómara and Díaz del Castillo on the other. For as Roa-de-la-Carrera writes, "They all considered the conversion of the native inhabitants of the Indies to Christianity a worthy endeavor, along with their submission to the authority of the crown.

It was after examining Spanish actions and their consequences that Las Casas and Benzoni expressed their condemnation" (p. 8).

What this book accomplishes is a new illumination of what Gómara was trying to achieve, what he was up against in his discursive environment, and why his ethical vision failed to reconcile the terrible contradictions of Spanish imperialism. At the center of his ethics was the notion of a necessary evil. But what necessity, we must ask, justifies this description of imperialism that Roa quotes (on p. 11) from Michel de Montaigne?

> So many towns razed, so many nations exterminated, so many millions
> of people put to the blade of the sword, and the richest and most
> beautiful part of the world turned upside down, for the transaction of
> pearls and pepper: mechanical victories.

Passages like this and Roa-de-la-Carrera's powerful and fluid analysis will lead some readers to come away realizing that there will never be a reconciliation of the discourse of wonder and the discourse of infamy. For as the last section of the book entitled "Gómara and the Destruction of the Indies" shows, the unconcealed histories teach us what the *Life* magazine list will never admit to, namely that in Mexico, the infamies still cry out at the wonders, drain them of their awe, and put redemption at bay.

— Davíd Carrasco

⇀ 𝕬cknowledgments ⇁

fter working so many years on a project whose focus and objectives have changed several times, it is difficult even to begin to recollect all the many people and institutions that have contributed to its completion. Although some undoubtedly may be overlooked, I will try my very best here to acknowledge them all.

I have greatly benefited from the help of Rolena Adorno and Anne J. Cruz—two generous senior colleagues who have supported and guided me over the last several years through the various challenges I have faced in my career. Both of them have gone out of their way to share their knowledge, experience, and wisdom with me when I needed it most. In addition, my admiration for their scholarly achievements has served as an important source of inspiration in pursuing my own research. I have found Anne's insights on gender issues and early modern Spanish culture particularly valuable. Rolena, in turn, has had a profound influence on the way I read colonial texts, but perhaps more importantly, she has taught me to develop a sense of respect for the authors I read no matter how distant they may seem from my contemporary sensibilities. Her sense and awareness of human dignity are exemplary.

Susan Schroeder and Davíd Carrasco, two extraordinary Mesoamerican scholars, have done much to make me feel at home in that area. Their respective work has taught me a great deal about the indigenous colonial experience and given me a deeper awareness of the value of indigenous cultural production in colonial times. I would also like to thank Davíd for the thoughtful foreword he has provided for this book.

In addition to Rolena, Anne, Susan, and Davíd, many other scholars have liberally shared their knowledge and advice with me over the years. Lucía Invernizzi Santa Cruz, Arcadio Díaz-Quiñones, Grínor Rojo, and Luis Vaisman not only taught me many things, but also greatly motivated me to continue my intellectual pursuits at various points in my career. Arcadio, in particular, introduced me to postcolonial theory and pushed me to engage with colonial studies from a more theoretical perspective. His comments have greatly shaped how I think about colonial writing.

Other people have offered helpful criticism concerning this project at one stage or another. I am deeply indebted to Ronald Surtz, Mary Beth Rose, Ciaran Cronin, Elizabeth Weber, and Christopher Maurer for their comments on various portions of the text. Two anonymous reviewers and the editorial board of the University Press of Colorado also provided useful observations and certainly helped make this a stronger book. Laura Furney was an excellent editor whose careful reading of the manuscript caught many errors and oversights and Daniel Pratt provided the wonderful layout and design.

Many other scholars and colleagues have influenced the progress of my research. I have found it intellectually rewarding to have encountered Raquel Chang-Rodríguez, James Muldoon, Ellen Baird, Luis Millones, Electa Arenal, José Antonio Mazzotti, Raúl Marrero Fente, José Antonio Rodríguez Garrido, Javier Villa Flores, Luis Fernando Restrepo, Lisa Voigt, Glen Carman, Monique Mustapha, María Cordero, and Hidefuji Someda in conferences, meetings, and other professional activities. In addition, my department colleagues Rosilie Hernández-Pecoraro, Ellen McClure, Klaus Müller-Bergh, and Margarita Saona at the University of Illinois at Chicago have been a constant source of encouragement.

I would also like to thank the librarians and staff of the Lilly Library, the Newberry Library, the New York Public Library, the John Carter Brown Library, Beinecke Library at Yale University, and the Firestone and Scheide Libraries at Princeton University. All of them went out of their way to be helpful and make every possible arrangement to facilitate my work. I feel extremely fortunate to have been able to consult their collections. A Lilly Library Mendel Fellowship allowed me to make considerable progress on my research. Norman Fiering, director and librarian of the John Carter Brown Library, welcomed me to his Fellows Luncheon Chats in the summer of 2002 and introduced me to a superb group of scholars. I found it stimulating to meet new colleagues, learn about their work, and receive insightful feedback on my own project.

The University of Illinois at Chicago has afforded me a vast array of opportunities and assistance to carry on my research. Funds from the Minority Grant and OVCR-AAH competition facilitated my access to a number of libraries and sources that proved essential to the completion of the task at hand. Most significant among my debts to the university was my year as a fellow at the Institute for the Humanities, where I was able to interact with colleagues from various disciplines who made this project more meaningful and enjoyable. I found it particularly enriching to work with Mary Beth Rose, Linda Vavra, Ciaran Cronin, John D'Emilio, Mindie Lazarus-Black, Susan Levine, Katrin Schultheiss, Daniel Scott Smith, and Daniel Sutherland.

I am most profoundly indebted to Scott Sessions for his invaluable contributions to the successful completion of this project. He has not only been a wonderful translator and editor, but also an intellectual companion who has pushed me to the best of my limits. I cannot count the hours we have spent not only on this project, but also discussing the field of colonial studies. He has been extremely generous in making readily available his knowledge and extraordinary writing skills throughout the process of bringing this work to fruition. This book would not be what it is without our continued dialogue.

Finally, I owe more than I can rightly express to the support of Gabriela, whose love and patience allowed me to weather all the trials and travails of this project. To her and our son Andrés I dedicate this book.

—SEPTEMBER 2005
CHICAGO, ILLINOIS

Histories
of Infamy

⮜ Introduction ⮞

Quae flagitia, ne amplius perpetrentur, cunctis rationibus iusto ac religioso principi providendum est, ut saepe dico, ne aliena scelera ipsi propter negligentiam in hoc saeculo infamiam, in altero pariant damnationem aeternam.

As I often say, a just and religious prince must by all means see to it that no greater outrages are perpetrated so that through negligence the crimes of other people do not bring him infamy in this life and eternal damnation in the next.[1]

—Juan Ginés de Sepúlveda, *Democrates secundus*

he Spanish historian Francisco López de Gómara (1511–ca. 1559) enjoys a prominent place as one of the most despised apologists of Spanish imperialism in the sixteenth century. His *Historia general de las Indias y Conquista de México* (General history of the Indies and Conquest of Mexico), first published at Zaragoza in 1552, told the story of the principal discoveries and conquests that Spaniards had carried out until that date.[2] Based on a wealth of written sources and testimonies of conquistadors, it soon became the most comprehensive and frequently cited treatment of the history and geography of the American territories colonized by Spain. The most notable feature of the *Historia general* today is arguably Gómara's attempt to provide a philosophically grounded solution to the ethical and intellectual dilemmas besetting Spanish colonialism in the New World. He put forth an emphatic defense of the conquest that presented Fernando[3] Cortés (1485–1547) as an exemplary model of military prowess, political leadership, and religious devotion. Gómara sought to persuade

European readers that the conquest was beneficial to the Indians and he proposed a political ideal of common good for both colonizers and colonized. He believed that the conquest was one of the greatest accomplishments in world history and commended its role in enabling the spread of the Christian gospel.

Taking up such a project was not as simple or straightforward as it might seem from a perspective familiar with the ideologies of post-Enlightenment colonialism. The writing of history within the humanist tradition provided well-established precedents for the political use of history, but the moral issues raised by the conquest of the New World made it difficult to provide a satisfactory account for the sensibilities of many of Gómara's contemporary readers. There was a well-known record of abuses that violated both the legal and moral standards of even those who considered colonization a legitimate enterprise. The issue for Gómara as a historian was not so much a forensic one regarding what the Spaniards had exactly done, or who was to blame for it, but rather a deliberative one about establishing the desirability of these pursuits. This involved assessing the good that could be attained by means such as conquest, settlement, and the subjugation of indigenous peoples. The question for Gómara, then, was how to present this history in a way that would allow him to tell his readers that, in spite of its devastation, the conquest of the New World was a worthwhile endeavor. In his attempt to produce an ethically persuasive argument in favor of Spanish imperialism, however, he failed. The purpose of my book is to examine the main issues that this failure raises in terms of the analysis of Spanish colonial writing. But before turning to the basic argument and organization of my text, I would like to discuss some rhetorical challenges confronting Gómara and his contemporaries.

Gómara was very well positioned socially and institutionally within Spain to take on such a propagandistic endeavor. As Cortés's chaplain, he was well acquainted with renowned humanist intellectuals, high-ranking royal officials, and members of the Spanish court. While he was in Cortés's service between 1540 and 1546, he had the opportunity to interview many conquistadors, peruse the maps and records of the House of Trade (Casa de Contratación), and access some of the accounts kept at the Council of the Indies.[4] In addition to his privileged connections, he brought his solid humanist learning and eloquence to the task of writing an account of Spanish imperial expansion in the New World.[5] The broad intellectual scope and concise elegant style of his

Historia general have made it a hallmark within the culture of Spanish imperialism.[6]

Paradoxically, as the *Historia general* became known throughout the Spanish possessions and Europe, it acquired notoriety for its unyielding portrayal of imperialism. Contemporary historians such as Gonzalo Fernández de Oviedo y Valdés (1478–1557) and Bartolomé de las Casas (ca. 1484–1566) heavily criticized it because Gómara elevated Cortés to the stature of a great leader and hero. Others who drew extensively upon his work in their own narratives often denounced Gómara. Bernal Díaz del Castillo (ca. 1495–1584) and Inca Garcilaso de la Vega (1539–1616) left compelling testimonies of the conquistadors' discontent about Gómara's disregard for the honor and merits of some individuals who served in Mexico and Peru. Pedro de la Gasca wrote to Charles V's counselor Willem van Male that although Gómara was a truthful man, he was misinformed about some events that had transpired during his tenure in office as viceroy of Peru.[7] When the grandson of Pedrarias Dávila (the infamous conquistador of Tierra Firme, Panama, and Nicaragua) brought suit against the royal chronicler Antonio de Herrera y Tordesillas (1559–1625) for soiling his grandfather's honor, he accused Herrera of following Gómara's narrative.[8] Even the Council of the Indies, which was in charge of colonial administration, banned the *Historia general* in Castile a year after its publication.[9]

The more people read, quoted, and paraphrased his work, the more Gómara fell into disrepute. In his famous essays "Des Cannibales" (On cannibals) and "Des Coches" (On coaches), the French moral philosopher Michel de Montaigne (1533–1592) questioned the popularized representations of Indian barbarism and criticized the conquest of the New World. There is evidence to suggest that his understanding of the Spanish conquests was based on the *Historia general* — Montaigne merely had a different take on the events.[10] Girolamo Benzoni (1519–ca. 1570) borrowed copiously from Gómara's account to condemn Spanish activities in the Americas in his *Historia del Mondo Nuovo* (History of the New World). The French translator of the 1588 Paris edition of the *Voyages et conquestes du capitaine Ferdinand Courtois* (Voyages and conquests of Captain Fernando Cortés), a translation of the *Conquista de México*, the second part of Gómara's *Historia general*, attempted to defend the author from the criticism he received for basing his account on oral sources, praising Spaniards, and attacking Indians. His basic reply to each of these points was that Gómara could not be blamed for doing what every other historian did. His discussion regarding Gómara's defamation of the Indians is most revealing:

> *Plus, il charge, dit-on, bien souue[n]t sur ces pauures Indie[n]s, en faisant accroire des choses d'eux, où ils ne penserent iamais, & ceux qui dient que Gomare afferme les Indiens estre descenduz de Cam, à l'occasion, comme ie pense, d'vn passage de son Histoire generale, ne font ils rie[n] accroire de luy? (1588, [5]r–v).*

> Moreover, he often attacks, it is said, these poor Indians, making up things about them that they would not dream of, and those who say that Gómara states that the Indians have descended from Ham, based, I believe, on a passage from his *Historia general*, are they not making something up about him?

The translator went on to transcribe and correct the translation of a passage in the *Historia general* where Gómara had stated that God may have permitted the hardship and servitude of the Indians in order to punish them for their sins. This reading clarified that Gómara had not said that *they* were descended from Ham, but rather that *Ham* had committed a lesser sin against Noah and *his* descendants had been condemned to slavery. This little vignette of French critics misrepresenting Gómara misrepresenting Indians clearly reveals how strongly negative the reaction was against him. As the translator's comments indicate, the historian's apologia for the conquest and his defamation of the Indians could not surmount the prevailing climate of hostility and mistrust in Europe toward Spanish imperialism.

Although it was one of the most widely read and translated histories of the New World in the sixteenth century, the previous examples reveal that the *Historia general* failed to convince many of its readers about the benefits of Spanish colonialism. The ethical and political problems created by Spain's imperial enterprise helped shape colonial writing in ways that merit further exploration. The impact of colonization on indigenous communities resulted in violent social changes, caused uncertainty about colonial administration in Spain, and gave rise to international condemnation. Recent critics of Spanish American colonial discourse, such as Peter Hulme (1986, 1994), José Rabasa (1993, 2000), Stephen Greenblatt (1991), and Walter Mignolo (1995), have shown how Spanish chroniclers supported European expansion by producing territorial representations that enabled the subjugation of native peoples. These analyses underscore the means whereby representations — like capital — could be reproduced and accumulated in order to create structures of social power (see Certeau 1986). But how effective were these mechanisms? What conditions did they require to be socially productive and are there plausible readings that reveal the limits of their efficacy?

Homi Bhabha (1994) convincingly argues that the contradictions and general ambivalence of colonial discourse ought to be considered its key enabling feature, as it allows for an efficient way of articulating the anxieties and desires underlying the colonizing project. Although the case of Gómara's *Historia general* in many ways confirms Bhabha's assertions, it also calls attention to the critical debate on the political liabilities of imperialism and the colonizing process that early modern Spanish colonial writing carried out within the nation-state. In other words, what discursive conditions made it possible for sixteenth-century readers to react critically to apologetic representations of the Spanish conquest such as Gómara's?

Unable simply to rely on hegemonic discourses, Spanish chroniclers attempted to figure a way out of the ethical impasses posed by the violence and destruction that went hand in hand with colonial expansion. Many of them lent their support to the imperial enterprise by deploying complex rhetorical devices that reinforced transatlantic power structures. They certainly conveyed expansionist desires in the ways they expressed wonder about the newness of the Indies, concealed the violence underlying the project, and reiterated key tropes embodying their colonizing moves. This raises the question of how these texts engaged their reading public and operated socially in the context of the cultural debate on colonization. Assessments of Spanish imperialism in the New World — whether written by Gómara, Las Casas, Benzoni, or others — reveal that the ideological premises of the discourse alone cannot account for their dispositions toward the enterprise.

Gómara provides a good example of the arguments promoting the colonial enterprise at the end of the first part of his *Historia general*:

> *Nu[n]ca jamas rey ny gente anduuo, y sujeto, tanto en tan breue tiempo, como la nuestra. Ny [h]a hecho ny merecido, lo que ella, assi en armas, y nauegacion, como en la predicacion del santo Euangelio, y conuersacion de idolatras. Por lo qual son Españoles dignissimos de alabança en todas las partes del mu[n]do"* (1552, 1:121v).

Never did a king and people go out and subject so much in such a short time as ours, and done and merited what ours have in arms and navigation as well as in preaching the holy gospel and the conversion of idolaters, for which Spaniards are the most worthy of praise in all parts of the world.

His claims about the greatness of Spanish achievements in the New World stress their unprecedented quality as a unique development in universal history. Temporal brevity and territorial expanse combine to convey a sense of wonder that makes Spain's imperial experience worthy of Gómara's praise. Later in the passage he acknowledges that laboring in the mines, fishing for pearls, and bearing heavy loads had killed many Indians, but he dismissed these evils by arguing that God had punished those responsible. Instead of inducing a thoughtless reader to admire the conquest, he was proposing a way of arriving at an ethical decision about its overall result.

Gómara's exaltation of the conquest had to contend with the moral resistance already awakened in public discourse. Although his assessment that the conquest had been something out of the ordinary would essentially remain undisputed, there were many who expressed their dismay at the acts that Spaniards committed in the New World. In the same year that Gómara first published his *Historia general*, Las Casas's *Brevísima relación de la destrucción de las Indias* (Brief account of the destruction of the Indies) was printed in Seville. The introductory section titled "Argumento del presente epítome" (Argument of the present summary) included a poignant overview of the crimes being perpetrated in the Indies:

> *Todas las cosas que han acaecido en Las Indias, desde su maravilloso descubrimiento, y del principio que a ellas fueron los españoles . . . han sido tan admirables y tan no creíbles en todo género a quien no las vido, que parece haber añublado y puesto silencio y bastantes a poner olvido a todas cuantas, por hazañosas que fuesen, en los siglos pasados se vieron y oyeron en el mundo.*
>
> *Entre éstas son las matanzas y estragos de gentes inocentes y despoblaciones de pueblos, provincias y reinos, que en ellas se han perpetrado, y que todas las otras no de menor espanto (1988–1998, 10:31).*

All the things that have happened in the Indies, since their marvelous discovery and from the beginning when the Spaniards went there . . . have been so admirable and so incredible in every way to one who has not seen them, that it seems to have obscured, silenced, and sufficiently made us forget all the many things, heroic as they were, seen and heard in past centuries.

Among these are the massacre and ruin of innocent peoples and the depopulation of provinces and kingdoms that have occurred there and are no less appalling than all the others.

This inversion of the discourse of wonder violently jolts readers out of their complacency to inform them of the slaughter and depopulation of Indians caused by the Spaniards. For Las Casas, the gravity of these evils vividly overshadowed any other deed in the context of human history and his inflammatory remarks were meant to stir the conscience of the king into taking action and stopping these atrocities. As Juan Ginés de Sepúlveda (1490–1573) had warned in his *Democrates secundus*: "As I often say, a just and religious prince must by all means see to it that no greater outrages are perpetrated so that through negligence the crimes of other people do not bring him infamy in this life and eternal damnation in the next" (1997, 133).

Imperialist stances were also challenged outside Spain as readers were able to develop critical perspectives concerning the impact of colonialism and question its essential claims. Although Girolamo Benzoni relied heavily on Gómara's *Historia general* for his *Historia del Nuovo Mondo*, he was quite capable of arriving at a completely opposite conclusion:

> *Essendo io andato per questo nuovo mondo per ispatio di anni quattordici, come disopra è detto, & hauendo letto le Historie che gli Spagnuoli hanno scritto delle imprese da loro fatte in questi paesi, trouo che in alcune cose si sono laudati vn poco più di quello che conuiene, & specialmente, che dicono, che sono degni di gran laude, perche hanno conuertiti, & fatti Cristiani, tutti gli popoli, & nationi, da loro conquistati, & soggiogati nell'India . . . come si direbbe per forma, chi dicesse, che'l fornaio ha cotto bene il pane. . . . Quanto più che nel Regno del Perù, & altri luoghi quantunque vi habbino publicato, che sono Cristiani figliuoli di Dio del cielo; per le dispietate crudelta, che hanno vsato fra di loro, mai non vi e stato ordine, che habbino voluto confessare tal nome (1969, 110r–v).*

After having been in this New World for a space of fourteen years, as previously mentioned, and having read the histories that Spaniards have written about the enterprise they conducted in these countries, I think in some things they have praised themselves a little more than what is appropriate, and especially when they say they are worthy of great praise for having converted and made Christians of all the peoples and nations they have conquered and subjugated in the Indies . . . as if one would say a baker has baked bread well. . . . Inasmuch as in the kingdom of Peru and in other places, although they have said they are Christians, children of the God of heaven, because of the impious cruelty they have inflicted among them, there is no way they would have wanted to confess such a name.

Benzoni observed that the religious goals of colonization were not being accomplished and the Spaniards' behavior was not conducive toward conversion. He was not criticizing the conquest on legal grounds as Las Casas did, nor did he share the Dominican friar's high regard for the Indians. Benzoni spoke of them as barbarians and uncivilized people, but it was his contempt for Spanish imperialism that led him to question Gómara's assumptions about the merits of its methods and results.

Gómara, Las Casas, and Benzoni each had his own different agenda, but none of them could avoid taking a stand on the injustices of colonialism. As there was no public consensus on the Spanish conquest, they could not expect their readers simply to submit to their rhetoric without pondering the weight of their arguments. In order to convince them, they had to engage in an ethical as well as ideological debate about the events they narrated. An ethical stance vis-à-vis the conquest would define what ends were worth pursuing and what means were adequate to achieve them, thus eliciting the kind of public criticism that we observe among Gómara's readers. The ideological affirmation of imperialism either through commonly accepted beliefs or through the discursive practices underwriting European expansion was not enough to legitimate Spanish action. Gómara, Las Casas, and Benzoni were all Roman Catholics (Gómara and Las Casas were even members of the clergy), and none of them questioned Spanish imperialism in principle. They all considered the conversion of the native inhabitants of the Indies to Christianity a worthy endeavor, along with their submission to the authority of the crown. It was after examining Spanish actions and their consequences that Las Casas and Benzoni expressed their condemnation.

The debate about colonization did not question fundamental beliefs about religion, nature, government, or society: the Europeans' assumption about the superiority of their religion and civilization remained unshaken. The issue concerned the proper way of going about colonization. The unprecedented nature of the conquest, which Gómara and Las Casas emphasized, suggests how intellectually unprepared Spain was to deal with the moral challenges of colonialism. The main problem was that the empire developed suddenly, spanned extensive regions, affected millions of people, and initiated profound changes. By the end of the first half of the sixteenth century, the enterprise had already undergone several stages of transformation. The ongoing ideological debate about colonization can be understood within the reconfiguration of social forces taking place in the process of expansion, but it is very difficult to identify clear-cut ideological divides in this period.

In this regard, Montaigne's skeptical reading of Gómara's *Historia general* is particularly enlightening. In "Des Cannibales" he warned his readers against "s'attacher aux opinions vulgaires" [becoming attached to popular opinions] and proposed that they judge things "par la voie de la raison" [according to the way of reason] (1998, 1:339). He argued that knowledge was altered by interpretation, but truth rested in the normal course of nature without art or human invention. Things such as letters, numbers, political power, servitude, wealth and poverty, and contracts had artificially led humankind astray from the natural order. On the other hand, he regarded cannibals as beings who had not been shaped by the human spirit and still lived in a state of nature. He thus concluded that European representations of Indian barbarism embodied prejudices toward cultural difference rather than an appreciation for the virtues of the soul. He was troubled by the course his world was taking so he used the case of cannibals to illustrate that his society's way of life was unnatural and corrupt.

Stephen Greenblatt (1991, 146–151) has argued that Montaigne was a "knight of non-possession" and that his "discourse on the New World turns not toward fantasies of ownership and rule but toward shame." Montaigne's ideological analysis of cannibals, however, did not assert Indian freedom or equality; it merely criticized European society for faults such as "la trahison, la déloyauté, la tyrannie, la cruauté" [treachery, disloyalty, tyranny, and cruelty] (1998, 1:351). He worried that the Indians' transactions with Europeans would bring about their ruin because they were learning negative values from their example (1998, 1:357, 3:197). Moreover, Montaigne took an overtly imperialist stance in "Des Coches," where he discussed the conquests of Mexico and Peru.

Regarding the Indians, he said their world was "si nouveau et si enfant qu'on lui apprend encore son *a, b, c*: il n'y a pas cinquante ans qu'il ne savait ni lettres, ni poids, ni mesure, ni vêtements, ni blés, ni vignes" [so new and so infantile that it is still learning its ABCs: no more than fifty years ago it did not know letters, weights, measures, clothing, wheat, or vines] (1998, 3:197). Montaigne's paternalistic appreciation of native peoples was based on the very same observations that Gómara had made about the things they lacked as societies, and reiterated a similar understanding of the improvements that colonization could bring to their lives.[11] As Tom Conley (1989, 251) has observed, in "Des Coches" Montaigne's discourse "continues to argue obliquely against colonial development and insists that European nations would do well to curtail deficit spending, arrest plunder of the New World, and regain a balanced economy that distributes wealth more evenly among its subjects." Montaigne presents us with an ethics of international exchange and redistribution of wealth, but this is not tantamount to a rejection of imperialist policies. His criticism of European society is actually addressing the changes needed in order to expand into other worlds.

Montaigne's criticism in "Des Coches" of the conquests of Mexico and Peru actually concerned the way in which they had been attained. Commenting on the advantages of the Spaniards over the Indians, he stated that "quant à la dévotion, observance des lois, bonté, libéralité, loyauté, franchise, il nous a bien servi de n'en avoir pas tant qu'eux" [as for devotion, observance of laws, kindness, liberality, loyalty, and frankness, it has served us well not to have as much of these qualities as they do] (1998, 3:198). He regretted that Spaniards had achieved their victories based on factors such as trickery and deceit, their unexpected arrival, and military technology, and asserted that if these disparities were removed, then there would have been no basis for all their victories. He did not question conquest or empire per se, instead he wished that the enterprise had fallen into hands that would have carried it out with higher virtue:

> *Que n'est tombée sous Alexandre, ou sous ces anciens Grecs et Romains,*
> *une si noble conquête, et une si grande mutation et altération de tant*
> *d'empires et de peuples, sous des mains qui eussent doucement poli et*
> *défriché ce qu'il y avait de sauvage, et eussent conforté et promu les bonnes*
> *semences que nature y avait produit: mêlant non seulement à la culture des*
> *terres et ornement des villes les arts de deçà, en tant qu'elles y eussent été*

nécessaires, mais aussi mêlant les vertus Grecques et Romaines aux
originelles du pays (1998, 3:199–200).

Why did such a noble conquest not fall upon Alexander, or upon
these ancient Greeks and Romans, and such a great mutation and
alteration of so many empires and peoples upon hands that would
have gently polished and cleared away what was savage, and
reinforced and promoted the good seeds that nature had produced
there: not only combining the arts here with the culture of the lands
and the adornment of towns, as had been necessary there, but also
combining Greek and Roman virtues with the original ones of the
country?

Montaigne understood that conquest was an endeavor worth pursuing
when it led to the betterment of the subject people. His emphasis on
virtue sets forth an ethical standard for the development of imperialism, instead of questioning the need for its existence. He argued that
the conquest had gone wrong because it gave priority to economic value
over the well-being of native communities:

Au rebours, nous nous sommes servis de leur ignorance et inexpérience à les
plier plus facilement vers la trahison, luxure, avarice, et vers toute sorte
d'inhumanité et de cruauté, à l'exemple et patron de nos mœurs. Qui mit
jamais à tel prix le service de la mercadence et de la trafique? Tant de villes
rasées, tant de nations exterminées, tant de millions de peuples passés au fil
de l'épée, et la plus riche et belle partie du monde bouleversée, pour la
négociation des perles et du poivre: mécaniques victoires (1998, 3:200).

On the contrary, we take advantage of their ignorance and
inexperience to incline them more easily toward treachery, lust,
avarice, and every sort of inhumanity and cruelty, after the example
and pattern of our ways. Who ever put such a price on the service of
commerce and trade? So many towns razed, so many nations
exterminated, so many millions of people put to the blade of the
sword, and the richest and most beautiful part of the world turned
upside down, for the transaction of pearls and pepper: mechanical
victories.

Montaigne's reading of Gómara offers us a lesson on the ethics of
imperialism. There is a limit to the actions that a civilizing mission can
justify, which is determined by the values that a society claims to uphold. The primacy of economic value cannot sustain the effort because

it defies the very principle upon which the subordination of one community to another is undertaken, that is, to attain a higher end. According to Montaigne, the New World should have been subjugated through virtuous qualities so that the ends and means would be consistent:

> *Nous tenons d'eux-mêmes ces narrations, car ils ne les avouent pas seulement, ils s'en vantent, et les prêchent. Serait-ce pour témoignage de leur justice, ou zèle envers la religion? Certes ce sont voies trop diverses, et ennemies d'une si sainte fin. S'ils se fussent proposé d'étendre notre foi, ils eussent considéré que ce n'est pas en possession de terres qu'elle s'amplifie, mais en possession d'hommes, et se fussent trop contentés des meurtres que la nécessité de la guerre apporte, sans y mêler indifféremment une boucherie. . . . Si que plusieurs de chefs ont été punis à mort, sur les lieux de leur conquête, par ordonnance des Rois de Castille, justement offensés de l'horreur de leurs déportements, et quasi tous désestimés et mal-voulus (1998, 3:204).*

> We have these accounts from their own selves, for they not only acknowledge them, they brag and preach about them. Is this a testament of their justice or zeal toward religion? Surely these ways are too different and contrary to such a holy end. If they intended to extend our faith, they would have considered that it is not enlarged from the possession of land, but from the possession of men, and they would have been overly content with the deaths brought on by the necessities of war, without indifferently adding carnage. . . . Thus many leaders have been punished with death, in the places of their conquest, by order of the monarchs of Castile, justly offended by the horror of their behavior, and almost all of them were disesteemed and disliked.

Montaigne rejected the conquest, for he did not find its methods defensible. Quite another thing was his view of the monarchs of Castile whom he portrayed as righteously concerned about justice. He understood that the excesses of the Spaniards were detrimental to the goal of evangelization and therefore he chose to condemn them. For Montaigne, interpreting the conquest was chiefly an ethical task, but his criticism did not compromise his sympathy toward the imperialist project of transforming the New World by means of European trade, civility, arts, and culture. He gave primacy to the end of "improving" the lives of indigenous peoples, for in its attainment he based the very principle of empire.

Montaigne's idealization of imperialism devised the rhetoric that would fashion more powerful and efficient discourses of colonization. When Gómara examined the ethics of the conquest, he gave thorough consideration to the injustices committed by the Spaniards.[12] His decision to support the conquest in spite of its drawbacks was a more direct way of confronting the problems posed by colonialism. His main difference with the French philosopher was that neither purity of soul nor consistency between ends and means concerned him. Montaigne's notion of imperialism was probably closer to the one formulated by Las Casas, whose projects of peaceful colonization relied on virtuous men developing bonds of friendship in order to attract the native inhabitants to the service of the monarchs. Gómara had rejected Las Casas's propositions as a naïve formulation that, although desirable, was unattainable. The ethical debate on means focused on the questions of how conquest should be carried out as a method of colonization (as in Montaigne's reading of Gómara) and whether the conquest was acceptable for making the Indians subjects of the Spanish crown (as in Las Casas's criticism in his *Brevísima relación*). The relative weight of the empire's political, economic, and religious goals was also at stake in these varied reactions to the accounts of colonization, but all three continued to be regarded as desirable forms of hegemony. The ideological divide between Gómara's pragmatism and Montaigne's emphasis on purity of soul reveals that the criticism of Spanish expansion led to the development of new principles of dominance that would come to life in the second wave of European imperialism.

This book seeks to explore why Gómara's *Historia general* failed to reconcile the contradictions of Spanish imperialism. Evaluating the efficacy of ideologies of colonization, it examines the main impediments he encountered in producing an ethically persuasive argument. I have organized four chapters thematically to focus on how he confronted the main problems he faced, namely, (1) his use of the historical genre for the creation of a hegemonic discourse; (2) his reinterpretation of Christian tradition to explain New World geography, ethnicity, and dominion; (3) his treatment of processes of discovery and conquest to construct a coherent narrative of colonization and articulate a colonizing mission; and (4) his deployment of political theory to present the injustices of the conquest as a necessary evil and to envision the creation of a colonial political community founded on the patriarchal authority of the conquistador.

On the uses of history, the first chapter analyzes how the changes in colonial policy during the 1540s imposed serious limitations on Spanish historians to promote apologetic views of the conquest. It examines how Gómara endeavored to use his *Historia general* to further the interests of his patron Cortés as well as the cause of the conquistadors in general. Gómara regarded histories of the Indies as a genre that would allow him to provide a comprehensive account of Spanish colonization for national and international audiences. The censorship of Oviedo and Sepúlveda for their negative statements concerning the capacity of the Indians made Gómara aware of the obstacles he faced within the intellectual and political climate of the time. Institutionalization in preceding decades had conferred an aura of authority on the genre, but at the same time it had created the condition of its own impediment as concern for the treatment of the Indians and the disputes about the legitimacy of the Spanish conquest intensified. With its moral and political obligations as a colonial power in question, Spain moved to strengthen the legal grounds of its claims to empire and limited the conquistadors' authority over the native population.

Hoping that his *Historia* would attain official recognition, Gómara sought to circumvent the prevailing contradictions in the field and create a form of hegemonic discourse. He proposed a formula of compromise that could give representation to the conflicting interests involved in imperial expansion. Gómara relied on Cortés's personal relations at the court as a powerful network to gain intellectual authority and effectively influence public opinion on colonial policy. He saw in Cortés a figure capable of conveying a notion of common good in colonial relations, but his efforts to put forth an imperialist agenda failed to persuade his readers. Gómara's history was censored, and although there is no documentation available to clarify the grounds of the prohibition, we know that the censorship practices of the time mainly addressed textual disagreements with legal and theological principles or served an arbitral role between conflicting parties. Gómara's account soiled the honor of some conquerors, and thus conflicted with the interests of many individuals who aspired to public recognition of their identities. Moreover, his formulation presenting Cortés as the embodiment of virtue and achievement failed to articulate an imperial mission because it could not reconcile the interests of the conquistadors as a collectivity with the crown's concern for legitimacy. The negative reception and prohibition of the *Historia general* suggest that his argument came at the end of an era, when it was no longer possible to reach a social consensus on conquest and colonization.

The story of Gómara's failure makes it necessary to more closely examine the ideological foundations grounding his historiographical project. Many scholars have called attention to the critical importance of territorial representations and "proto-ethnographic" discourse to account for the efficacy of Spanish colonial discourse. Chapter 2 examines Gómara's use of Christian conceptions of universal history, world geography, and cultural diversity as a justification for colonization. Departing from Nicene interpretations of the Roman Empire as divinely ordained to facilitate the spread of Christianity, he could articulate the meaning of the discovery of the Indies within the providentialist view of history centered on the redemption of humankind. Gómara was able to assert Spain's sovereignty in the New World by reinterpreting Christian theories about the unity of the earth, the common descent of mankind from Adam and Eve, and Noah's resettlement of the world after the Flood. He draws a parallel between Noah's alleged exploration of the Mediterranean—naming and partitioning among his sons the three continents known to the ancients—and Spanish explorations unveiling the existence of the Indies. Spanish legal discourse on dominion in the works of Juan López de Palacios Rubios and Francisco de Vitoria was based on Noah's donation of territory and the consent of his descendents in the occupation of the continents. Relying on the notion of Noah's universal dominion, Gómara was able to narrate the pope's partition of the world between the Spaniards and the Portuguese as a legitimate act of donation. Recurrently weaving these notions into his narrative of exploration and conquest, he used sacred history to formulate a historical and geographical discourse in support of Spanish territorial claims.

Putting forth an interpretation of the nature of the Indians and their place in world history was also essential for justifying imperial expansion. Gómara explained human diversity by the existence of branches of human descent, which, having a common lineage, also shared basic traits in morals, civility, and religion. Assuming a monogenetic stance on the origin of the Indians allowed Gómara to articulate a narrative of imperial policy toward them. Based on a stern condemnation of their ways of life, Gómara's geocentric, providentialist discourse provided an explanation for the subordination of native communities to the Spaniards within the divine plan of human redemption. Beginning his work with a reflection on man's desire to learn the secrets of the world because of its diversity, Gómara links the foundations of Spanish expansion in Christian tradition to a passage in the second book of Esdras that relates knowledge and the exercise of dominion over the world. Their common thread was that the diversification of human lineages brought about impiety among men, but Ezra stated that Israel would inherit the world as the chosen people. In this light, Gómara's analysis of indigenous capacity in terms of civility and moral disposition presents them as a lineage gone astray from the path of salvation. His Eurocentric understanding of cartography and human history tied the debate to the theological foundations of Spanish dominion in the New World, the very same grounds on which Spanish legal theorists had contested the conquest and colonial institutions such as the *encomienda*. Using this Christian framework, Gómara sought to resolve the contradictions haunting the imperial project on the issues of dominion and the nature of the Indians.

Gómara also sought to provide a way of articulating the goals of Spanish expansion within a well-defined imperial mission, but to do so he needed to construct an account that reconciled the incompatibilities among the various objectives organizing Spain's activities in the New World. Focusing on the empire and its narratives, Chapter 3 studies Gómara's attempt to overcome the lack of social consensus and conflicting interests of the diverse sectors involved in colonization. A critical issue was to deal with the historiographical record about the discovery of the Indies, which made it difficult to give a sense of coherence to Spain's imperial history. He adjusted his own narrative to articulate a story of the empire's beginnings that would account for the colonization project. Gómara tried to show how the discovery had allowed the Catholic Monarchs to set forth a principle of colonial difference defining Spain's mission in the Indies. He interpreted colonization as a mechanism for material and cultural exchange, reiterating this logic throughout his account of exploration and conquest in other regions. He employed this narrative of exchange to show how the various goals of the colonial enterprise could transform the New World and consistently lead to the common good of Spaniards and Indians.

Exchange served as a powerful instrument to encompass and conceptualize the processes of discovery, conquest, evangelization, and economic exploitation of the Indies. Gómara's reliance on colonial difference to account for the dynamic of intercultural relations between Spaniards and Indians, however, would ultimately expose the moral and political shortcomings of colonization. Gómara's account suggests that the subordination of Indians in imperial encounters resulted from a clash between their knowledge systems and those of their invaders. He relied on the protocols of warfare established in the royal instructions to explain how conquistadors interacted with Indians in these situations, but the legal changes that the crown implemented in the procedures of war carried negative implications for previous conquests. The main problem was that Spaniards had used a document called the Requirement as a legal instrument legitimating the use of force. Gómara, in turn, reframed the protocol as the preaching of a sermon, thus he avoided explaining how the major conquests could have been conducted shortly before on the basis of an already obsolete legal procedure. Using the topos of the *savage critic,* he availed himself of indigenous voices to criticize the Spaniards, but only to place the blame for colonial violence on their resistance or misguided collaboration. The Indians fail to develop adequate responses to the Spaniards in Gómara's account, mainly because they lack the moral resources to generate effective modes of resistance against their conquerors. Gómara implied that the disparity between Indians and Spaniards was ultimately to blame for the evils of the conquest. At the same time, however, this difference helped him explain the kind of benefits colonization could bring for both Spain and the Indies.

The fourth and final chapter discusses the ethical foundations of imperialism. Conquest raised the issues of justice and morality within the state because the plunder that soldiers carried out in other nations was objectionable in principle to Christians. The early church fathers such as Augustine and Lactantius made this clear when criticizing the Skeptics' argument that justice and wisdom were not compatible. This is the underlying philosophical issue that Spanish colonial discourse confronted when determining whether the Spanish monarchs could justly colonize the Indies. In fact, the basic legal principle guiding war and governance in the Indies was based on the premise that the monarch and his subjects engaged in colonization must endeavor to extend the faith in those regions and not dominate them or enrich themselves. The historiographical record on colonization, however, revealed that the Spaniards had in fact been motivated by greed and committed grave injustices against the native populations of the Indies. Gómara took on the task of showing that the conquistador's pursuit of self-interest was compatible with a notion of common good in colonial relations, arguing that peaceful approaches to evangelization were doomed to fail. He presents the insatiable desire for riches and the lust of the conquistador as the main condition determining how the colonization process unfolded in the New World. He highlights the conquest of Mexico, however, as an exception and a model of how the conquistador could channel his greed and masculinity in accordance with Christian principles of empire. Articulating the Spanish conception of honor, he puts forth a patriarchal notion of colonial order where the economic, military, and sexual activities of the conquistador served to maintain the stability of the social system.

Gómara addresses the negative aspects of colonization in order to propose the necessary changes for a just society in the New World. Focusing mainly on the rebellions of Peru, he critically examines the consequences in the Indies of the reforms promoted by Las Casas. Gómara's willingness to accept the evils of colonialism results from his optimism about the social reforms carried out by the crown in the mid-sixteenth century. Applying the concepts of *conditional action* and *self-sufficiency* from Aristotle's *Politics*, Gómara was able to construct the idea of a colonial political community where Spanish imperialism brought improvements to Indian life by reorganizing the structures of tribute and labor in their communities. He understood that this could be achieved through a shift from acquisition to exchange, where the surplus value of the colonial economy would provide for Spanish households. In turn, through property and enterprise, the new structures of taxation would help liberate the Indians from pre-conquest forms of subjection. Gómara's solution for the ethical contradictions of the colonial enterprise, however, could not overcome international criticism and an emerging anti-Spanish discourse, now known as the "Black Legend." Despite his attempts to rally his readers in support of Spain's imperial expansion, his efforts clashed with the political agendas and ethical standards of the day.

Gómara's lack of success is a revealing example of the conditions undermining discourses of domination. The debates about the justice of the conquest were far from redeeming Spanish colonialism, rather they deterred people from accepting the acts carried out by the conquistadors. Outrage over the crimes committed by the Spaniards against the Indians appear in the public record as early as 1524 or 1525, when Peter Martyr (Pietro Martire d'Anghiera, 1456–1526) condemned the enslavement of the Lucayos (the native inhabitants of the Bahamas) in his *Decades*. Most of the writers who have become part of the canon of colonial writing did not consider it contradictory to simultaneously expose these crimes *and* support Spanish imperialism. This discursive economy created the impediments that would plague subsequent histories of the Indies. As concern for the well-being of the Indians mounted, figures such as Las Casas were able to effectively argue against the legality of the entire process of colonization. Gómara's praise of the conquest was an ill-timed effort to set forth an ideology capable of mobilizing support for transatlantic power structures. The crucial role of international criticism in challenging the claims and assumptions of these accounts illuminates how colonial discourse encountered its own limitations to establish more influential and efficacious ideological foundations.

NOTES

1. Unless otherwise indicated, all translations of quoted passages were done by Scott Sessions.

2. Gómara organized his *Historia general de las Indias y Conquista de México* into two parts. The first part contains an explanation of world geography, the location of the Indies, a narration of Columbus's discoveries, and the colonization of Hispaniola, followed by an account of the most important explorations and conquests organized region by region. It concludes with miscellaneous notes on topics such as Indian slavery, the Council of the Indies, the colonization of the Canaries, the route to the Indies, and a "Praise of Spaniards." In the second part, the conquest of Mexico is framed within Fernando Cortés's biography, beginning with his birth and ending with his death. Gómara traced his path through Santo Domingo, Cuba, and Mexico, as well as his expedition to Honduras and his trips back and forth to Spain. He also included detailed descriptions of Aztec life, which are still considered valuable sources for the study of Mesoamerican cultures.

3. Also known as Hernando or Hernán, I have chosen to use Fernando because this is the name most frequently employed in his letters (Cortés 1993, 159, 309, 310, 451, 454) and by nearly all of his contemporaries.

4. For more information on Gómara's biography and connections, see Lewis (1983, 21–67) and Ramos (1972, 111–145).

5. Regarding Gómara's achievements in the *Historia general,* see Lewis (1983, 312).

6. Gómara's style has been commended by scholars such as Raúl Porras Barrenechea (1941), Ramón Iglesia (1942), José Durand (1952), Rolf Eberenz Greoles (1979), and Robert Lewis (1983, 1986).

7. A commentary on this letter can be found in Lewis (1983, 294–295).

8. On this lawsuit, see Roa-de-la-Carrera (2001) and Chapter 1 that follows.

9. The causes for the prohibition are unknown; for a more detailed analysis, see Chapter 1.

10. In "Des Coches," Montaigne's discussion of the Spaniards' reading of the Requirement combined Gómara's accounts of incidents taking place, respectively, with the lord of Cenú (Colombia) and with the lord of Tabasco (Mexico). He also followed Gómara's version of the conquests of Mexico and Peru, and his condemnation of Spanish boasting is likely a reaction to the "Praise of Spaniards" chapter in the *Historia general*. His description of Indian ways of life in "Des Cannibales" also closely matches those provided by Gómara. For a discussion about the relation between Montaigne and Gómara, see Bataillon (1959) and Conley (1989). On "Des Coches," see Conley (1992, 135–162).

11. Tom Conley (1989, 252) states that "Montaigne fashions his experience of the Indian other through the productive alterity of his textual means. These essays refuse to arrogate the figure or the rights of the other into its own discourse." Similarly, María Antonia Garcés (1992, 156–157) argues that although Gómara was Eurocentric and unwilling "to examine the foundations of his knowledge of the world," in Montaigne "America appears as a point of departure for a radical inquiry into difference." In contrast, Aldo Scaglione's analysis of Montaigne's treatment of the myth of the Noble Savage shows that he "remains essentially the humanist who uses the theme of the Indian . . . to confirm the humanists' myth of modern man as a moral and psychological pigmy" (1976, 68). Michael Ryan (1981, 520–521) contends that the humanists were not shaken by the exotic because diversity was intelligible for them within the Christian and Platonist traditions. He also suggests that skeptics like Montaigne confronted diversity as a problem in relation to the overwhelming availability of texts, not to challenge their own Eurocentric biases.

12. Jonathan Loesberg (1983, 255–256) has suggested that Gómara himself had created the conditions for Montaigne to read his text in an inverted way, arguing that Gómara's interest in creating a "formal order" in his account was situated above any concern for the contents involved. I would argue, however, that the possibility of inversion existed because Gómara openly discussed the problematic aspects of the conquest.

CHAPTER 1

Gómara and the
Politics of Consensus

HISTORY AS INFLUENCE:
THE EMPEROR AND THE CONQUEROR

n 1541 Fernando Cortés joined Emperor Charles V's campaign to capture Algiers on the Mediterranean coast of North
Africa. After the siege of the city had scarcely begun, a storm
destroyed 140 of the 450 vessels transporting the imperial
troops. The forces defending the city had fiercely attacked the besieg-
ers, whose firearms had been rendered inoperable by the rain. In view
of the peril, the fleet's commander, Andrea Doria, sent word to the
emperor to retire his troops and went to await him at Cape Matifou.[1]
Charles, who was commanding the expedition, met with the members
of his council of war, who decided withdrawing the imperial troops
was their best course of action. Willing to put his military skill to the
test, Cortés offered to take Algiers with a group of Spanish and Italian
soldiers who had besieged the city, but he was unable to change the
emperor's decision to lift the siege and abandon the undertaking.

Gómara, who claimed to have been there on that occasion, later expressed his surprise at the lack of consideration that the offer from a soldier as experienced as Cortés received. In his account of the incident, Gómara evoked the situation that the conquistador already had faced in 1519, when he scuttled his ships and with a few hundred men launched the conquest of Mexico. He added that Cortés's plan had the support of the men engaged in the siege, but he was excluded from the council and could not make his voice heard by the emperor (1552, 2:139r).

This brief episode ended the military career of Cortés and initiated the unsuccessful legal campaign for his "vassals and privileges," which he would only abandon shortly before his death in December 1547. Ten years after the failed siege of Algiers, Gómara completed his account of the episode in the *Historia general*. Although the conquistador failed to attain greater recognition as a military leader in his life, the public voice of the historian could confer higher honors upon him. His exclusion from the war council must have taught Gómara that Cortés's reputation had its limits. His determination to assume a leadership role in Algiers took on a parodistic resonance of his old exploits in Mexico. The lack of consideration that Cortés received from the emperor suggests the little esteem Charles held for the accomplishments of Spaniards in the Indies. Girolamo Benzoni would use the same episode in his *Historia del Mondo Nuovo* to diminish the heroic image of the conquistadors in the Indies. Stating that they had fought "brutti animali, & proprie bestie Occidentali" [brutish creatures and typical western beasts], he quoted the commentary of a Spanish noble on Cortés's proposition: "questa bestia pensa d'hauer à fare co[n] i suoi Indianelli, doue diece huomini à cauallo bastano à rompere venticinque mila" [this beast thinks he is dealing with his little Indians, where ten men on horses are enough to defeat twenty-five thousand] (Benzoni 1969, 50v–51r). The reputation that Cortés had gained in the conquest of Mexico could only give him recognition in accordance with the value the crown gave to conquistador service in the Indies.

Gómara chose to praise the wars carried out by the Spaniards to conquer the native populations of the Indies. Like other Europeans of his time, he held the conviction of the Spanish conquistadors' intellectual and military superiority over the Indians, but at the same time he considered that the services they had lent to the king had great merit. Gómara argued that the colonization of the New World had been as beneficial to the Spaniards as for the Indians; but his history of the

Indies loudly echoed the interests of Cortés's heirs and, at least in theory, those who were reaping the benefits of the conquest and indigenous labor. However narrow the group of people whose views it represented, the significance of the *Historia general* lies in the part it played in framing—rhetorically and conceptually—the cultural debate concerning the history of the Indies. Many aspects of the text are questionable and do not stand up to critical scrutiny in view of the documentary record, but the *Historia general* offers valuable insights into the central historical problems raised by Spanish imperialism in the New World.

Gómara's historiographical discourse reveals his strong desire to give coherent expression to the conflicting interests that took part in governing the Indies. In writing the *Historia general*, he relied on the efficacy of historical discourse to illuminate the character of relationships that had developed between Spain and the New World and to shape its future. In his dedication of the *Historia general*, Gómara explicitly suggested to the emperor the principle that should govern his policy with respect to the Indies: "Justo es pues que vuestra majestad fauorezca la conquista, y los conquistadores, mirando mucho por los conquistados" [It is just for your majesty to favor the conquest and the conquistadors, closely looking after the conquered] (1552, 1:[*ii*]v). Favoring the conquistadors meant protecting the privileges that they had attained in the wars of conquest, especially their authority over the native population, whereas looking after the conquered meant no more than protecting Indians from suffering further injuries than those already inflicted. Such a suggestion was not inappropriate at the time inasmuch as history, which was viewed in this tradition as a *magistra vitae* or "teacher of life," offered a mirror in which a prince could observe his own actions and decide on the most adequate courses of action to follow.[2] In light of the political function of advice or propaganda recognized in the writing of history, Gómara's historiographical activities also constituted a means of service to the emperor. When promoting the interests of individuals such as Cortés in the intellectual realm, however, he transformed his historiographical activities into a vehicle of social action. Inasmuch as the *Historia general* attempted to solicit the emperor's favor for the conquistadors, Gómara's intervention to define the place of the conquerors and the conquered in the colonies takes on less of an advisory role than that of an advocate. His advocacy requires him to design a way of providing political solvency to his historiographical practice within the context of imperial Spain.

The conditions in which the history of the Indies as a genre could exert influence upon colonial politics derive from the modes of inquiry that served to produce representations of the New World. Knowing the colonized territories was a matter of reconnaissance, occupation, military control, economic exploitation, evangelization, and political reorganization. The most obvious example of the intimate relationship between intellectual life and the activities of colonization can be seen in the case of the House of Trade, the institution in charge of supervising commerce and navigation between Spain and her overseas possessions. Clarence Haring (1964, 298–314) has shown that the House of Trade directed the production of knowledge necessary to support the maritime activities that sustained the operations of expansion and communication in the colonial world. Navigation and commerce in the Indies established the problems and objectives that guided the development of Spanish cartography and naval science in the sixteenth century. These intellectual activities, in turn, provided the training, means of evaluation, principles, and tools with which maritime operations were conducted. The development of Indies historiography was nurtured by the world of explorers, conquistadors, missionaries, and royal officials employed in the colonial government (Sánchez Alonso 1941–1950, 1:359). Given that the administration of the colonies had to arbitrate between conflicting goals, the formulation of the Indies as a subject of knowledge came to reflect the contradictions created in the process of colonial expansion. The conquistadors, missionaries, and royal functionaries who actively dedicated themselves to lobbying for laws, privileges, concessions, and royal favors provided the narratives that would then be employed in historical discourse. In like manner, the historical genre acquired a relevance of its own vis-à-vis the social practices of the colonizing process.

The main questions here are how the historiographical discourse of the Indies developed and what kind of social presence did it achieve in the emerging empire. Rather than simply widening the thematic repertoires of history, the new writings made intelligible the emergence of a system of colonization in the New World. Given that the intellectual problem of the Indies was formulated in relation to the experiences and necessities of colonial expansion, it is essential to situate this historiography within this social context. The production of the *Historia general* provides an excellent case to examine the institutional mechanisms that gave rise to the locus of the historian of the Indies in the creation of a New World empire.

HISTORIOGRAPHY AND EMPIRE-BUILDING

When the *Historia general* first came out in 1552, it appears that the history of the Indies already was consolidated as a discursive practice. For Gómara and his contemporaries, writing a history of the Indies meant relying on a certain tradition. As a field of intellectual activity, the genre enjoyed a kind of established social presence and included figures recognized in the world of books as well as in the public sphere. In terms of subject matter, it was an area rich in materials, tasks to be realized, and issues that required explanation. Histories of the Indies served the cultural function of formulating cognitive relationships with the New World through concepts, representations, and accounts. In this regard, they also served an important role in the political and administrative realms. Gómara recognized the development of a discourse concerning the Indies as a response to the needs of the reading public. In his *Anales,* among the events of 1535, he noted: "Publica G[onzal]o Hernandes de Ouiedo la primera parte de la historia gen[era]l y natural de Indias, que fué bien receuida" [Gonzalo Fernández de Oviedo publishes the first part of the *Historia general y natural de las Indias* (General and natural history of the Indies), which was well received] (Gómara 1912, 231). When writing his *Historia general,* Gómara will consider the demand for such an account as one of the conditions in which his text would manage to achieve social and cultural efficacy.

We know that Gómara had begun working on the *Historia general* by 1545. In the dedication of his *Crónica de los Barbarrojas* (Chronicle of the Barbarossas), he announced that he was composing the other work "para que venga á noticia de todo el viejo mundo el mundo nuevo, y sepan todos tantas cosas, tan extrañas y admirables como en él hay, las quales no se entienden bien segun su grandeça" [so that the New World would come to the notice of all the Old World, and everyone would know such things, as strange and admirable as exist there, which are not well understood according to their grandeur] (Gómara 1853, 337).[3] Gómara hoped that his history would have an impact on European perceptions of the Indies. In the front matter of his work he included a small section addressed "A los trasladores" (To translators), where he noted:

> *Algunos por ventura querran trasladar esta [h]istoria en otra lengua, para que los de su nacion entiendan las marauillas, y gra[n]deza de las Indias. Y conozcan que las obras ygualan, y aun sobrepuyan, a la fama que dellas anda por todo el mundo* (1552, 1:[ii]r).

Some by chance might wish to translate this history into another language, so that those of their nation may understand the marvels and grandeur of the Indies. And they would know that the works equal, and even surpass, their reputation, which travels throughout the world.

Gómara thought that his work would have international appeal and should be written for readers interested in understanding "the marvels and grandeur of the Indies." Moreover, he supposed that there would be translators wishing to prepare a Latin edition and he concluded his remarks with a warning that he was composing one of his own "para que no tomen trabajo en ello" [so they should not take up working on it]. Gómara wanted to present the New World to both vernacular and erudite readers. From his perspective, the Indies had a public image or, in his own words, a "reputation . . . throughout the world," which made it necessary to relate the most precise information about its geography and history. The *Historia general* came to satisfy a public interest for information about the human and natural realities of the Indies.

Gómara attempted to carve out a space for his history of the Indies in the public sphere. He has been characterized as a historian who was highly conscious of the literary and historical world of his time (Merriman 1912, xxvii–xxxiii; Lewis 1983, 73, 103–125). The kind of prestige that the historical genre held for him may be appreciated in some of the annotations he made in his *Anales* about historians of the period. When relating the death of King Ferdinand the Catholic (1516), instead of discussing the life of the monarch, he provided a list of his chroniclers and pointed out Jerónimo Zurita as the best historian of his reign (Gómara 1912, 191).[4] On various occasions, Gómara included certain entries related to the activities of historians among the events of the year, such as the completion of a certain text or the appointment of certain chroniclers.[5] This shows that Gómara considered the writing of history to be an event shaping his contemporary world — so much, in fact, that in his *Anales* he managed to present himself as a historical figure:

> *Nace Fran[cis]co Lopez en Gómara domingo de mañana, que fué dia de la Purificación de nuestra Señora que llaman Candelaria, el qual hiço estos años, y las guerras de mar de nuestros tiempos, y la historia de las indias con la conquista de México, y piensa otras obrillas, y pues lo ha trabajado es razon que lo goçe en compañia de tantos buenos varones (1912, 182).*

Francisco López is born in Gómara, on a Sunday morning, the Day
of the Purification of Our Lady they call Candelaria, the man who
wrote these Annals, and the Naval Wars of Our Times, and the
History of the Indies with the Conquest of Mexico, and is
considering other shorter works, and because he has worked hard at
it, it is reasonable for him to enjoy the company of such fine men.

The attention that Gómara devoted to history as an intellectual activity among the key events of the sixteenth century suggests that he
oriented the production of his own discourse to interact with other
historians. In addition to making himself a public figure, in the writing
of history he found a means of participating in the political life of the
state.[6] This is particularly evident with respect to his historiographical
practices, which gave him a privileged space for political action and
confrontation. Among the events that established the main discursive
precedents on the subject matter of the Indies, Gómara in his *Anales*
(1912, 248, 258) records the efforts of Las Casas to contradict Sepúlveda's
justification of the conquest and to block the publication of Oviedo's
Historia general y natural. This confrontation of ideas and accounts motivated him to advance a principle of social good to guide imperial policy
in the New World. When Gómara suggested that the emperor should
"favor the conquest and the conquistadors" in the dedication of the
Historia general, he was taking a position as to which form of colonial
government was best. His dedication clearly explains the kind of civil
service that his work intended to offer:

> Y ta[m]bien es razon que todos ayuden, y ennoblezcan las Indias, vnos con
> santa predicacio[n], otros con buenos co[n]sejos, otros con prouechosas
> granjerias, otros con loables costu[m]bres y policia. Por lo qual [h]e yo
> escrito la [h]istoria (1552, 1:[ii]v).

> And it is also reasonable for everyone to help and ennoble the
> Indies, some with holy preaching, others with good advice, others
> with profitable enterprises, others with laudable customs and
> policy, which is the reason why I have written the *Historia*.

His attitude with respect to the diffusion of his work is consistent
with the tone of humanist historiographical practice oriented toward
the development of an elaborate rhetorical style and the promotion of
the interests of individuals, families, or communities.[7] Among the enor-

mous variety of texts written on themes related to the New World during this period, history was the genre that had the most literary prestige and cultural impact. Genres like the letter, the *relación,* or even the collections of travelers' accounts could only provide fragmentary glimpses of the Indies, but writing history made it possible to present an overview of the different regions of the New World and their historical development. This overarching perspective, with its capacity for assembling, summarizing, and interpreting events, gave the genre political utility. In the case of Italian humanism, the propagandistic potential of history was commonly put to the service of principalities and city-states, fulfilling a public function important enough for many political leaders to commission them (Hay 1977, 99). There is no doubt that the kind of diffusion and appeal that history enjoyed made it a strategic genre for defining and debating the modes of relationships that had been developing between Spain and the New World.

Gómara hoped that his *Historia general* would serve to promote the kind of evangelical, administrative, and economically exploitive activities that from his perspective of history helped to ennoble the Indies. His strategy for making his discourse influential is based on the kind of relationship that he established within the historiographical tradition. His method of positioning himself in the historiographical practice of his time rested on two main characteristics that had developed in the genre up until that moment: the type of authority that its authors achieved as public figures, and the complete absence of a work that presented a sufficiently comprehensive view of the conquest of the New World. Nowhere is this more clearly evident than on the back of the *Historia general*'s title page where he provided a list of "[h]istoriadores de Indias" [historians of the Indies] (1552, 1:[i]v), including Peter Martyr, Gonzalo Fernández de Oviedo y Valdés, Fernando Cortés, and Francisco López de Gómara.

This list heading the front matter of the *Historia general* offers a good indication with respect to the possible criteria for forming a historiographical canon of the Indies in the sixteenth century. It also permits us to understand the way in which Gómara intended to situate himself before this tradition in order to compose his *Historia general.* To the list of authors' names who could be considered historians of the Indies, Gómara added a brief annotation about the works they had written:

Pedro Martyr de Angleria clerigo Milanes escriuio en Latin la [h]istoria de Indias en decadas, que llama Oceanas, hasta el año de mil y quinientos y veinte y seys.

Fernando Cortes escriuio al Emperador sus cosas en cartas.

Gonçalo Fernandez de Ouiedo, y Ualdes, escriuio el año de mil y quinientos y treynta y cinco la primera parte de la general, y natural [h]istoria de las Indias.

Francisco Lopez de Gomara, clerigo, escriue la pressente [h]istoria de las Indias, y conquista de Mexico, en este año de mil y quinientos, y cinquenta y dos (1552, 1:[i]v).

Pietro Martire d'Anghiera, Milanese cleric, wrote in Latin the history of the Indies in decades, which he calls *Oceanas,* up to the year 1526.

Fernando Cortés wrote about his things to the emperor in letters.

Gonzalo Fernández de Oviedo y Valdés, in 1535, wrote the first part of the *Historia general y natural de las Indias.*

Francisco López de Gómara, cleric, writes the present *Historia de las Indias, y conquista de Mexico,* in this year 1552.

Gómara's comments here distinguish the works according to the range of information their authors provided about the Indies. Martyr covered events "up to the year 1526," Cortés wrote about "his things," Oviedo had written "the first part," but Gómara offered a comprehensive work. The subject had a certain relevance for Gómara, for in his dedication he explained to Charles: "Intitulola a vuestra majestad, no porque no sabe las cosas de Indias mejor que yo, sino porque las vea juntas con algunas particularidades tan aplazibles [*sic*] como nueuas, y verdaderas" [I dedicate this to your majesty, not because you do not know the affairs of the Indies better than I, but because you may see them together with some particularities as pleasing as they are novel and true] (1552, 1:[*ii*]v). The promotional significance that this kind of comprehensive perspective could have is reaffirmed in the way that subsequent editions continued to present the work to the public. The long title of these editions emphasized that the work presented a complete picture of the history of the Indies to date: "Primera y segunda parte de la historia general de las Indias con todo el descubrimiento y cosas notables que han acaecido dende que se ganaron [h]a[s]ta el año de 1551" [The first and second part of the general history of the Indies with all the discovery and notable things that have occurred since they were acquired up until the year 1551] (1553a, 1:[*i*]r).[8]

Along with purporting to supply a comprehensive view of the conquests, Gómara's annotated list of authors constructed the canon of the history of the Indies based upon each text's authority and importance. His list distinguished between the works of authors who achieved the title of historian and those of other writers who also gave accounts of discoveries and conquests, but were not considered worthy of mention. After the list, Gómara went on to state his criteria of inclusion and exclusion in the canon:

> *Estos autores [h]an escrito mucho de Indias, y impresso sus obras, q[ue] son d[e] substa[n]cia. Todos los demas, q[ue] anda[n] impressos escriuen lo suyo, y poco. Por lo qual no entran en el numero de [h]istoriadores. Que si tal fuesse todos los capitanes, y pilotos que dan relacion de sus entradas y nauegaciones, los quales son muchos, se dirian [h]istoriadores (1552, 1:[i]v).*

These authors have written much about the Indies, and published their works, which are substantial. All the others who have been published write about their own, and little, therefore they do not enter into the number of historians. If that were the case, all the captains and pilots who gave accounts of their incursions and voyages, who are many, would be called historians.

The authors Gómara considered historians were those whose printed works stood out for the richness of their writing and the range or depth of their subject matter. Meanwhile, the other authors who "write about their own, and little" — that is to say, those who had reported on events limited to a particular expedition — did not make the list. His implicit way of configuring the canon of the genre established a correlation between the position of authority of those who received the title of historians and their intellectual weight within the tradition.

The inclusion of Cortés, in particular, suggests a way of understanding the canon of the history of the Indies centered principally on the prestige that such texts could acquire from a social perspective, for his *Cartas de relación* (Letters of relation) were thematically rather limited. The idea of presenting Cortés as a historian of the Indies could be explained by the reception that his *Cartas* enjoyed in Europe. There is considerable evidence that Cortés's *Letters* were perceived in their moment as narratives of "substance" from the point of view of their style and content. On the one hand, the *Cartas de relación* were published in a

Latin edition translated by Pietro Savorgnano, who praised Cortés's narration of the conquest of Mexico.[9] Savorgnano had titled the text *Praeclara Ferdina*[n]*di Cortesii de Noua maris Oceani Hyspania Narratio Sacratissimo ac Inuictissimo Carolo Romanoru*[m] *Imperatori semper Augusto, Hyspaniaru*[m] *& c*[hristianorum] *Regi* (The admirable narration of Fernando Cortés concerning the New Spain of the Ocean Sea, addressed to the most holy and triumphant Charles, emperor of the Romans, forever august, king of the Spaniards and Christians). Its dedication to Pope Clement VII reveals that Savorgnano thought highly of the narrative as well as the content, which he compared to the acts of Hannibal and Alexander the Great (Cortés 1524, [*ii*]r). On the other hand, the prestige of the conquistador's text is already clearly expressed in the edition's colophon, which suggests that Fernando, *infante* of Spain and archduke of Austria, provided Savorgnano with the Spanish text and entrusted its translation to him (R. Commissione Colombiana 1892–1896, part 3, vol. 2:326–328).[10]

The aforementioned list of historians of the Indies shows that Gómara was positioning himself politically and institutionally in the Spain of Charles V. This would explain his association with Cortés, who, in spite of not having had the favor of the crown in some of his affairs, nevertheless enjoyed a certain political presence in the Spanish court and had become a public celebrity. Oviedo presented Cortés as a figure of authority in his *Historia general y natural*:

> El marqués, después que vino de las Indias . . . se fué a la corte de Su
> Majestad, e fué muy bien rescebido e aceptado del Emperador, e continuó su
> corte, como señor de estado, e con muy buena casa e auctoridad, e con
> muchos gastos (1992, 4:265).

> The marquis, after he arrived from the Indies . . . went to the court of
> His Majesty, and was very well received and accepted by the
> Emperor, and remained in his court, as a lord of state, and with a
> very fine household and considerable authority, and with many
> expenses.[11]

The aura of authority and social importance that Cortés seems to have enjoyed from the status he had acquired explains, at least from Gómara's perspective, how his *Cartas de relación* could have warranted a degree of prominence in the historical genre comparable to that of the works of Martyr and Oviedo, both of whom wrote about the Indies as royal chroniclers. The significance of this appeal to the authority of tradition rests on the conditions of production that define the relationship the genre maintained with Spanish imperial practices.

IN THE SERVICE OF THE KING:
HISTORIANS AND ADMINISTRATORS

Histories of the Indies came to play an instrumental role in the administrative arrangements of the colonial regime mainly because their authors had strong links to the crown. Peter Martyr, in particular, came to perceive the genre as an activity through which it was possible to exercise considerable intellectual influence in the political realm. Martyr's success as an author is quite apparent, for in the sixteenth century his work was widely used as a source on the subject.[12] The prominent place that he came to occupy in the affairs of the New World since the reign of the Catholic Monarchs also demonstrates his presence as an intellectual figure in the public sphere. The historians Oviedo, Las Casas, and Gómara not only saw him as one more author who had written about the Indies, they also referred to him as a figure of authority. Las Casas claimed that Martyr was the most reliable early historian of the Indies and that Spaniards who had returned from there informed him about everything "como un hombre de auctoridad" [as a man of authority] (1988–1998, 3:348, 4:1474). Gómara, in spite of criticizing him, attributed to Martyr the importance of being the first to write about matters of the Indies "en estilo" [in style] (1552, 1:25v). Oviedo, who accused him of being an "auctor de lo falso" [author of the false], still considered him an "hombre grave e de auctoridad . . . que se osó escrebir al Papa e a los reyes e príncipes extraños" [important man of authority . . . who dared to write to the pope and to foreign kings and princes] (1992, 1:14).[13] Moreover, all three recognized his various positions as prothonotary apostolic, a member of the Council of the Indies, royal chronicler, and the abbot of Jamaica.[14]

The elevated institutional stature that historians of the Indies bestowed upon Martyr set the tone of the genre at least until the moment Gómara wrote his *Historia general*. Although Martyr does not seem to have received a commission from the monarchs to write about the Indies, there is sufficient evidence that he wrote his *Decades of the New World* from an official position. Las Casas saw a very definite relationship between Martyr's position on the Council of the Indies and his historiographical activities. In his *Historia de las Indias* (History of the Indies) he said that Martyr "se le presentaban las cosas que de nuevo acaecían y iban destas Indias" [was presented things that just happened and came from these Indies], and added "Esto se hacía porque, por aquel tiempo [en] que esto escribía, era del Consejo de Indias" [This was done because, at the time he wrote this, he was on the Council of the Indies] (1988–1998, 4:1474). Martyr's political influence as a historian of the Indies and a royal advisor, no doubt, was enormous if one takes into account that the king and his advisors did not have direct contact with the Indies. Even though Martyr had never been there either, he tried to inform himself about everything that was happening through the testimony of Spaniards who were returning from the New World. He managed to gather as much information about the Indies as possible at that time, thus his *Decades* were able to greatly shape the image that the king and his colleagues on the Royal Council were formulating about the colonies.

The task of chronicler of the Indies lent a kind of service to the crown that chroniclers of other Spanish kingdoms could not match. Oviedo insisted in his *Historia general y natural* on the importance of writing based on personal experience, assuming that telling the truth was the service that history rendered to the king and his council: "Y si dijeren que al Rey e a su Consejo se sirvió así, como esos doctos cronistas lo apuntaron, no todas veces sabe el Rey por tales cartas todo lo que consuena con la verdad" [And if they say that this served the king and his council, as these learned chroniclers note, the king does not always learn through such letters everything that conforms with the truth] (1992, 4:271). The context of this statement is his criticism of Peter Martyr and Bernardo Gentile, for even though they wrote in a "buen estilo" [good style], they were not sufficiently concerned with the quality of the information that they used in their writings.[15] Oviedo's concern was based on a concrete administrative problem, for until they began to name functionaries who already had served in the New World, the major difficulty that confronted the Council of the Indies was the lack of knowledge its members had about the lands they had to govern (Merriman 1962, 3:622). The distance and lack of contact with the Indies of those in charge of their administration caused an enormous responsibility to fall upon the historian who was instrumental in mediating their relationship with the New World. Historians like Oviedo and Las Casas would systematically question the veracity and propriety of previous accounts because of the influence these representations of history could have on future decisions made by the king's functionaries.

The relationship between the history of the Indies and the administrative world clearly surpassed the traditional function of monitoring the conduct of kings and advising by way of example (Carbia 1934, 17–25). The *licenciado* Juan de Ovando y Godoy ordered the official creation of the position of chronicler of the Indies in 1571 after an inspection of the Council of the Indies in which he discovered that it was nearly impossible to get reliable information about the New World (Carbia 1934, 97–103). There are sufficient reasons, however, to suggest that creating this official position did nothing more than legally formalize a kind of historiographical practice that already found itself relatively institutionalized during the reign of Charles V. The task of writing histories of the Indies had been carried out by royal chroniclers like Martyr, who undoubtedly enjoyed the backing of the crown in the production of their writings.[16] After Martyr's death, the crown appointed Antonio de Guevara as chronicler of Castile with the task of continuing to write the chronicle of the Indies begun in the *Decades*. Although he never wrote a single line to fulfill his commission, the appointment reveals that the crown was institutionalizing the genre. A royal *cédula* of December 7, 1526, made the position official and ordered that all of Martyr's papers be put in Guevara's possession so that he could carry out this work (Carbia 1934, 76; Keniston 1958, 276). This kind of legal assistance was also given to Oviedo when he was named royal chronicler (August 18, 1532) with the support of the Council of the Indies.[17] None of this occurred in Gómara's case, but he may have intended to join the list of Indies historians through unofficial means.[18] Insofar as he operated within a more or less established tradition of histories of the Indies, Gómara could aspire to occupy a position among those who had served the crown or gained influence with their writings. It is not possible to determine if he tried to be named chronicler or not, but the *Historia general* contributed to others perceiving him in this manner.[19]

In the time between Martyr and Oviedo the history of the Indies had achieved a more defined profile within the colonial administration. Beginning with the publication of the first edition of Oviedo's *Historia general y natural* in 1535, the genre assumed a very precise informative function within the institutional apparatus, playing a major role in defining the modes of colonial relationships between Spain and the Indies. Oviedo thought that the importance of the service he provided the crown required the assistance of legal instruments as he explicitly pointed out to his readers:

> [T]engo cédulas y mandamientos de la Cesárea Majestad para que todos sus gobernadores e justicias e oficiales de todas las Indias me den aviso e relación verdadera de todo lo que fuere digno de historia por testimonios auténticos, firmados de sus nombres e signados de escribanos públicos, de manera que hagan fe. Porque, como tan celosos príncipes de la verdad e tan amigos della, quieren que esta Historia Natural e General de sus Indias se escriba muy al proprio (1992, 1:13–14).

> I have *cédulas* and orders from the Caesarian Majesty for all his governors, justices, and officials throughout the Indies to give me information and true account about everything that may be worthy of history by authentic testimonies, signed with their names and notarized by public scribes, in a manner that would establish faith. For, as such zealous princes and friends of the truth, they want this *Natural and General History of their Indies* written quite properly.

Oviedo gave his historiographical activity the dignity of a juridical process, which he made clear to the reader when declaring that he relied upon legal instruments to obtain sworn testimonies before notaries and then utilized them in writing his history. The parallel that he established with juridical systems of proof went further than the analogy in the preceding passage. Oviedo explicitly declared that the procedures he employed to summon information from royal officials had legal validity. The function that these methods fulfilled in his history was that of providing a guarantee of truth to the readers for whom history was their access to information about the New World. In the case of the functionaries on the Council of the Indies who had to make legislative decisions or arbitrate lawsuits and petitions originating in the Indies, Oviedo's production strategy seemed particularly appropriate for the circumstances.

The council's original proposal to the emperor on May 7, 1532, had been for Oviedo, then located on the island of Hispaniola, to travel around the Indies gathering materials to send to Spain, but the chronicler would negotiate the conditions of his position and obtain the crown's authority to summon depositions from "all its governors, justices, and officials throughout the Indies" on December 15, 1532.[20] With an annual salary of thirty thousand *maravedíes,* he set out to write a history of the Indies that aspired to achieve the status of juridical truth. The relationship that Oviedo's historiographical practice established with the colonial administration was so important that his appointment as chronicler stipulated that the Council of the Indies had to see "antes que se imprima ni publique lo que escribiere" [what he wrote before it was printed and published] (Tudela 1992, cxviii). The work was in fact examined and amended by the council before its publication as revealed in the colophon of the first edition and the "carta missiua" that Oviedo addressed to Cardinal Francisco García de Loaysa, the emperor's confessor and president of the Council of the Indies (1535, 191v–193r).

The influence that a historian like Oviedo could have in administrative and governmental tasks was complex and made it indispensable for the Council of the Indies to review the work, because those who directed these affairs from Spain wanted to have the last word on the image they were projecting to the public. Oviedo implicitly recognized the preeminence and authority of the council in matters of government when he declared that "que lo que toca a la gobernación, no es lo que principalmente se me manda escrebir, ni su Cesárea Majestad quiere saber de mí, pues su Real Consejo de Indias asisten tan grandes e señalados varones" [what concerns governance is not mainly what I am ordered to write, nor does his Caesarian Majesty want to learn from me, for such great and outstanding gentlemen serve on his Royal Council of the Indies] (1992, 1:226). Nevertheless, the influence that Oviedo could exercise on colonial administration through his *Historia general y natural* is based on the ignorance of the members of the council and their distance from the New World. This is precisely what Oviedo told the council president in his "carta missiua":

> [S]i en esto hobiere descuido, visto está qué tales andarán las ovejas si los pastores a quien fueren encomendadas no fueren cuales los han menester. E tanto es mayor el peligro, cuanto el camino es más luengo, y Vuestra Señoría Reverendísima tan apartado de lo ver, e tanta dubda como ocurre en saberse acá la verdad (1992, 1:6).

> If sufficient care is not given the matter, it is clear that the sheep will wander about if the shepherds are not up for the task. And the peril is so much greater, for the journey is longer, and Your Most Reverend Lordship is so far away to see it, and so much uncertainty occurs here for the truth to be known.

The administrative backing that Oviedo enjoyed while writing his *Historia general y natural* guides the course of his historiographical activity. His conception of the art of writing history was based on a guarantee of truth whose foundation was a complementary combination of the legal framework of the production of his discourse and his personal experience in the Indies. Oviedo made this abundantly clear in the preface of the first edition of his *Historia general y natural*:

> [E]l capitan Gonçalo herna[n]dez de Ouiedo & valdes: alcayde de la fortaleza de la ciudad de sancto Domingo de la ysla Española & cronista de la sacra cesarea & catholica magestades del emperador don Carlos quinto de tal nombre rey de España: & de la serenissima & muy poderosa reyna doña Juana su madre nuestros señores. Por cuyo mandado el auctor escriuio las cosas marauillosas que ay en diuersas yslas & partes destas Indias & imperio de la corona real de Castilla: segun lo vido & supo en veynte & dos años & mas que ha que biue & reside en aquellas partes (1535, [i]v).

> Captain Gonzalo Fernández de Oviedo y Valdés, *alcalde* of the fort of the city of Santo Domingo on the island of Hispaniola, and chronicler of the Holy Caesarian and Catholic Majesties of Emperor *don* Charles V, king of Spain, and of the most serene and very powerful Queen *doña* Juana, his mother, our lords. By whose order the author wrote about the marvelous things that exist in the different islands and parts of these Indies and empire of the royal crown of Castile: according to what he saw and learned in the twenty-two years or more that he has lived and resided in those parts.

The role that historiographical discourse played at that time in relation to the colonial administration was one of presenting a view of what had happened in the Indies. This did not mean that history was defining government policies any more than in the general sense of promoting the interests of certain sectors. The historian's power to narrate events was significant, but his ability to influence royal officials depended on his skill at gaining public recognition. In Oviedo's case, the *Historia general y natural* appears to have had a favorable reception in the Council of the Indies and considerable literary success with the public (Amador de los Ríos 1851, lxiv; Gómara 1912, 231; Las Casas 1988–1998, 5:1856–1857). It is difficult to determine the degree of authority that the *Historia general y natural* achieved, but the words of Pedro Mexía (1497–1551), who was appointed cosmographer of the House of Trade in 1537, confirm the prestige that Oviedo's position as royal chronicler conferred to him. In his *Historia del emperador* (History of the emperor), published around 1547–1551, Mexía wrote that the

Indies "se avían conquistado y traydo a conosçimiento de la Fe. E hoy día lo están, por la manera que Gonçalo Hernández de Oviedo, coronista de las cosas de Yndias, lo escriue largo; al qual yo me rremito en este propósito" [had been conquered and brought to the knowledge of the Faith, and are today, in the manner that Gonzalo Fernández de Oviedo, chronicler of the things of the Indies, writes at length, to whom I defer in this matter] (1945, 351). The authority that Oviedo had as "el coronista que tiene espeçial y particular cuydado de las cosas de Yndias" [the chronicler who has special and particular care of the matters concerning the Indies] (Mexía 1945, 113) shows how his work could consolidate certain views of the Indies and influence someone as prominent as Mexía among Spanish intellectuals at that time.

Oviedo initially relied on his advantageous position to develop an influential historiographical practice, but between 1535 and 1548 political conditions had changed. The first part of the *Historia general y natural* (books 1–19) was published in 1535 in Seville and reprinted with modifications and additions at Salamanca in 1547 and Valladolid in 1557. As previously noted, Gómara mentioned two events in his *Anales* that were related to this work: the positive reception it had in 1535 and Las Casas's attempt to "estoruar la Historia General y Natural de Indias, que Gonçalo Hernandes de Ouyedo coronista mostró al Consejo Real de Castilla para la imprimir" [block the *Historia general y natural de Indias* that the chronicler Gonzalo Fernández de Oviedo showed the Royal Council of Castile in order to publish it] in 1548 (Gómara 1912, 231, 258). Although Oviedo did not mention the incident in his writings, Gómara may have been referring to an attempt to publish the second part of the *Historia general y natural* (books 20–38). Oviedo had planned to publish the second part around 1542, according to a letter he sent to Viceroy Antonio de Mendoza (Tudela 1992, cxxxiii). It is possible that he may have presented a version of his manuscript, containing the first and second parts, to the Council of the Indies around 1548, for the 1547 Salamanca edition only includes the first. At this time Oviedo declared that he hoped to publish the "primera parte, acrescentada y enmendada" [first part, enlarged and amended] and the second, while he would continue working on the third (Oviedo 1992, 1:142; Tudela 1992, cxxxix–cxl). If he had really submitted the second part, it is quite possible that the council had not yet agreed to approve its publication. In any case, Las Casas was in Spain between 1547 and 1556 and had good reason to interfere with the *Historia general y natural*.

CONTESTED HISTORIES IN A
CHANGING DISCURSIVE LANDSCAPE

Gómara intended to create an authoritative account of the conquest of the Indies, but he had to contend with a contested field and changing politics. This situation is well exemplified in Las Casas's criticism of Oviedo. Las Casas considered the *Historia general y natural* dangerous mainly because of the images that Oviedo propagated with respect to the conquest, the *encomienda*, and the Indians. In his *Historia de las Indias*, Las Casas was greatly concerned about the impact that Oviedo's characterizations of the Indians might have on his readers. The problem for Las Casas was the kind of authority that Oviedo's work was acquiring among the European public:

> *Levántoles a éstos destas islas y a otros munchos y a todos los destas Indias falsísimos testimonios, cierto, infamándolos de grandes pecados y de ser bestias; porque nunca abrió la boca, en tocando en indios, sino para decir mal dellos. Y estas infamias han volado cuasi por todo el mundo, como ha días que temerariamente publicó su falsa historia, dándole el mundo crédito, el cuál él no merecía por sus falsedades grandes y munchas que dixo destas gentes. Pero el mundo no considera más de que se ponga en molde (1988–1998, 5:1856–1857).*

> He raised the most false testimonies against those of these islands and many others throughout these Indies, in fact, accusing them of great sins and of being beasts, for he never opened his mouth, with respect to the Indians, except to speak ill of them. And these infamies have spread nearly throughout the world, in as many days since he recklessly published his false history, the world giving him credit, which he did not deserve for his great and many falsities that he said about these people. But the world believes nothing more than what is put in print.

The question of the capacity of the Indians had a central importance in the debates concerning the justice of the conquest and the treatment of the indigenous population. The debate was evolving throughout the first half of the sixteenth century, but around 1548, when Oviedo may have presented his work to the council for its approval, it had acquired enormous importance in the political realm.

The debate directly affected the aspirations of the Spanish conquistadors and settlers to become lords. The expectation of the Spaniards was to receive an *encomienda* in return for the services they had rendered to the crown in the conquest and colonization of the Indies. The *encomienda* system had its roots in medieval Spain where the war of territorial expansion was formalized through royal concessions of territorial jurisdiction, vassals, and titles of nobility (Elliott 1984a, 156–158; Lockhart and Schwartz 1983, 19–22).[21] Whatever service Spaniards had lent to the crown, time-honored Spanish custom mandated their subsequent reward in compensation for their efforts. Recompense in war normally consisted of the right to a share of the spoils after sacking a city. In the Indies, the crown preferentially granted *encomiendas* or *repartimientos* as incentives for its vassals to conquer and settle territory. The Indian *encomiendas* placed certain indigenous communities under the authority of a conquistador or a settler who had the responsibility of seeing to their evangelization and received the right to extract tribute in labor or goods from them.[22] In this sense the *encomienda* satisfied a dual necessity: it permitted the organization of native labor and evangelization,[23] and it served to compensate the activities of conquest and settlement of the new territories. But as soon as the attacks on the capacity of the Indians fell into discredit, the advisability of maintaining the *encomienda* regime was put into question.

The indigenous situation began to receive closer attention as soon as accusations of injustices committed in the conquests and *encomiendas* surfaced. The mistreatment and abuses endured by the Indians at the hands of the Spaniards became a serious concern when the pattern of their demographic decline had become evident.[24] The experience of colonization contradicted the idea that the native population could derive some benefit from being submitted to the authority of the conquistadors. John Elliott (1984b, 304–310) has stated that agitation concerning the well-being of the indigenous population reached its peak when Charles V returned to Spain in 1541 and did not culminate until 1550 in the long debate in Valladolid between Las Casas and Sepúlveda.[25] The importance that this debate had for historiographical discourse fundamentally rests in the fact that it transformed the conditions within which forms of textual authority could be established. The historiographical treatment of questions referring to the Indians and the conquests had to delicately navigate between the pressures of the conquistadors and *encomenderos,* the campaigns of those who advocated indigenous freedom and the abolition of the *encomienda,* and the complicated situation of a colonial administration incapable of implementing effective solutions to the problems that the process of colonization presented.

Oviedo's *Historia general y natural* attempted to legitimate the territorial dominion that Spain exercised over the New World, the plundering of indigenous territories that had been carried out in the conquests, the subjection of the native population to the service regimen of the *encomienda* and, in some cases, Indian slavery. Concomitantly, although he criticized the excesses of some conquistadors and *encomenderos,* he fundamentally tried to justify the destruction of the indigenous population and present the conquest of the Indies as a process that had produced great benefits for the New World. Oviedo's argument is based in part on the opinion concerning the capacity of the Indians that Las Casas had attempted to combat:

> *Porque, en la verdad, segund afirman todos los que saben estas Indias (o parte dellas), en ninguna provincia de las islas o de la Tierra Firme, de las que los cristianos han visto hasta agora, han faltado ni faltan algunos sodomitas, demás de ser todos idólatras, con otros muchos vicios, y tan feos, que muchos dellos, por su torpeza y fealdad, no se podrían escuchar sin mucho asco y vergüenza, ni yo los podría escrebir por su mucho número y suciedad (1992, 1:67).*

> Because, in truth, according to what everyone who knows these Indies (or part of them) says, in no province of the islands or the mainland, which Christians have seen up to now, have there lacked or are there lacking any sodomites, the rest all being idolaters, with many other vices, and so ugly, that many of them, for their stupidity and foulness, could not be heard without much disgust and shame, nor could I write about them for their great number and filthiness.

Based on this representation of the Indians, Oviedo could interpret the destruction of the native population as divine punishment and justify the need for the *encomienda* and native slavery. At the same time, he was conscious of the objections that had been raised against these kinds of colonizing practices and he had to deal with them. Nevertheless, he maintained his position and testified negatively about "el ser y capacidad de los indios" [the condition and capacity of the Indians] before the Council of the Indies on at least two occasions, at Toledo in 1525 and Medina del Campo in 1532.

Oviedo figured that, given the conflicting opinions that existed among the missionaries of different religious orders, he could support his negative assessment of the Indians based on his personal experience. For him it was fundamentally a question of conscience until an official decision was reached among the theologians who advised the crown:

> Así que yo me remito a estos religiosos dotos, después que estén acordados. Y entre tanto, esté sobre aviso quien indios tuviere, para los tratar como a prójimos, e vele cada cual sobre su conciencia (1992, 1:68).

> Thus I defer to these learned religious, until after they come to an agreement. And in the meantime, whoever possesses Indians should be on his guard, in order to treat them as neighbors, and each one tend to his own conscience.

The position adopted by Oviedo recognizes the importance that the decisions of theologians and legal scholars had on the public conscience. These theological and juridical resolutions came to alter the idea of what constituted a good conscience in both public and private spheres with respect to the treatment of the Indians. In the 1540s, these new conditions changed the way authors could write about the Indies.

Openly expressing his support of the conquest, Gómara's intervention attempted to maintain the old status quo after the confrontation had already reached its turning point. The struggle sustained before theologians and lawyers by various missionaries initially led to continued vacillation in the legislation and policies adopted with respect to the Indians. Their efforts to stop the abuses were met by opposition from corrupt royal officials, some of whom had an economic stake in *encomiendas* or were accepting bribes from Spanish settlers.[26] In spite of Las Casas's successful 1519 confrontation with Juan de Quevedo in defense of Indian freedom and Cardinal Adrian of Utrecht's similar intervention in the Spanish court the following year, powerful interests still managed to subvert Charles V's 1520 order to abolish the *encomienda*. In subsequent years, further negative legislative effects resulted from testimonies attacking the Indians' capacity made before the Council of the Indies by *fray* Tomás Ortiz in 1525 and *fray* Domingo de Betanzos in 1533 and 1545. Their accusations helped the council's president, Cardinal Loaysa, secure the revocation in 1525 and 1534 of some royal decrees aimed at eliminating Indian slavery (Gómara 1552, 1:117v–118r; Hanke 1974, 11–13, 18–19; Adorno 1992b, 49–50). These negative characterizations of the native inhabitants, however, began to lose their political and rhetorical efficacy as the intellectual debate over the Indies changed.

By the time Gómara met Cortés in the siege of Algiers, the ideologies that supported the previous policies in the Indies were already loosing their persuasive force. In the period between 1537 and 1549, the objections against Indian slavery, the *encomienda,* and the conquests had acquired such importance that earlier views of colonization were no longer tenable within the social consensus. Rolena Adorno (1992b) has shown that around the middle of the sixteenth century, broad generalizations, whether positive or negative, gave way to a more differentiated approach based on situations and conditions in specific locations. The first important change came when *fray* Bernardino de Minaya solicited the intervention of Pope Paul III in favor of the native population in 1537. The result of Minaya's efforts was the proclamation of the bulls *Altitudo divini consilii, Veritas ipsa,* and *Sublimis Deus,* where the ecclesiastical jurisdiction over the Indians was upheld, their enslavement was condemned, and opinions stating that they were irrational and incapable of receiving the Christian faith were classified as heretical. The papal bulls were accompanied by a pastoral letter setting the penalty of excommunication for those who persisted in the practices condemned in the bulls. J. H. Parry (1940, 27–29) states that, upon his return to Spain, Minaya was sent to prison and Charles solicited the revocation of the bulls that threatened royal authority over the Indies. Minaya's incarceration and the petition for revocation show the degree of concern with which the crown received Paul III's bulls, whose major effect was to provide an answer to the kind of questions that somebody like Oviedo would have previously deemed a matter of conscience.

The interplay of interests and value systems had also changed in the process, thus creating new constraints for the historian. The *visita* or inspection of the Council of the Indies and the promulgation of the New Laws in 1542, abolishing the *encomienda* and prohibiting the Spaniards' utilization of Indians for personal service, suggest that reaffirming imperial authority required a political formula of compromise with the papal decrees of 1537.[27] According to Anthony Pagden (1990b, 6), one of the fundamental concerns of the crown was to show its adherence to the ethical and political principles of Christianity. For a crown that based its rights over the Indies in the Alexandrian bull of concession (1493), the most appropriate course of action from a political perspective was to proceed in harmony with Paul III's bulls or, if this was not possible, try to obtain their revocation through proper channels. Although the questions concerning Indian slavery and their capacity to receive the faith were settled by these decrees, the debate drifted away from the theological realm into the problem of deciding the best mode of governing the Indians and incorporating them into Christian society.

Gómara also faced other factors that contributed to changing the strategic situation of the discourse. The position that many conquistadors and colonial administrators continued to sustain in the face of the New Laws placed them in difficult political terrain. The resistance of *encomenderos* in Mexico and the rebellion of conquistadors in Peru had led to the revocation in 1545 of the laws eliminating the *encomienda*, but Las Casas had managed to transform the debate from the topic of the capacity of the Indians to the treatment they received from the Spaniards (Adorno 1992b). If he accused them of violating the rights of the Indians, the rebellion in Peru completed the polarization of the conquistadors against the royal authorities.[28] The colonists' crimes not only were a liability to the emperor's political authority, they were an outrage against the very social system that the crown was attempting to establish in the New World. Their resistance to carry out the crown's ordinances clearly placed in doubt their capacity to oversee the integration of the native population into colonial society. The *encomenderos'* failure to secure their grants "a perpetuidad, con jurisdicción civil y criminal sobre los indios" [in perpetuity, with civil and criminal jurisdiction over the Indians], and the monarch's suspension of the conquests in 1550 reveal that the position of the conquistadors and *encomenderos* had lost credibility before the crown.[29]

Establishing a hegemonic discourse within governmental and administrative circles presented serious difficulties for Gómara, even when deploying forms of textual affiliation to create a sense of intellectual authority. Spanish discourses on colonization could accommodate polemic or compromise, but they could not achieve authority or consensus. An example of this is Sepúlveda's *Democrates secundus* (ca. 1544), a treatise composed by the prestigious Aristotelian scholar at the request of Cardinal Loaysa in order to justify the conquest and the right of the conquistadors to have *encomiendas*. In spite of the fact that his *Democrates secundus* had been commissioned by Loaysa, who was president of the Council of the Indies at the time, permission for its publication was denied by the institution. Sepúlveda appealed the decision to the Council of Castile, which appointed a commission of theologians who also decided against it. The text circulated in the court in manuscript form and, according to Sepúlveda, received the approval of everyone who read it, but it never achieved the backing of the crown to render "service to God and the king" that Loaysa hoped it might (Hanke 1974, 61–64). His *Apologia pro libro de justis belli causis* (Defense of the book on the subject of just war), subsequently published in Rome in 1555, defended his *Democrates secundus,* but it was banned and confiscated by order of the Council of the Indies (León Pinelo 1629, 66).

The lack of a well-established discourse of colonization is apparent in the outcome of the Valladolid debate, which did not settle the question of whether it was appropriate to identify the conquest with the values of the empire (Adorno 1988). The seven treatises that Las Casas published in Seville in 1552 proposed a disassociation between Spanish imperial claims and the conduct of the conquistadors.[30] By that time it was already evident that the Indians had an established position as subjects of the crown who should benefit from the colonial relationship between Spain and the Indies, rather than just being objects of economic exploitation. It was in response to this controversy that Gómara proposed a concept of common good consisting of recompensing the conquerors and, at the same time, protecting the conquered. This idea of colonial government was founded on an equilibrium between distributive justice (granting favors to the conquistadors for their services) and commutative justice (guaranteeing the good treatment of the indigenous population) and therefore called attention to the ways and means of achieving justice in the New World. The way in which the *Historia general* discusses the realization of colonial ideals in the Indies undoubtedly responds to the conditions set by the debate. Moreover, by referring his readers to Sepúlveda for the justification of the conquest Gómara was searching for a way out of the ideological stalemate constraining the empire.

Gómara confronted the difficult task of influencing public views where others had failed. The debate over the nature of the Indians, which a decade earlier Oviedo merely left to the individual's conscience, had become stained by political pragmatism and ideological struggle. When Las Casas questioned and rejected the assumptions of Oviedo's defamatory discourse, he attributed his opinions to the self-interest of an owner of Indian slaves (1988–1998, 5:2384). Although Las Casas (1988–1998, 4:1326–1335, 1523, 1527, 5:1855–1861, 2381–2401) supported his refutation of Oviedo's ideas with historical argumentation, the discursive context also had changed. These conditions framed the way Gómara understood his position vis-à-vis the historiographical tradition of the Indies and how his own practice could achieve political and intellectual viability. The manner in which he strategically situated himself in the discourse is revealed by his portrayal of Cortés as the model conquistador. Therefore, it is necessary to examine their relationship in order to explain Gómara's method of intellectual production and the ways in which his writing interacted with forms of political activity during the reign of Charles V.

THE AUTHORITY OF DISCOURSE: THE *HISTORIA GENERAL* AND THE WORLD OF FERNANDO CORTÉS

Gómara was entering a contentious arena when he started writing the history of the conquest. He evidently knew of the impediments confronting him, and it is likely that he went to Aragon to obtain the royal imprimatur for his work in order to circumvent the censorship within the kingdom of Castile. He likely sought to disseminate his history in order to influence public views of the conquest and help create a hegemonic discourse on colonization. The contradictions of Spanish imperialism must have been daunting, but Gómara's project sought to draw its strength from featuring Cortés as the charismatic hero of the conquest. Gómara's remembrance of the deceased conqueror served to further the honor of his family by creating an exalted portrait of his merits, virtues, and accomplishments. Given that political action took place in networks of personal relations within a patrimonial system, Gómara was negotiating his personal stake not only in the history of the conquest, but also in the politics of empire, which most often were played out in the court.

Gómara's historiographical project, therefore, must be understood in relation to the intellectual atmosphere and practices of the courtesan world. Although his position in the Spanish court is not clearly known, various documents describe him as a "clérigo, rresidente en la corte de sus Magestades" [cleric, resident in the court of their Majesties].[31] Less opaque is the manner in which the courtesan environment shaped the character of Gómara's historiographical activity. His first encounter with this world occurred during his stay in Italy (possibly between 1531 and 1541), where he witnessed events in the papal court and had contact with political and intellectual figures such as Olaus Magnus (1490–1557) and Diego Hurtado de Mendoza (1503–1575).[32] Gómara conducted his historiographical activity as a form of service that he attempted to render by treating topics of interest among the figures of social, intellectual, or political authority associated with the court of Charles V. For example, in his *Anales* he consistently listed events and information primarily relevant to the great political concerns of the crown or other incidents that would attract the attention of the court. Topics that continually reappear include the dangers presented by the Ottoman Turks, events occurring in the Indies, the conflicts between Spain and France (first between Ferdinand of Aragón and Louis XII of France, then between Charles V and François I), and the heresy of Martin Luther. This way of approaching historiographical practice is evident in the way Gómara presented his *Crónica de los Barbarrojas* to *don* Pedro Álvarez de Osorio, the marquis of Astorga. In order to explain why it was important to write about the Barbarossa corsairs, he appealed to the kind of presence that the problem of Ottoman aggression had in the political consciousness of the period:

> ¡Ojalá tan fáçilmente se pudiese remediar como llorar, proveer como leer! Muy bien tiene entendido todo esto el Emperador nuestro Señor, y ha procurado ya y aun probado el remedio dello. . . . [N]i puede entender ansi ligeramente una cosa como esta que requiere costa, poder y consejo (1853, 334).

> O if it could be as easily remedied as crying [or] dispatched as reading! The emperor, our lord, has understood all this very well and has already provided and even proven its remedy. . . . Nor can he take lightly something like this which requires expenditure, power, and counsel.

The positions that Gómara took on matters concerning the intellectual and political environment he encountered at the court fundamentally derived from his experience while working in the service of Cortés. He had probably met the marquis in Algiers while taking part in Charles V's aborted 1541 expedition and continued in the conquistador's service until his death.[33] This relationship must have had a fundamental impact on Gómara's career if we follow the opinion of Robert Lewis (1983, 30–31) who suggested that his presence in Charles V's court resulted from his association with Cortés. At least this is undoubtedly correct with respect to his activities as a historian, for Gómara was already serving as Cortés's chaplain when he began to write his early works. He understood his historiographical activity within the framework of his working relationship with the conquistador, as is evident in the dedication of his *Crónica de los Barbarrojas*. He explained to the marquis of Astorga that he wrote to "hacer[le] serviço . . . porque habeys tomado deudo con el marques del Valle, cuya historia yo escrivo, casando á Don Alvaro Perez de Ossorio vuestro hijo mayor con su hija mayor Doña Maria" [do him service . . . because you have become an in-law of the marquis of the Valley, whose history I am writing, your oldest son *don* Álvaro Pérez de Osorio being married to his oldest daughter *doña* María] (1853, 332).

Gómara's relationship with the conquistador and his relatives also influenced the positions he took in the *Historia general*. One document explicitly states that Martín Cortés, the primogenitive heir of the marquis, paid him for writing the second part of the *Historia general,* or the *Conquista de México*.[34] After Fernando Cortés's death, Gómara continued working in the service of his son Martín for at least twelve more years. The payment that he gave him for the *Historia general* suggests that Gómara had received the commission to write the work from the marquis before his death in 1547 or else Martín Cortés subsequently commissioned it to leave a record of his father's services to the crown.[35] In either case, it is important to note that the work served in a sufficiently explicit way to give prestige to the name of Fernando Cortés and promote the interests of his family. The *Conquista de México* not only exalted Cortés the individual, it also emphasized the value of his services to the emperor and presented them as one of the foundations of the colonial empire. Gómara's account served his patron's interests in such a specific manner that it may have had some legal utility for the family at the time of reclaiming recompense from the crown.[36]

The degree to which the *Historia general* served Cortés's interests was evident to contemporary historians as well. The best-known case of this is that of Bernal Díaz del Castillo who reacted against the way that Gómara had lauded Cortés's role in his account of the conquest of Mexico. Rolena Adorno (1988) has shown that Díaz's criticism of the *Conquista de México* was mediated by his own personal interests, but it most certainly was motivated by Gómara's treatment of Cortés and the conquest. Similar reactions can also be found among historians whose economic interests were not directly affected by the account. Oviedo probably had Gómara's *Historia general* in mind when he said that he had "visto algunos memoriales o acuerdos escriptos por algunos aficionados suyos, a quienes se les encomendaría que escribiesen en su alabanza, o ellos, por su comedimiento, harían por complacer a sus subcesores, o por cualquier causa que a ello les moviese" [seen some memorials or remembrances written by some fans of his, who were commissioned to write in praise of him, or they, out of courtesy, would do it to please his descendents, or for any other reason that moved them] (1992, 4:265). In a similar manner, Las Casas (1988–1998, 5:1870, 2251, 2256, 2382, 2466–2472) thought that Gómara's narrative in the *Historia general* was influenced by his position in Cortés's service as "su capellán y criado después de marqués" [his chaplain and servant after becoming the marquis]. Because of the way Gómara presented Cortés, Las Casas supposed that the composition of the work owed a substantial debt to the conquistador's collaboration:

> *Así que Gómara muncho se alarga imponiendo a Cortés, su amo, lo que en aquellos tiempos no sólo por pensamiento, estando despierto, pero ni durmiendo, por sueños, parece poder pasarle. Pero como el mismo Cortés, después de marqués, dictó lo que había de escribir Gómara, no podía sino fingir de sí todo lo que le era favorable; porque, como subió tan de súpito [sic] de tan baxo a tan alto estado, ni aun hijo de hombre, sino de Júpiter, desde su origen quisiera ser estimado.*
>
> *Y así, de este jaez (y por este camino) fue toda la historia de Gómara ordenada, porque no escribió otra cosa sino lo que Cortés de sí mismo testificaba; con que al mundo – que no sabía de su principio, medio y fin cosa – Cortés y Gómara encandilaron (1988–1998, 5:1871).*

Thus Gómara greatly extends himself, attributing to Cortés, his master, what in those times not only could seemingly come into his mind while awake, but also asleep in his dreams. But as Cortés himself, after becoming a marquis, dictated what Gómara had to write, he could not but make up everything that was favorable to him; for rising so suddenly from so low to such a high status, he wished his origin to be esteemed as not just a son of man, but of Jupiter.

And thus in this manner (and in this way) all of Gómara's *Historia* was put together, because he did not write anything other than what Cortés himself testified, so that Cortés and Gómara blinded the world, which knew nothing about his beginning, middle, and end.

The comments of Las Casas and Oviedo suggest the extent that Gómara's praise of Cortés conformed to the image that the conqueror and his descendants wanted to disseminate. The public function of his *Historia general* specifically was to promote Cortés's desire to appear as a "man of status" in the Spain of Charles V. The concept of service that guided Gómara's composition operated within the limited social, political, and intellectual scope of his patron's personal interests. The servile relationship that he had with Cortés was the condition of production that defined the economy of enunciation of his discourse within the framework of courtesan culture. In his dedication to Charles, he assumed that he could coherently represent the interests of Cortés as an individual, the conquistadors as a collectivity, and the crown as an institution, along with the common good of the Indies. By 1552, however, it was impossible to talk about conquistadors, Indians, friars, advisors, governors, and *encomenderos* in a general manner without compromising, in one way or another, the stakes of the different individuals involved. The political viability of Gómara's discourse fundamentally rested on the receptivity that certain sectors of the court had toward the position and values that the conquistador embodied.

Over the course of his life, Cortés had managed to secure the amity of individuals of influence and authority in the court of the emperor. His marriage to *doña* Juana de Zúñiga—the daughter of the count of Aguilar, *don* Carlos Arellano—had guaranteed him a certain social prestige and presence in the court. This relationship also gave political solvency to his position, at least from the perspective of Gómara, who suggests that his father-in-law and his father-in-law's brother were "fauorecidos del Emperador" [favored by the emperor] (1552, 2:114r). Along with the count of Aguilar, Cortés's influential political allies in the court included the admiral of Castile and the duke of Béjar (Madariaga 1986, 488). These alliances validated the emperor's favors and mercies to Cortés such as the title of "Marquis of the Valley of Oaxaca" and certain other personal gestures that granted him certain distinction (Madariaga 1986, 523–526). Given the importance of familial ties and personal relationships in political practices at that time, the individual figure of Cortés could easily be subsumed within the position of a sector of the court operating within the kingdom's social structures of political participation.

It is important to clarify, however, that these relationships based on familial alliances did not give Cortés real political power, but merely a more efficient way of furthering his interests and more direct access to the crown.[37] John Elliott (1990, 86–99) has shown that beginning with the reign of the Catholic Monarchs the nobility lost prescriptive political power and the weight of the government began to fall upon the lawyers and secretaries who served as crown officials. This bureaucratization of governmental power in part explains the limitations that confronted Cortés when soliciting royal favors and his interest in creating alliances with important colonial administrators. Because the marquis associated with influential individuals, Gómara and his contemporaries could identify with him as a social subject in the political process of colonial government.[38]

Two such individuals whose friendship Cortés enjoyed were Cardinal Loaysa and Francisco de los Cobos (Gómara 1552, 2:139r). As important members of the colonial administration they held opinions similar to the marquis on issues such as the conquest and the *encomienda.* Cobos was the emperor's secretary and a member of the Council of the Indies. In 1522 he was appointed *"fundidor y marcador mayor"* of the mines of Yucatán, Cuba, Coluacán, and New Spain, a charge whose jurisdiction in 1527 extended from Florida to Panuco and from Darién up to the Gulf of Venezuela (Keniston 1958, 72, 104, 105). In 1534 he managed to get his son Diego named chancellor of the Indies, a responsibility previously held by the grand chancellor, Mercurino Gattinara (Keniston 1958, 149). Loaysa was the emperor's confessor, the head of the Dominicans in Spain, and president of the Council of the Indies from its official creation in 1524 until his death in 1546.[39] He was also the one who encouraged Sepúlveda to write his *Democrates secundus* to justify the conquest and the *encomienda* around the time when he and others were seeking the revocation of some of the New Laws. The friendship that Cortés had with these men reinforced his position as a paradigmatic figure representing the common interests of a sector of the court and the colonial government that supported or was benefiting from the conquest. In fact, Sepúlveda (1997, 66–69) presented Cortés as a model of prudence and utilized the conquest of Mexico as an example to show how the native inhabitants were *natura servi* (slaves by nature) and therefore should be subjugated by the Spaniards.

The environment of the court at the time of the *Historia general*'s composition was undoubtedly a political space of familial relationships, personal interests, and strategic alliances. This atmosphere of courtly relationships and activities made it possible for Gómara to construct a discourse of service centered on the figure of Cortés. Surely it was a form of political elitism that could only have some degree of efficacy within a limited segment of readers. The corrections that Las Casas (1988–1998, 5:1871) made to Gómara concerning the humble origins of Cortés were intended to neutralize the kind of public appeal that Cortés could have as "not just a son of man, but of Jupiter." The *Historia general* paid less attention to Cortés the individual than to what he could represent publicly in the context of political change in the middle of the century. The deaths of Loaysa in 1546 and Cobos and Cortés the following year brought an end to the symbolically most prestigious characters of the process of colonial expansion that Spain had conducted since the 1520s. While working on his *Historia general*, Gómara also witnessed, either directly or indirectly, the censorship of Sepúlveda's *Democrates secundus*, the successful interventions of Las Casas in the Council of the Indies, the suspension of the conquests, and the Valladolid debate. It is quite probable that Gómara may have wanted to see in Cortés a figure capable of representing the collective interests of the conquistadors and a notion of common good under colonial rule.

Gómara's position in the *Historia general* can be coherently interpreted by relating his work to the practices of intellectual production of the courtesan environment in which he operated. He surely participated in the "Academia de Cortés," which brought lawyers and members of the political and ecclesiastical hierarchy together to discuss such varied topics as "la eternidad del alma" [the eternity of the soul], "la diferencia del hablar al escribir" [the difference between speaking and writing], "cual debe ser el cronista del príncipe" [who should be the prince's chronicler], and "la diferencia de la vida rústica a la noble" [the difference between the noble life and the rustic life].[40] The period of the Academia's activity coincides with the period in which the revocation of the New Laws was discussed and Sepúlveda composed his *Democrates secundus*. The years were marked by an atmosphere of political and intellectual tension generated by the debates concerning the nature of the Indian, the justice of the conquest, and the right of the conquistadors to keep and bequeath their *encomiendas* to their heirs. Lewis Hanke (1974, 60) has said that the debate concerning "the true capacity of the Indies . . . became more and more heated after the issuance of the New Laws of 1542, and the revocation in 1545 of the law that would have phased out the *encomienda*." These are also the years in which Cortés was embroiled in litigations for "his vassals and privileges" (Gómara 1552, 2:139r; Madariaga 1986, 551–556).

Demetrio Ramos (1972, 113) suggests that in these meetings were present, among others, two central figures for contemplating this courtesan context of intellectual production: Sepúlveda and Mexía. The royal chronicler Mexía was also well known as a humanist for his *Silva de varia lección*. Sepúlveda had acquired notoriety in the Indian debate with his *Democrates secundus* and his active pressure to propagate his ideas (Hanke 1974, 62–64). Gómara's approach to writing his *Historia general* may share the kind of political and intellectual conceptualization of the New World found in these other authors' works. In his chapter entitled "Loor de españoles" (Praise of Spaniards), Gómara openly expressed his allegiance to the *Democrates secundus*:

> *Yo escriuo sola, y breuemente, la conquista de Indias. Quien quisiere ver la justificacio[n] della lea al dotor Sepulueda, coronista del Emperador, que la escriuio en latin dotissimamente. Y assi quedara satisfecho del todo (1552, 1:121v).*

> I write only, and briefly, about the conquest of the Indies. Anyone who would like to see the justification for it should read Doctor Sepúlveda, the emperor's chronicler, who wrote most eruditely about it in Latin. And thus you will be completely satisfied.

In deferring to Sepúlveda's work, Gómara clearly intended to establish a kind of textual affiliation that appealed to the political and intellectual circles of the court in which Sepúlveda had remained active (Hanke 1974, 62). As a space of intellectual production the familial meetings of the Academia de Cortés and the courtesan environment in general no doubt stimulated the articulation of political concerns with the instruments of the humanist and learned culture of the time. The political elitism revealed in the *Historia general*'s transparent exaltation of Cortés finds its legitimation in the sophistication of the intellectual culture surrounding it. The narrative that Gómara employed in his account of the conquest of Mexico echoed the argument of Sepúlveda (1997, 66) concerning the qualities of "prudentia, ingenio, magnitudine animi, temperantia, humanitate, et religione" [prudence, ingenuity, magnanimity, moderation, humanity, and religion] that legitimated the conquest, but above all it demonstrated the military, legal, and political prowess of Cortés the individual. Using this kind of representation to give social vitality to his patron's public image, Gómara attempted to serve a sector in whose public preeminence he saw the most perfect realization of his social ideals as well as the realization of the common good under the Spanish empire of the Indies.

THE LIMITS OF CONSENSUS: GÓMARA UNDER ATTACK

Sepúlveda's *Democrates secundus* helped Gómara define a theoretical framework to support his vision of the New World from the ethical and juridical point of view. In this way, he successfully achieved a certain rhetorical efficacy at the same time that he situated himself polemically and intellectually in relation to the controversy over the conquest. Gómara's move is comparable to one that Pedro Mexía contemporaneously made in his *Historia del emperador* when he deferred to Oviedo's authority to confirm that the Christian faith had been brought to the Indies. This practice of citation that both Gómara and Mexía employed in support of their texts, however, did not rest on any discursive consensus concerning the impact of the conquest in the New World. Therefore, Gómara was unable to establish a form of intellectual authority over the Indies through the mechanisms of textual affiliation. For as Oviedo's deference to the king's theologians aptly demonstrates, juridical and theological debates greatly conditioned the social communicability of the discourse. Anyone narrating or reading about Spanish discoveries and conquests in the Indies around 1552 had to contend with a wide spectrum of confrontation over the nature of the native population and the justice of the conquest.

The publication of the *Historia general* addressed the dominant ideological vacuum afflicting the imperial enterprise. Not only had the legitimacy of its methods been publicly challenged, the role of the conquest in facilitating evangelization had been called into question. The influence that friars like Las Casas were acquiring over the course of the century can be related to the increasingly greater urgency to find a more effective way of integrating the native population within Christian society. The failure of colonial society to achieve these objectives had damaging consequences from the political perspective. In this way the polemical context in which the *Historia general* appeared greatly undermined the possibility of an uncritical reception and encouraged skepticism and mistrust among its readers.

The *Historia general* was prohibited on November 17, 1553, in the city of Valladolid, just one year after its publication. The *cédula*, countersigned by Juan de Samano, secretary of the Council of the Indies,[41] on behalf of Prince Philip ordered the book's seizure in the kingdoms of the crown of Castile (Pérez Pastor 1895, 93–97; Medina 1958, 262–265; CDIU 1885–1932, 14:126, 240). Two copies of the decree were immediately sent to the House of Trade—one to the treasurer Francisco Tello and the other to other officials there. The *cédula* ordered them to conduct an inspection of the fleet that was anchored at San Lúcar de Barrameda and to "no dexar ni consentir pasar ninguno de los dichos libros a las dichas Yndias y hagáis todas las diligencias que ser puedan para saver si en la flota que está presta . . . se llevan algunos de los dichos libros" [not let or allow any of the said books to pass to the Indies and make all possible diligence to know whether the fleet that is ready . . . is carrying any of the said books] (Lewis 1983, 317–318). The order applied to all cities and towns in Castile, but today the register of the decree's application is kept in the city of Seville. The prohibition forbidding the printing, sale, possession, and reading of the *Historia general* dictated:

> *Sabed que Francisco López de Gómara, clérigo, ha hecho un libro intitulado, "La Historia de las Indias y conquista de México," el qual se ha impreso, y porque no conviene quel dicho libro se venda ni lea ni se impriman más libros, sino los que están impresos se recojan y traigan al Consejo Real de las Indias de Su Magestad, vos mando á todos é á cada uno de vos, según dicho es, que luego que ésta veáys os informéys y sepáis qué libros de los susodichos hay impresos en esas ciudades, villas y lugares, é todos aquellos que halláredes, los recojáis y enviéis con brevedad al dicho Consejo de las Indias (Medina 1958, 264–265).*

> Know that Francisco López de Gómara, cleric, has written a book titled *La Historia de las Indias y conquista de México*, which has been published, and because it is not suitable for the said book to be sold or read or more books printed, but rather those that are printed are to be collected and brought to the Royal Council of the Indies of His Majesty, I order you all and each one of you, according to what is said, that as soon as you see this inform yourselves and know what printed copies of the aforementioned book exist in these cities, towns, and places, and all those that you find, gather and send them quickly to the said Council of the Indies.

The decree was effectively transmitted by means of public proclamation. On January 8, 1554, the *licenciado* Villagómez of the Council of the Indies appeared in Seville before the notary Luis de Varsuto, who had twelve booksellers declare what editions of the work they had sold and to whom. The next day a proclamation that prohibited "tener ni vender ni imprimir ni leer" [possessing, selling, printing, and reading] Gómara's *Historia general* was read in the plaza of San Francisco and on the docks of the city (Medina 1958, 262–264). The efforts to suppress the work were not limited to the diligence of council officials in 1553 and 1554. A *cédula* issued in Madrid on September 26, 1562, ordered the *corregidor* of the city of Soria to seize Gómara's papers associated with the *Historia general*, inventory them, and bring them to the Council of the Indies (Medina 1958, 266). A second *cédula* similar to the earlier prohibition was issued in Bosque de Segovia on August 7, 1566, this time countersigned by Francisco de Eraso, secretary of the Council of the Indies.[42]

Extant documentation does not reveal the reasons for the prohibition, nevertheless a plausible explanation could be found if one considers that the institution actively dedicated to bringing this about was the Council of the Indies. Although many theories on the reasons behind the prohibition exist, none of them is particularly compelling.[43] The policies of censorship afoot in the kingdoms of Castile shed little light on the possible reasons for the *Historia general*'s prohibition. Robert Lewis (1983, 325–326) thought that Gómara overlooked some step in the process of gaining the necessary approval for his work; however, the basic procedure established by the Catholic Monarchs in 1502 was to require a royal license authorizing publication (Elliott 1990, 225–226). The first edition had a *licencia de impresión,* or royal imprimatur, authorized by Prince Philip for the kingdoms of the crown of Aragón. The *privilegio de impresión,* or publication rights, included at the end of the work stated that "nos visto primero el dicho libro por algunas personas doctas, y hauida relacion dellas, que dicho libro es vtil, y trata fielmente la dicha [h]ystoria de las Indias, conquistas de Mexico, y descubrimientos dellas, y de las costumbres de los naturales" [we first had the said book examined by some learned persons and received their report that the said book is useful, and treats faithfully the said history of the Indies, the conquests of Mexico, and their discoveries, and the customs of the natives] (1552, 2:[140]r). The license approving its publication had been awarded by the archbishop of Zaragoza, *don* Hernando de Aragón (1552,

2:[*i*]v).[44] In addition to his authority for granting the imprimatur as archbishop, he had sufficient influence to have provided the position of chronicler of the kingdom of Aragón in 1548 to a historian of the stature of Jerónimo de Zurita. If the work had the support of "learned persons," one would have to assume that the problems arose after the *Historia general* was published.

The question becomes whether the work had been reviewed by the Council of the Indies before its publication, as Lewis argued on the basis of a royal *cédula* that stated:

> *a Nos se a hecho relación que algunas personas han hecho e cada día hazen libros que tratan de cosas de las nuestras Yndias e los han hecho e hazen ynprimir sin nuestra licencia. Y . . . a nuestro servicio conviene que tales libros no se ynpriman ni vendan sin que primero sean vistos y examynados en el nuestro Consejo de las Yndias (1983, 325).*

> It has been reported to us that some persons have composed and each day compose books that deal with matters concerning our Indies and have been written and printed without our permission. And . . . it suits our service that such books not be printed and sold without first being seen and examined in our Council of the Indies.

It is important to remember, however, that this *cédula* only appeared in 1556, three years after the *Historia general*'s prohibition. Lewis's argument calls attention to the preponderant role that the Council of the Indies had in the censorship of the *Historia general.* His explanation suggests that there were some points of conflict between the book and imperial policy, specifically Gómara's siding with the *encomenderos* of Peru and Mexico, his glorification of Cortés, his treatment of the vices and virtues of the Indians, and his support of forced conversion (Lewis 1983, 324).[45] Lewis concluded that the council did not want the *Historia general* circulated in the Indies "no doubt because they considered it a dangerous, inflammatory book which would feed the fires of dissent and discontent" (1983, 324). Nevertheless, even though Lewis presented convincing arguments suggesting that Gómara's *Historia general* may have displeased members of the Council of the Indies, this does not necessarily explain its censorship.

One could likewise speculate that the council may have performed an arbitral function in the banning of Gómara's *Historia general* if one considers that the prohibitions of Oviedo's *Historia general y natural* and

Sepúlveda's *Democrates secundus* were solicited by Las Casas. The cases of Oviedo and Sepúlveda would suggest that criticisms of the conquest and colonization of the Indies were getting the attention of the colonial administration. Given the affiliation of the *Historia general* with the *Democrates secundus,* Las Casas could have easily argued that Gómara's work contained ideas harmful to the Indians' well-being. The Council of the Indies had participated in censorship activities at least since the prohibition against Cortés's *Letters* in 1527. Rolena Adorno and Patrick Pautz (1999, 2:5–9) have cited a *cédula* from the Council of the Indies dated June 1, 1527, that explicitly states that Pánfilo de Narváez had solicited the prohibition because he claimed that Cortés's *Letters* had damaged his reputation. A short time later, however, Francisco Núñez got the same council to cancel the prohibition and order Narváez to return the original *cédula* and proceedings to the court. This case posed a conflict of interest among the conquistadors with respect to their honor. The Council of the Indies performed an arbitral function in this dispute similar to one it might have played if Las Casas had solicited the *Historia general*'s removal from circulation.

Other evidence, however, suggests that beginning in 1550 the council was actively occupied in censoring works about the Indies and that its members were concerned about the social detriment that certain writings on the topic could cause. In this same year a council decree ordered the "gobernador de Tierrafirme tome los libros que hubiere en aquella provincia de los que el Doctor Sepúlveda hizo imprimir sobre cosas tocantes a las Indias sin licencia y los envíe al gobierno" [governor of Tierra Firme to seize the books in the province about matters concerning the Indies that Doctor Sepúlveda published without permission and to send them to the government] (CDIU 1885–1932, 20:212). This same decree was addressed to Peru, New Granada, Hispaniola, and New Spain and included instructions that the officials of Seville were not to allow their passage to the New World. It is also appropriate to remember that the *cédula* of 1556 stipulated that "[n]o se impriman libros tocantes a las Indias sin licencia y los impresos se tomen" [no books about the Indies are to be printed without permission and those printed are to be seized] (CDIU 1885–1932, 20:209). This policy of censorship could be interpreted as a reaction to the dominant ideas among theologians and legal scholars with respect to justice in the conquest and the treatment of the native population. The problem was that authors' statements often contradicted doctrinal and legal principles.

Such is the case with the censorship of Las Casas's treatises published in 1552 and 1553 where he debated the legal foundations of the empire and strongly criticized the conquest and the *encomienda*. Although most of these texts were printed without royal licenses, there is ample evidence that they were examined by theologians, royal functionaries, and members of the court.[46] The censorship of one of these treatises, the *Confesionario*, is particularly interesting because it left Las Casas's criticisms of the conquest and the *encomienda* intact. Las Casas figured that all the conquests carried out in the Indies had been illegitimate and therefore the conquistadors and *encomenderos* were obligated to make restitution for the damages and loss of goods that the Indians had suffered. The *Confesionario* contained rules on how confessors could grant absolution to those who had benefited from the conquest. The bibliographer Antonio de León Pinelo (1629, 62–64) explained that the Council of the Indies ordered the treatise to be seized because of the first and fifth rules, but he added that after its revision the treatise was approved. Based on what may be inferred from the corrections added to the printed edition, the problem for the council involved a legal technicality in the procedures that the confessor had to follow in order to demand from the penitent a public writ obligating the restitution of the goods acquired in the conquest. Once these points of canonical law concerning restitution were corrected, the text received its approval. The censorship of the *Confesionario* reveals that Las Casas's statements about the illegitimacy of the conquest were irrelevant to the council's censors, but discrepancies between the text and the law (even if there were only a few passages) could occasion its removal from circulation.[47]

The *Historia general*'s prohibition is better explained by its affiliation with Sepúlveda's *Democrates secundus* and its position with respect to the juridical problems of the conquest and the treatment of the Indians. León Pinelo simply stated that the *Historia general* "[e]s historia libre i esta mandada recoger por cedula antigua del Co[n]s[ejo] Real de las Indias" [is free history and is ordered to be seized by an old Royal Council of the Indies *cédula*] (1629, 70). Ramón Iglesia and Robert Lewis have interpreted León Pinelo's comment as a reaction to Gómara's support of the conquistadors against the crown; however, it is more probable that the banning of the text was due to its failure to reflect the juridical and theological principles that supported the construction of the empire. The meanings of the word *libre* in the *Diccionario de autoridades* (1726–1739, 4:399) that are applicable to León Pinelo's statement are "licencioso, poco modesto, atrevido y desvergonzado" [licentious, of little modesty, insolent, and shameless] and a "persona que dice ù hace lo que le parece, sin reparar en inconvenientes" [person who says or does what he thinks, without considering the consequences]. Gómara could have been seen as an author who said what he thought "without considering the consequences," for at the end of his *Historia general* he had explicitly embraced Sepúlveda's *Democrates secundus*, despite the fact that it had been prohibited by both the Councils of the Indies and Castile.

The *Historia general* continued to be reprinted in Spanish for only a couple years after the prohibition. It was published in Zaragoza by Agustín Millán in 1552 and 1553, and by Millán in conjunction with Pedro Bernuz in 1554 and 1555; in Medina del Campo by Guillermo de Millis in 1553; and in Antwerp by Martin Nucio and by Hans de Laet in 1554.[48] It is appropriate to note that out of all these editions, only the one published in Medina del Campo omitted the *privilegio de impresión*. The two Antwerp editions alluded to a *privilegio* on the back of the title page, with Nucio's version citing a royal privilege undersigned by P. de Lens. If the prohibition affected only the kingdoms of the crown of Castile, then there was no reason for the authorities to prohibit the editions of Aragón and Antwerp. Nevertheless, Spanish editions of the *Historia general* were only printed between 1552 and 1555, but Italian, French, and English translations of the work continued to be printed throughout the rest of the century.[49] Gómara's *Historia* would not reappear in Spanish until 1749 in the *Historiadores primitivos de las Indias Occidentales* (Early historians of the West Indies) series originally compiled by the Spanish historian Andrés González de Barcia Carballido y Zúñiga (ca. 1654–1723).[50]

The efforts of the Council of the Indies to suppress the *Historia general* contributed more to discrediting the work than to containing its diffusion. When the bibliographer Nicolás Antonio (1672, 334) indicated that Gómara's account was considered unreliable, he mentioned Bernal Díaz del Castillo's criticisms as well as the council's prohibition. Although the *Historia general* achieved a limited number of printings, it became well known among contemporaries and its Spanish editions continued to circulate even beyond the sixteenth century. When Martín García was sent by the *corregidor* of Soria to look for Gómara's papers, he declared to have found in the possession of Pedro Ruiz, the historian's nephew, the edition of the *Historia general* published by

Agustín Millán. Then he added that "el cual dicho libro, por ser público é notorio y haber muchos en muchas partes de como él, se le quedó en poder del dicho Pedro Ruyz" [the said book, for being common knowledge and well known and there being many other copies like it in many places, was left in the possession of the said Pedro Ruiz] (Medina 1958, 268). Additional evidence of its circulation can be found in the lists of books that Luis Padilla imported to New Spain in 1600 and that Juan de Sarria brought to sell in Cuzco in 1606, which have been transcribed and discussed by Irving Leonard (1992, 247–257, 296–300, 360–384, 395–400).[51]

Gómara was the subject of harsh and extensive criticism not only on the part of people such as Las Casas who questioned the legitimacy of the conquest, but also by the conquistadors and their descendents interested in justifying it.[52] The most severe attacks came from Bernal Díaz del Castillo, who commented about the perplexity he felt when reading the *Historia general* while writing his own *Historia verdadera de la conquista de la Nueva España* (True history of the conquest of New Spain). Not only was he embarrassed by its "gran retórica" [grand rhetoric], but also it seemed that "desde el principio y medio hasta el cabo no llevaba buena relación, y va muy contrario que lo que fue e pasó en la Nueva-España" [from the beginning and middle to the end it was not a good account and runs quite contrary to what went on and happened in New Spain] (1982, 33a–34a). Díaz fundamentally rejected Gómara's characterization of the overwhelming strength of the conquistadors over the Indians. Part of the problem was that the image of great massacres tarnished the conquest, but also downplayed the effort and work that the conquistadors contributed to overcome the difficulties that the undertaking presented them. A second point that figures prominently in Díaz's commentary on the *Historia general* is that "toda la honra y prez della la dio sólo al marqués don Hernando Cortés, e no hizo memoria de ninguno de nuestros valerosos capitanes y fuertes soldados" [all the honor and glory for it he only gives to the marquis *don* Fernando Cortés, and he does not remember any of our valiant captains and strong soldiers] (1982, 36a).

When Díaz insists that Gómara's account is flawed, he accuses him of "sublimar" [exalting] the deeds of Cortés and altering the actions, the circumstances, or the actors (1982, 35a–36a). His irritation with the *Historia general* is so pronounced that he says that after setting two gentlemen straight on a few points concerning Cortés's entry into Saltocan, they "juraron que avían de romper el libro e [h]istoria de Gómara que tenían en su poder, pues tantas cosas dize fuera de lo que pasó que no son verdad" [decided that they had to tear up Gómara's book and history, which they had in their possession, for so many things he says happened are not true] (1982, 337b). The points where Díaz accuses the *Historia general* of falsities are numerous, but ultimately they concern defending the honor of the conquistadors or condemning passages that questioned the legitimacy of the conquest. As Rolena Adorno (1988, 242–243) has demonstrated, these two aspects of the collective history of the conquistadors represented a threat to their economic well-being in their claims for favors. In either case, the fundamental issue was that Gómara's account prejudiced the conquistadors or, in Díaz's words, because it was "tan lejos de lo que pasó es en perjuicio de tantos" [so far from what happened, it is in prejudice of so many] (1982, 35a). In fact, in the chapter he dedicated to his criticisms of Gómara's *Historia general,* Díaz explicitly stated that "su majestad sea servido de conocer los grandes e notables servicios que le hicimos los verdaderos conquistadores" [his majesty would be served in knowing the great and notable services that we, the real conquistadors, rendered him] (1982, 35a).

Criticisms of the *Historia general*'s veracity were common among eyewitnesses of the episodes it narrated, primarily because Gómara had accepted versions of the events that some conquistadors had given him without corroborating them. Observations on the poor quality of information that Gómara got from oral accounts are found in Díaz's *Historia verdadera* (1982, 35a); Viceroy Pedro de la Gasca's 1553 letter written to Willem van Male, an advisor to Charles V (Lewis 1983, 294–295); and the Inca Garcilaso de la Vega (1944, 2:266). The Inca attempted to refute Gómara's statements about idolatry among the Incas and some episodes of the conquest of Peru. One of his concerns was to restore the honor of his father for his role during the revolt of the conquistadors of Peru in assisting the rebel leader Gonzalo Pizarro in the battle of Huarina. Likewise he defended the honor of Pizarro's aid, Francisco de Carvajal, whose imprisonment and death he felt Gómara had narrated in an offensive manner. After impugning Gómara's less than decorous observations on Carvajal, the Inca related in his *Historia general del Perú* (General history of Peru) an incident between Gómara and a conquistador who accused him of not having fulfilled his responsibility as a historian:

[E]s assí que un soldado de los más principales y famosos del Perú, que vino a España poco después que salió la historia de Gómara, topándose con él en Valladolid, entre otras palabras que hablaron sobre este caso le dixo que por qué havía escrito y hecho imprimir una mentira tan manifiesta no haviendo passado tal. Con éstas le dixo otras palabras que no se zufre ponerlas aquí. A las cuales respondió Gómara que no era suya la culpa, sino que de los que davan las relaciones nacidas de sus passiones. El soldado le dixo que para eso era la discreción del historiador, para no tomar relación de los tales ni escrevir mucho sin mirar mucho, para no disfamar con sus escritos a los que merecen toda honra y loor. Con esto se apartó Gómara muy confuso y pesante de haver escrito lo que levantaron a Carvajal (1944, 2:266).

It is in this manner that one of the most important and famous soldiers of Peru, who came to Spain shortly after Gómara's *Historia* was published, running across him in Valladolid, among other words they spoke about this case, asked him why he had written and published such a manifest lie when no such thing had happened. Along with these words he told him others that do not bear to be set down here, to which Gómara responded that it was not his fault, but rather that of those who gave him accounts born of their passions. The soldier told him that for this reason it was the discretion of the historian not to accept the account of such people and not to write much without much regard, so as not to defame with his writings those who deserve all honor and praise. With this Gómara was left quite confused and regretful for having written what they leveled at Carvajal.

The soldier accused Gómara of having defamed some conquistadors whose reputations he had shown little consideration for in his account. The case cited by the Inca suggests that the problem the conquistadors had with the *Historia general* mainly was that Gómara had favored certain versions of the events without considering the impact of his account on the reputations of other conquistadors.

These readings of the *Historia general* clearly reveal the centrality of honor in colonial Spanish discourse. In fact the concept was at the heart of the patriarchal ideology of colonization, because it determined the royal favors to which a conquistador could aspire in recompense for his services. Honor, or reputation, not only offered social prestige to the conquistador, it played a large part in determining his economic future. Royal favors were awarded according to a principle of distributive justice that granted "galardones e renumeraçiones de los buenos e virtuosos trabajos e serviçios que los [h]om[br]es fazen a los reyes e prínçipes e a la cosa pública de sus reynos" (Columbus 1996, 262) [rewards and re-munerations of the good and virtuous works and services that men perform for kings and princes and the public welfare of their king-doms] (1996, 72).[53] The conquistadors had a financial stake in represen-tations of the conquest, for the more prominent their services to the king appeared, the greater the reward to which they could aspire. Like-wise, any action that might stain a conquistador's record of services could damage his personal interests.

In the cases of Bernal Díaz and Garcilaso de la Vega, their concern for honor was related to their own solicitations in Spain to obtain mer-cies from the king. Díaz had testified before the Council of the Indies in the debates over the perpetuity of the *encomienda* in 1550 and returned with royal decrees granting him certain favors (Hanke 1974, 59; Adorno 1988, 251). The Inca said he had presented himself before the *licenciado* Lope García de Castro, who rejected his petition because of the inci-dent related by Gómara in the battle of Huarina. When the Inca at-tempted to dispute the circumstances of the event, the *licenciado* re-sponded: "Tienénlo escrito los historiadores ¿y queréislo vos negar?" [Historians have written this, and you wish to deny it?] (Vega 1944, 2:216). The credit Gómara took away from the conquistadors for their services to Spain or the evil deeds he attributed to them had an impact on the response of royal officials or the king himself to the social and economic aspirations of the conquistadors or their heirs.

The rejection and condemnation that the conquistadors or their de-scendants leveled at the *Historia general* reveal that writing Indies his-tory was seen primarily as a space in which to advance the interests of individuals who aspired to the recognition of their values and identi-ties in the cultural realm. In the history of the Indies, however, the honor of the conquistadors and that of the monarchs were not always compatible.

The contradiction between the two intensified around the begin-ning of the seventeenth century. As the main thrust of the conquest came to an end and the crown faced international criticism for its im-perialist policies, the values and identities of the conquistadors lost social currency within Spanish colonialism. The weight that these con-ditions had in historical discourse are evident in the lawsuit that *don* Francisco Arias Dávila, the count of Puñonrostro, brought against the chronicler Antonio de Herrera y Tordesillas in the Council of the Indies around 1602–1610 for his treatment of Pedrarias Dávila in his *Historia general de las Indias Occidentales* (General history of the West Indies). The count presented his quarrel against Herrera as a case of damage to his honor:

> [E]n lo que trata de Pedrarias Davila, mi Abuelo, pone munchas cosas yndignas de hystoria tan grave, e de lo que merescen los servycios de mi Abuelo, fechos en España e en las Indias; porque pone muchas cosas en perxuycio de su [h]onrra, fynxiendo pryncipalmente al Hystoriador de Hernando Cortés, a quien los demas quél alega syguieron, siendo todo lo que disce tan contrario de la verdad, como consta por los prevylexios de las mercedes que los antebesores [sic] de Vuestra Maxestad le fyscieron, en remuneracion de sus servycios, ques a lo que más se [h]a de creer (CDIA 1864–1884, 37:76).

> Concerning Pedrarias Dávila, my grandfather, he writes many things unworthy of such serious history and of what the services of my grandfather performed in Spain and in the Indies merit; because he writes many things in prejudice of his honor, mainly copying Fernando Cortés's historian, whom he alleges everybody else followed, everything he says being so contrary to the truth, as is clear by the privileges and favors that the ancestors of His Majesty did him, in remuneration of his services, which is what has to be more believed.

The count wanted Herrera to revise some statements about his grandfather that, he argued, were not consistent with his services and prejudiced his honor. At stake here was simply his reputation as a servant of the king. Puñonrostro in fact employs the royal favor as proof that Pedrarias Dávila had rendered good service to the king. It is significant, however, that he would link Herrera's treatment of his grandfather to Gómara's *Historia general*.[54] That the count thought he could use "the historian of Fernando Cortés" to discredit Herrera suggests the problematic place that Gómara's work had come to have in historical tradition.

Herrera refused to change his *Historia* so as not to compromise the credibility of his account, arguing that Spain's honor before foreign nations was a stake. He repeatedly insisted that he did not follow any historian but rather the papers that were given to him (CDIA 1864–1884, 37:106–108). His evidence contained a detailed refutation of the memorial presented by the count in which each point was supported primarily by specific references to the royal papers to which he added what was established in historiographical texts.[55] His handling of such texts was based on a concept of tradition that established no one authority, but rather a condition of factual guarantee in his historiographical practice. When Herrera said "la tradyscion ansi lo tiene" [tradition considers it so] (CDIA 1864–1884, 37:117), he was referring to establishing a consensus in different texts only with respect to the facts. Among the authors he cited are figures of such diverse opinions concerning the conquest as Martyr, Oviedo, Las Casas, Gómara, Benzoni, and Theodor de Bry. That Herrera would consider them all as indispensable sources demonstrates that the European criticisms of Spanish imperialism had undermined the moral authority of the historian in the representation of the conquest. In this new economy of enunciation focused on removing infamy from Spain and its monarchs, the *Historia general* resonated only because it corresponded in certain facts with other historical accounts.

Herrera needed to compare the accounts already circulated about the conquest, including authors who had criticized the Spaniards' activities in the New World, because it was the only way that he could gain the trust of his readers. The reason why the tradition was important for Herrera was related only to the integrity of the facts and contents of the history. The difference of opinions that the authors he cited held with respect to the conquest did not matter. Herrera felt responsible to this tradition because any other way would compromise his mission as a historian to convince foreign nations that the monarchs and their advisors had justly conducted their affairs in the Indies. The point for Herrera, however, was not to debate whether injustices had been committed, but rather to determine who was responsible:

> *Vease pues, si atentas las santysimas ynstruciones e ordenes questos Catholicos Reyes dieron, es más xusto que las culpas e pecados que se cometieron contra los yndios, caigan sobrellos, o sobre las personas que non las complieron (CDIA 1864–1884, 37:142).*

See then, considering the most holy instructions and orders that these Catholic Monarchs issued, whether it is more just that the transgressions and sins committed against the Indians would fall upon them, or upon the persons who did not carry them out.

Herrera thought that if he changed his *Historia,* then it would lose credibility before foreign nations and Pedrarias's transgressions would fall upon the Catholic Monarchs and the "nation" because it would not be clear that he had failed to carry out royal instructions. Herrera's response gave precedence to defending the honor of the monarchs and the Spanish nation. For Herrera, the object of history was justice, therefore the historian's practice consisted of examining the way in which the monarchs and different members of the community had tried to carry out the Alexandrian bull of donation and tended to the governance of the Indies for the common good. In other words, what mattered to him was evaluating the realization of the social ideals expressed in juridical discourse.

In 1603 the count had reached an agreement with Herrera in order to "moderar algunos afectos con xustas condyciones" [moderate some affects with just conditions; that is, tone down his language where appropriate], but the count wanted changes of content, which Herrera refused, stating that "tocar en el fecho non lo fará, antes se dexará fascer mil pedazos" [changing the facts he will not do, he would rather be cut into a thousand pieces] (CDIA 1864–1884, 37:320). After examining the case, the resolution of Sobrino and López de Bolaños found that Herrera, "escrebiendo cada cosa que la falló, a nadie fasce agravio en lo quescribe" [writing everything as he found it, does not affront anyone in what he writes] (CDIA 1864–1884, 37:327). This decision subjected the composition of the account to a group of legal principles to ascertain its "degree of certainty" and whether it offended others. On the first point, the count's claims were too general for determining that the chronicler's statements were false, while Herrera's responding proofs supported the veracity of the specific facts that he related. With regard to the central issue in the case, once it was established that a sufficient degree of certainty existed with respect to the facts, then no offense was recognized.

Gómara's project of constructing an authoritative narrative of colonization in the *Historia general* appeared at a time when the focus on conquests had given way to a concern for integrating the indigenous population within the colonial social system. The limitations that kept his *Historia general* from achieving an influential role in imperialist Spanish culture lay mainly in the fact that it revealed the contradictions existing between the historical record and the political obligations that the crown had assumed as a colonial power. The difficulties that Spaniards confronted when interpreting the violence in the colonizing process could not be sufficiently addressed through representations of human history or imperialist ideological formulations. Examining the ways in which the colonial discourse confronted the moral failings of the enterprise of the Indies sheds light on the cultural mechanisms of denial and the inherent ideological weakness of the colonizing project. The conditions that had initially made histories of the Indies politically and socially influential within imperial Spain were shattered by the demand for a coherent answer to the ethical challenges posed by conquest and colonization.

NOTES

1. Andrea Doria was a veteran of naval campaigns against the Turks. In 1532 he led the fleet that captured Coron, Patras, and the castles protecting the entrance to the Gulf of Corinth. The following year, under the direction of Álvaro Bazán, he managed to disperse the Turkish fleet in Lepanto. On Charles V's struggle against the Turks in the Mediterranean, see Merriman (1962, 3:288–351).

2. The idea of history as the teacher of life comes from Cicero's *De oratore* (1959–1960, 2:36): "Historia uero testis temporum, lux ueritatis, uita memoriae, magistra uitae, nuntia uetustatis, quam uoce alia nisi oratoris immortalitati commendatur?" [History, true witness of the times, beacon of truth, giver of life to memory, teacher of life, messenger of antiquity, whose voice but the orator's could ensure its immortality?]. This didactic function of history was turned into an attractive tool of political reflection by advising rulers through the example of past events. Royal chronicler Lucio Marineo Sículo used this Ciceronian concept to explain the political utility of history: "La qual como sea por testimonio de muchos maestra de la vida humana, testigo de los tiempos passados, conseruadora de la memoria, mensajera de la verdad, por cierto da mucha causa de deleyte y de honesta vtilidad a los gra[n]des principes y señores, y generalmente a todos los hombres deseosos del saber" [The one which is, according to the testimony of many, the teacher of human life, witness of times past, keeper of memory, messenger of truth, certainly the cause of much delight and honest utility for great princes and lords, and generally to all men desirous of knowledge] (1539, [3]r). On the didactic role of history, see Rómulo Carbia (1934, 21–23) and Walter Mignolo (1982, 77, 94).

3. Gómara tells the marquis of Astorga more precisely that he is composing "la [h]ystoria de vuestro consuegro" [the history of your son's father-in-law], Cortés, but because he conceived the *Conquista de México* as an integral part of the *Historia general de las Indias*, it should be considered part of the same project.

4. The list seems sufficiently exhaustive: "Fueron sus coronistas fray Juan Bauprista Mantuano, Ao. de Palenzia, Antonio de Nibrixa, Pedro Martir milanes, fray Bernardino Gentile de Scicilcia, Hernando del Pulgar, Tristan de Silua, Gracia Dei gallego, Hernando de Riuera, y Carualjal. Escriuieron tambien algo Andres Bernal, Gco. Frz. de Ouiedo, y otros, empero escriue mejor que todos Geronimo Çorita en la historia que nombra de las empresas del Rey Don Fernando el Catholico" [His chroniclers were fray Juan Bautista Mantuano, Alonso de Palencia, Antonio de Nebrija, the Milanese Peter Martyr, *fray* Bernardo Gentile of Sicily, Hernando del Pulgar, Tristán de Silva, the Galician Gracia Dei, Hernando de Rivera, and [Lorenzo Galíndez de] Carvajal. Andrés Bernál[dez], Gonzalo Fernández de Oviedo, and others wrote some, but Jerónimo Zurita writes better than all of them in the history that he calls *Las empresas del rey don Fernando el Católico* (The enterprises of King *don* Ferdinand the Catholic)] (Gómara 1912, 191).

5. Although Gómara's discussion of the historians of his time in the *Anales* is by no means comprehensive, the events that he covers in the text (1912, 166, 187, 231, 233, 235, 244, 248, 258, 263) include the dispatch of Peter Martyr to Egypt in 1501; the completion of the histories of Pedro Bembo in 1513, Paolo Giovio in 1544, and Marco Guazzo in 1551; the publication of Oviedo's *Historia general y natural* in 1535; the appointment in Rome of Juan Ginés de Sepúlveda as chronicler in 1536, and in Spain Florián de Ocampo in 1539 and Jerónimo Zurita in 1547; and the interventions of Las Casas against the publication of Sepúlveda's *Democrates secundus* in 1546 and Oviedo's *Historia general y natural* in 1548.

6. The service of humanist historians in positions of a political character is well established. Moreover, history itself constituted a form of civil service to the extent that it could be utilized to stimulate loyalty to a king or show the justice of a cause (Barnes 1962, 100; Gilbert 1965, 218–219; Hay 1977, 89; Breisach 1994, 154–155).

7. On this aspect of humanist historiography, see Gilbert (1965, 203–235) and Hay (1977, 89).

8. The editions of Agustín Millán at Zaragoza (Gómara 1553a) and Guillermo Millis at Medina del Campo (1553b) are the first to modify the original title of 1552. Gómara must have approved the change because it is retained in the revised and enlarged editions published by Millán with Pedro Bernuz at Zaragoza (1554a, 1555), and in Antwerp by Jan Steels (1554b, 1554c), Martin Nuyts (1554d, 1554e), and Hans de Laet (1554f, 1554g). Subsequent Italian translations would keep this variant title, but it disappears in the French and English editions. On the editions of the *Historia general* and its variants, see Wagner (1924).

9. The Latin edition was published in Nuremberg in 1524. See JCBL (1980, nos. 524/1, 5, 8), Sabin (1868–1936, nos. 16947–16948), Harrisse (1866, nos.

125–126), Sanz (1960, nos. 933–934, 937–938), Medina (1958, nos. 70–71), and Church (1951, nos. 53–54).

10. The colophon of the text makes it clear that the printing occurred in Nuremberg when the *infante* Fernando presided over the Imperial Assembly in 1524 (Cortés 1524, 49r). Subsequently, the *infante* presented a copy of Savorgnano's translation to Carlo Contarini, patrician and ambassador of Venice (R. Commissione Colombiana 1892–1896, part 3, vol. 2:345). Contarini said that, when he gave him the copy, the *infante* had shown him a series of objects from New Spain that Charles V had sent to him. Among these items were plumes, skins, religious paraphernalia, and a mosaic tablet with images of the native gods. If Charles had sent him all these items, surely he would have included a copy of Cortés's *Cartas de relación.*

11. Pedro Mexía's *Historia del emperador* (History of the emperor) corroborates this statement: "bibió muchos años en grande honrra y estimaçión, ganada y meresçida por su persona, que verdaderamente fué señalada, y meresçió que su fama sea çelebrada, como lo será, en los tiempos venideros" [he lived many years in great honor and esteem, attained and merited by his persona, which truly was outstanding, and deserved that his fame be celebrated, as it will be, in the times to come] (1945, 115).

12. Martyr's *Decades of the New World* were both criticized and consulted by historians of the Indies such as Oviedo, Las Casas, and Gómara. In fact, Paolo Giovio cites it as his source on matters concerning the Indies in his *Historiarum sui temporis* (1550, 252–254) and it remained a relevant authority at least until 1580 when it was used in the *Historia de las Indias Occidentales,* which was prepared for the sultan Murad III (Elliott 1992, 88). The importance of Martyr's *Decades* in the sixteenth century has been emphasized by Parry (1981, 34) and Hirsch (1965, 41).

13. Here Oviedo does not mention Martyr by name, but undoubtedly he is referring to him because he will reiterate the same criticism explicitly in other parts of his *Historia general y natural* (1992, 2:82–83, 4:267–268, 271). Moreover, Martyr's *Decades* were specifically addressed to Popes Leo X and Clement VII, and King Frederick III of Naples, the cardinal of Aragón's uncle.

14. Oviedo calls him "el protonotario Pedro Mártir" [the prothonotary Peter Martyr] and mentions that he and Bernardo Gentile were "historiógrafos de Su Magestad" [historiographers of His Majesty] (1992, 4:271). Gómara mentions him as the first abbot of Jamaica in the *Historia general* (1552, 1:25v) and as "cronista de los Reyes Católicos" [chronicler of the Catholic Monarchs] in the *Anales* (1912: 191). Las Casas, in turn, was present when he was made a member of the Council of the Indies (1988–1998, 4:1474, 5:2047, 2198). On the positions occupied by Martyr, see Thacher (1903, 1:3–33) and Alba (1989).

15. Bernardo Gentile appears in Gómara (1912, 191), who mentions him in the *Anales* as "Bernardino Gentil" among the chroniclers of King Ferdinand the Catholic. See also Merriman's note 6 in Gómara (1912, 44–45).

16. Martyr's appointment as royal chronicler probably was related to his activity of writing about the Indies in his *Decades*. Francisco Esteve Barba (1964, 67) thought that the position of chronicler of the Indies existed since 1526, the year in which Martyr died and Guevara received the commission to continue his work. As previously discussed, however, the testimony of Las Casas suggests that Martyr also conducted his historiographical activity with some institutional backing.

17. On Oviedo's appointment as royal chronicler, see Carbia (1934, 76–78), Esteve Barba (1964), and the extensive study of Tudela (1992, cxviii–cxix).

18. With regard to Italian historiography, Felix Gilbert (1965, 218–219) states that an individual could be appointed to the position of royal chronicler with the charge of completing some kind of specific historiographical commission or as recompense after the fact. This was likely the case in Spain with Gómara.

19. In 1563 the *bachiller* Juan Ruiz referred to Gómara as "coronista de su magestad" [chronicler of his majesty] in a letter granting power of attorney. Robert Lewis (1983, 54–55) has suggested that Ruiz was thinking about the *Anales;* however, there is no evidence of this. It is more likely that Gómara, if anything, merely had the public's unofficial recognition as "chronicler of his majesty" from his *Historia general,* the only one of his works that was published. Ruiz was a cleric from the town of Gómara and served as one of the executors of López de Gómara's will. In this power of attorney letter Ruiz authorized Pedro Moreno to recover money from debts that had not been paid to Gómara. A copy of the document may be consulted in Lewis (1983, 359–369).

20. On these *cédulas*, see Tudela (1992, cxviii–cxix).

21. John Elliott (1984a, 155) also considers relevant the *donatários*, or proprietary titles, used by the Portuguese to compensate individuals who served the crown in the occupation and development of certain territories. The system was employed in Madeira and the Azores in the fifteenth century, and then in Brazil, which in 1534 was still divided into twelve hereditary captaincies.

22. On the *encomienda* in the colonization of the Indies, see Gibson (1966, 48–67), Haring (1947, 42–74), Simpson (1982), Elliott (1984a, 162–171, 188–196), and Lockhart and Schwartz (1983, 68–73, 92–96). Slavery also served to punish native resistance and provided a stimulus to colonization in the case of the Caribbean. See Palencia-Roth (1993).

23. The *encomienda* guaranteed the subordination of the Indians to the colonial process because it offered a system of coercion whereby they were subjected to the authority of the monarchs; they would serve as the workforce in mining, agriculture, and the Spaniards' personal service; and they would be evangelized by the missionaries.

24. Ernst Schäfer has suggested that one of the causes motivating Charles V to make major legal and institutional reforms in the government of the Indies

in 1542 was the Cortes of Valladolid's request for him to "remediar las crueldades que se hacen en las Indias contra los Indios, porque dello será Dios muy servido y las Indias se conservarán y no se despoblarán, como se van despoblando" [remedy the cruelties that are committed in the Indies against the Indians, because God will be greatly served and the Indies will be preserved and not depopulated, as they continue being depopulated now] (1935, 61–62).

25. See also Hanke (1974), Zavala (1988, 255–318), and Adorno (1992b).

26. The most renowned case is that of Diego Beltrán, a member of the Council of the Indies who accepted gifts and money from Cortés, Diego de Almagro, Hernando Pizarro, and Gonzalo de Olmos (Schäfer 1935, 64).

27. On this *visita* and the New Laws, see Schäfer (1935, 61–70).

28. Events in Peru concerned the crown even before the conquistadors' rebellion. Schäfer (1935, 62) stated that the emperor had been closely following developments since 1540, when the proceedings against the Pizarro brothers for the death of Diego de Almagro began.

29. According to Lewis Hanke (1974, 57–61), Las Casas and *fray* Rodrigo de Andrada played a central role in this process. They got the Council of the Indies to postpone its decision about the concession of rights in perpetuity to the *encomenderos* in 1550. Also, their recommendation in 1543 of revoking conquest permits was echoed in the Council of the Indies' suggestion of July 3, 1549, to suspend them and the emperor's order of April 16, 1550, which put the suspension into effect.

30. The objectives of these treatises basically were (1) to affirm the rights of the monarchs of Castile concerning the Indies, (2) to show the illegitimacy of the conquests in relation to the legal foundations of the empire in the New World, and (3) to obtain the elimination of the *encomienda*. Fray Domingo de Soto prepared a summary of the controversy titled *Aqui se contiene vna disputa o controuersia* (Here is contained a dispute or controversy) and printed in Seville by Sebastián Trugillo in 1552 (JCBL 1980, no. 552/9). On the Valladolid debate, see Hanke (1974, 67–71) and Adorno (1992b, 58–62).

31. These documents dated 1553 and 1558 refer to debts that Martín Cortés, the marquis of the Valley, had deferred to him as a form of payment. Transcriptions of them may be consulted in Lewis (1983, 332–348, 354–357).

32. Olaus was elected archbishop of Sweden in 1544 and was well known for his *Carta marina* (Map of the sea) [1539] and *Historia de gentibus septentrionalibus* (History of the northern peoples) [1555]. In the *Historia general*, Gómara calls him "Olao, Godo, arçobispo de Upsalia" [Olaus, the Goth, archbishop of Uppsala] and says he had long conversations with him in Bologna and Venice (1552, 1:4v). *Don* Diego Hurtado de Mendoza, in turn, had a long intellectual and political career. Gómara refers to him as a "varon notable y señalado en estos reynos en letras y negoçios" [notable gentleman, distinguished in these kingdoms in letters and business matters] (1853, 430). They had stayed together

in 1540 when *don* Diego was the ambassador of Spain in Venice (1539–1546). On this period of Gómara's life, see Lewis (1983, 28–31).

33. For a more detailed discussion of the relationship between Cortés and Gómara, see Lewis (1983, 31–35).

34. The commission received by Gómara is documented in an order of payment that the second marquis of the Valley, Martín Cortés, made out to Gómara in Madrid on March 4, 1553. A transcription of the document may be consulted in Lewis (1983, 330).

35. Gómara was working on the *Conquista de México* at least by 1545, when he mentions this work in a dedication to the marquis of Astorga (1853, 332–333).

36. The best example of this is the failure of Inca Garcilaso de la Vega to obtain mercies for his father's services around 1561, discussed later in this chapter.

37. Salvador de Madariaga (1986, 524) thinks that Charles V came to consult Cortés about matters concerning the Indies. It is difficult to determine if the conquistador managed to achieve such a degree of political authority with the emperor, but the contemporary testimony of Sepúlveda (1987, 142) indicates that Charles was present at one of the meetings in which Cortés recounted his experiences in the New World.

38. The political aura that Cortés had acquired increased when he returned from New Spain in 1540. The Council of the Indies sent representatives to receive him and reserved him a seat among the great magistrates when he attended its sessions (Madariaga 1986, 550).

39. On the roles of Loaysa and Cobos in the council, see Merriman (1962, 3:621–662). On Cobos and his influence in Charles's government, see Keniston (1958).

40. Information about the Academia de Cortés is scarce and comes from Pedro de Navarra (1565, 42r–43r). Its treatment in secondary sources is also limited (Madariaga 1986, 556–557; Ramos 1972, 113–114; Lewis 1983, 33–34).

41. Schäfer (1935, 38–39) has shown that Juan de Samano was official secretary beginning in 1513 under the orders of Lope de Conchillos, was appointed to the Council of the Indies in 1519, and was already "Secretario para los negocios de las Indias" [secretary for the transactions of the Indies] in 1522, a position he held until his death in 1558.

42. According to Schäfer (1935, 369), Francisco de Eraso was secretary of the council between 1559 and 1570.

43. Roger Merriman (1912, xvii–xix) stated that Gómara's extravagant elegies of Cortés displeased the crown. Merriman thought that Charles wanted to diminish the conquistador's prominence and limit his power in the territories he had acquired. Henry Raup Wagner (1924, 29–30) suggested that the prohibition could merely have been against the Medina del Campo edition, which lacked

the *privilegio,* and that Cortés's relatives may have requested the recall of earlier editions. Ramón Iglesia (1942, 119–133) returned to Merriman's theory, adding Gómara's criticisms of Charles V's ingratitude, the *Historia general's* liberty of judgment with respect to colonial policies, and Las Casas's possible intervention. Marcel Bataillon (1956), on the other hand, interpreted the *Historia general's* prohibition as an effort of the crown to neutralize Cortés's political influence in New Spain. His argument is based on a comparison of three prohibitions recorded in the *Copulata de leyes de Indias* against Cortés's *Letters* in 1527 and against Gómara's *Historia* in 1553 and 1566 (the latter, Bataillon argued, coincided with the conspiracy of the second marquis of the Valley, Martín Cortés, in Mexico). The hypothesis of the conflict between the crown and the conquistadors— particularly Fernando Cortés—as a social group, however, does not completely explain the prohibition. See the critical commentary on each of these theories in Robert Lewis (1983, 317–326).

44. Hernando de Aragón was the grandson of King Ferdinand the Catholic and had been raised in the court. He became the archbishop of Zaragoza in 1539 at the insistence of Charles V, and Philip II named him viceroy of Aragón in 1566. See Colás Latorre, Criado Mainar, and Miguel García (1998).

45. Ramón Iglesia (1942, 120–129) offered a very similar reading concerning possible conflicts that the *Historia general* posed with respect to imperial politics.

46. In the "Argumento" (Argument) of his *Brevísima relación de la destrucción de las Indias,* Las Casas explained that he had composed the text at the request of the court after he had related the massacres conducted by the conquistadors (1988–1998, 10:31). Then, in the work's prologue, Las Casas (1988–1998, 10:32– 33) stated that he had presented a version of the text to the archbishop of Toledo, who presented it to Prince Philip. At the time of publication the text was not only previously known in the court, but the printing itself was done to present the text to the prince. See also Wagner (1967, 107–120).

47. In her examination of the censorship of Jerónimo Román's *Repúblicas del mundo,* Rolena Adorno (1992a) has demonstrated that the Council of Castile ignored the petitions of the Council of the Indies in 1575 to seize the book and remove some objectionable passages. Taking into account the second publication of the work in 1595 with royal permission, she convincingly concluded that "[s]tern condemnations of the conquistadors were evidently not a matter that merited royal concern" (1992a, 817).

48. There were five printings in all, although the number increases when counting the editions that basically have the same typeset but a different title page (JCBL 1980, nos. 552/22, 553/30–31, 554/28–32, 555/29).

49. The first foreign-language editions published in the sixteenth century include Italian translations by Agustino Cravaliz published in Rome in 1556 (JCBL 1980, no. 556/22) and by Lucio Mauro in 1557 (JCBL 1980, nos. 557/22 and 565/26); French by M. Fumée in 1568 (JCBL 1980, no. 568/10) and by

Guillaume le Breton in 1588 (JCBL 1980, no. 588/35); and English by T. Nicholas in 1578 (JCBL 1980, no. 578/41). The Italian translations were regularly reprinted from 1556 until the late 1570s and then in 1599; the French, from 1568 to 1588; and the English only once (1596) before the end of the century. On Cravaliz's translations see Lucia Binotti (1992).

50. Barcia's series played a central role in the incorporation of Gómara's text into the colonial canon. Bibliographical references of this edition are found in JCBL (1980, no. 749/29) and, for a detailed description of its contents, Sabin (1868–1936, no. 3350).

51. Padilla's list mentions one copy of the *Historia* and the protocol of Francisco Dávalos lists two copies among Sarria's books (Leonard 1992, 373, 400).

52. Las Casas's criticisms are found in his *Historia de las Indias* (1527–1559), those of Díaz in his *Historia verdadera* (ca. 1550–1568), and those of the Inca in his *Comentarios reales* (1609), *Historia general del Perú* (1617), and his annotations in the margins of his personal copy of Gómara's *Historia*. A wider debate concerning these historians' criticisms is found in the works of Ramón Iglesia (1944, 77–96, for Díaz; 1942, 130–152, for Las Casas, Díaz, and the Inca), Joaquín Ramírez Cabañas (1943), José Luis Martínez (1981), Robert Lewis (1986), Rolena Adorno (1988, 241–245), and José Antonio Rodríguez Garrido (1993). It is also relevant to consider the synthesis that Lewis (1983, 294–297) presents on sixteenth- and seventeenth-century opinions about Gómara's *Historia*.

53. Christopher Columbus, in his *Libro de privilegios* (Book of privileges), talks about these royal favors as granting nobility, honor, and mercies together: "[E]ntre los otros galardones e renumeraçiones que los reyes pueden fazer a los que bien e lealmente les sirven, es honrarlos e sublimarlos entre los otros de su linage, e los ennobleçer e decorar e honrar, e les faser otros muchos bienes e graçias e mercedes" (1996, 262) [Among other rewards and remunerations that kings can give to those who well and loyally serve them, is the honor and exaltation of them above others of their lineage, and ennoblement, decoration, and honor of them, as well as the conferral on them of many benefits, gifts, and favors] (1996, 72).

54. One of Herrera's refutations leaves no doubt that he was referring to Gómara: "Quando al Coronista de Cortés, que disce la parte contraria que su Agüelo tobo con una soga a la garganta, nunco [*sic*] tal se a fallado, nin Gómara xamás estobo en las Indias" [Regarding Cortés's chronicler, whom the opposing party says that his grandfather had a rope to his neck, this has never been established, nor was Gómara ever in the Indies] (CDIA 1864–1884, 37:271–272).

55. According to the Colegio Hispano-Boloniense's classification of the report, Herrera employed three types of evidence: the papers and letters of the

bishop of Chiapas, the bishop of Darién, and two religious who wrote to the king; what the histories say; and "los papeles, cartas, libros e escripturas que se fallaron en los Archivos de los Secretarios que subcedieron en los Rexistros e Protocolos de las Indias, e en los Archivos del Colexio de San Gregorio de Valladolid" [the papers, letters, books, and writings that are found in the Archives of the Secretaries who succeeded in the post of the Registries and Protocols of the Indies, and in the Archives of the Colegio de San Gregorio in Valladolid] (CDIA 1864–1884, 37:101–103).

CHAPTER 2

Territories of Redemption
⇒ in the New World ⇐

GEOGRAPHY AND CULTURE IN THE COLONIAL WORLD

rancisco López de Gómara dedicated his *Historia general* to Emperor Charles V, whom he addressed as "don Carlos Emperador de Romanos[,] Rei de España, señor de las Indias, y nueuo Mundo" [*don* Carlos, emperor of the Romans, king of Spain, lord of the Indies and the New World] (1552, 1:[*ii*]v). His addition referring to the Indies and the New World departed from the official protocol established by Chancellor Gattinara to accompany Charles's name after his imperial election in 1519.[1] In reality, it was unnecessary to refer to the emperor as "lord of the Indies" because it was common knowledge that the New World was considered part of Castile. John Elliott (1989, 7–8) explains that the title of empire was appropriately applied to the Holy Roman Empire, but the expressions "empire of the Indies" and "emperor of the Indies" only began to acquire currency in the seventeenth century. As Oviedo suggested in his *Historia*, "estas Indias, como en otras partes está dicho, son de la corona e ceptro real de Castilla, e no del imperio Cesariano" [these Indies, as it is said elsewhere, belong to the crown and royal scepter of Castile, and not the Caesarian empire] (1992, 4:103). The imperial title created by Gómara identified the territorial dominions of Charles instead of the legal bonds that defined the relationship between the emperor and his vassals.[2] It also presented the possession of the Indies as an aspect of the emperor's political grandeur. Referring to Charles as "lord of the Indies" was a way of reminding the king of his commitment to Spanish imperial expansion in the New World at a time when the legal foundations of the conquest and its consequences were in question. Gómara attempted to prove that the society created by the conquistadors in the Indies was a desirable reality according to the Christian view of man and history.

Gómara's imperialist rhetoric responded to the necessities created by Spanish colonialism in the Indies. He understood the region subjected by Spaniards to be the size of Africa, Asia, and Europe combined. His use of the familiar reference of empire allowed him to emphasize the significance of the power that the crown acquired over the enormous territories of the New World. The multitude of peoples and lands subjected to the dominion of the monarchs of Castile not only gave them prestige, it also put them in the position of carrying out social transformations that could have a radical impact on human history. The concept of empire, with its historical connotations in European tradition, could transmit the idea of the creation of an *oikoumene*, that is, a world community controlled politically by a central power. Empires traditionally extended over peoples in a known and shared world, but the empire of the Indies of which Gómara spoke extended over distant lands. This kind of territorial configuration of the world demanded a discourse of imperial construction that provided a persuasive verbal formulation to support what the conquistadors and settlers had already brought about in action. In what follows I will examine Gómara's discourse concerning the territory and diversity of the peoples of the New World, particularly the specific rhetorical possibilities that he came to explore in order to promote Spanish imperialism.

That Gómara begins his dedication of the *Historia general* by calling Charles V's attention to the importance of the discovery of the Indies is less an expression of astonishment than an attempt to define them territorially from a political and religious perspective. Without introduction or explanation, Gómara simply says that it was one of the central events in the history of humankind: "Muy soberano Señor la maior cosa despues d[e] la criacion del mundo, sacando la encarnacion, y muerte, del que lo crio, es el descubrimiento de Indias. Y assi las llaman mundo nueuo" [Very sovereign lord, the greatest thing after the creation of the world, excepting the incarnation and death of the one who created it, is the discovery of the Indies. And thus they are called the New World] (1552, 1:[*ii*]v). The statement is an invitation to think about the implications of the discovery from the perspective of Christian historiographical tradition. The dominant providentialist view at this time saw the salvation of humankind as the main purpose of human history. Gómara ranked the discovery second only to the creation of the world and the sacrifice of Christ—two evidently fundamental events in the divine plan for the salvation of humanity in Christian tradition. More than expressing excessive enthusiasm for the discovery of the Indies, he was situating it within the framework of the larger narrative about the conversion of humanity to Christianity,[3] thus directing the attention of his reader toward human history in a universal sense.

Gómara does not make explicit in the dedication the reasons why he suggests that the discovery of the Indies occupied such an elevated place in the providential plan, leaving the reader the task of filling in the blanks. His statement, however, should not be taken lightly inasmuch as it implies an interpretation of the consequences of Spanish imperial expansion in the ultimate destiny of humanity. This move is significant because it suggests a change of perspective with respect to the way in which other European authors of that time situated the discovery in relation to universal history. Among humanist authors, the genre of universal history was dominated by Jacopo Filippo Foresti's *Supplementum supplementi chronicarum* (first published in 1483), Marco Antonio Sabellico's *Enneades* (1498–1504), and Hartmann Schedel's *Liber chronicarum* (1493) (Breisach 1994, 159). All of these works presented an account of human history from the beginning of the world up to the time of their composition, but only the *Supplementum* (beginning with the 1503 edition) and the *Enneades* discussed the topic of the discovery. Both Foresti and Sabellico based their works on models of Christian history derived from Saint Augustine, Saint Jerome, and medieval tradition (Dannenfeldt 1954, 99; Barnes 1962, 102–103); however, they did not interpret the discovery as part of the divine plan for redemption. They also did not regard the Columbian voyages as a milestone in Christian history, although they included them among the deeds of the Catholic

Monarchs, whom they presented as model Christian rulers. The significance of the discovery for these authors was limited to its association with the capture of Granada in the same year.[4] Gómara, on the other hand, led the reader to think about the discovery as a monumental event in the common history of humanity.

The philosophical perspective of Christian historiography permitted one to imagine an account that reduced the history of all the different peoples inhabiting the world under a universal scheme. Arnaldo Momigliano has shown that the appearance of Christian historiography in the fourth century CE suggests the development of a philosophy of history that did not exist in pagan tradition (1963, 83–87). Pagan historiography was filled with authors, such as Herodotus, Thucydides, Polybius, Plutarch, Livy, Sallust, Caesar, Tacitus, and Suetonius, who were principally concerned with the political and military actions of Greece and Rome. Christian historians like Origen, Lactantius, Eusebius of Caesarea, Saint Jerome, Saint Augustine, and Paulo Orosio sought to confront the criticisms of their pagan contemporaries, who blamed Christians for the ills of the Roman Empire. Incorporating the Jewish and Christian traditions into their historiographical discourse allowed them to operate within a wider temporal framework and to embrace a different interpretive perspective that was consistent with their values. Momigliano suggested that for the first time Christian historians thought in terms of a universal history because it was necessary to teach their converts the divine plan for the redemption of humanity.

The colonization of the New World posed narrative problems similar to those that the first fathers of the church had faced, particularly because both told a story in which providence intervened in human events in order to facilitate the realization of the divine plan. Origen refuted the notion that the spread of Christianity caused the Roman Empire's decline, arguing that Rome could not have survived because of its false gods, and attributed the Pax Romana to the birth of Christ (Breisach 1994, 80–81). The incorporation of the Roman Empire into the Christian view of universal history took shape in the Latin world with Saint Jerome's translation and amplification of Eusebius's *Chronicle*. Beginning with Eusebius, Christian historians recognized the Roman Empire as part of the divine plan for the diffusion of Christianity. Pagan and Christian histories became intertwined in the Council of Nicaea in 325 CE, when the emperor Constantine, of whom Eusebius was an advisor, declared Christianity as the religion of the empire.[5] In this way, the history of an empire that dominated vast territories became essential for interpreting the way in which the Christian God made his will prevail in human history—exactly the kind of framework that Gómara suggested in his dedication to Charles V.

Gómara particularly emphasizes the magnitude and diversity of the New World: "Y no tanto le dizen nueuo por ser nueuamente hallado, quanto por ser grandissimo. Y casi tan grande como el viejo, que co[n]tiene a Europa, Africa, y Asia. Tambien se puede llamar nueuo por ser todas sus cosas diferentissimas de las del nuestro" [And it is not so much said to be new for being newly discovered as for being enormous, and almost as large as the old, which contains Europe, Africa, and Asia. It could also be called new for all its things being so different from ours] (1552, 1:[*ii*]v). The referents that allow him to examine the unity of human history presuppose the political integration of geographical space as a way of resolving the obstacle of diversity. Just as the Roman Empire had enabled the integration of extensive territories under the same religion, the conquest now made the spread of Christianity possible in an area the size of Europe, Africa, and Asia. The difference of the Indies from the known world, however, constitutes the point of departure for the dynamics of future developments. Gómara establishes two essential points in his theory concerning New World diversity: first, the animals and plants "son de otra manera . . . siendo los elementos vna mesma cosa alla, y aca" [are of another kind . . . the elements being the same there and here]; second, "los [h]ombres son como nosotros, fuera del color, que de otra manera bestias, y mostruos serian. Y no vernian, como vienen de Adam" [the men are like us, outside of their color, otherwise they would be beasts and monsters and would not come, as they do, from Adam] (1552, 1:[*ii*]v). Thus the two worlds share the same historical origin and a common genealogy, although the forms of their "things" differ.

The diversity of plants and animals in the New World is revealed in the existence of species that are distinct from those found in the Old World. In the case of human beings, Gómara is unable to say they are a different species, for this would exclude their link to Adam as a common ancestor and relegate them to the level of beasts. Emphasizing the genealogical link between the native population and Adam leads to situating the topic of New World difference in the account of the common origin and proliferation of man. Gómara expresses the native inhabitants' difference in terms of their customs, civilization, and religion:

[N]o tienen letras, ni moneda, ni bestias de carga, cosas principalissimas para la policia, y viuienda del [h]ombre. . . . Y, como no conoscen al verdadero Dios, y señor, estan en grandissimos pecados de idolatria, sacrificios de [h]ombres viuos, comida de carne humana, habla con el diablo, sodomia, muchedumbre de mugeres, y otros assi (1552, 1:[ii]v).

They have no letters, money, or beasts of burden, the most important things for the civility and livelihood of man. . . . And, as they do not know the true God and Lord, they remain in the greatest sins of idolatry, live human sacrifices, eating human flesh, speaking with the devil, sodomy, herding women, and the like.

Fundamentally, these are generalizations aimed at presenting the Indians in a state of degradation that equates human diversity with moral transgression and the rupture of the link between humans and the divinity.

Gómara's reading of the universal history tradition is favorable to the conquest, for he presents it as a means for facilitating the diffusion of Christian values and restoring the unity of the human family. Immediately after explaining the differences between the New World and the Old, Gómara adds that the Indians, who are subjects of the king, have been converted to Christianity. Placing the problem of human diversity at the center of his reflection allows him to establish the foundation for his narrative scheme in order to define the meaning of the imperial enterprise:

El trabajo, y peligro, vuestros Españoles lo toma[n] alegremente, assi en predicar, y conuertir, como en descobrir, y conquistar. . . . Quiso Dios descobrir las Indias en vuestro tiempo, y a vuestros vassallos, para que las conuertiessedes a su santa lei, como dizen muchos [h]ombres sabios, y christianos. Començaron las conquistas de Indios, acabada la de Moros, porque siempre guerreassen Españoles contra infieles (1552, 1:[ii]v).

The work and peril your Spaniards gladly take on, preaching and converting, as well as discovering and conquering. . . . God wanted you to discover the Indies in your time, and your vassals, so that you would convert them to his holy law, as many wise and Christian men say. The conquests of Indians began after that of Moors, so that Spaniards could always wage war against infidels.

Gómara reads the coinciding events of the end of the war in Granada and the beginning of the conquest of the Indies as a sign of God's providential design for Spain. The construction of an overseas empire implied assuming a mission in service of the divine plan with the institutional approval of the church: "Otorgo la conquista, y conuersion, el papa" [The pope granted the conquest and conversion] (1552, 1:[*ii*]v). The process of papal mediation, conquest, and conversion of the Indians mentioned by Gómara, as well as the king's dominion over the Indies, makes sense from the global perspective embodied in the imperial emblem, as he explains to the emperor: "Tomastes por letra plus vltra, dando a entender el señorio del nueuo mundo" [You took as your motto *plus ultra,* meaning the lordship of the New World] (1552, 1:[*ii*]v).

The reflections in Gómara's dedication to the *Historia general* cover a series of topics such as the history of humankind, the novelty of the Indies, the difference of worlds, native customs, the transformation of the New World, and the mission of the empire. Gómara ends by making a call for favoring the conquest and collaborating in the imperial enterprise—the reason why he has composed his work. The dedication offers an elaborate outline of the principles that give coherence to his work. In a manner similar to the Roman Empire, Gómara's Spaniards were able to bring about a task of political unification that would facilitate the general conversion of those who would become subjects of the empire in the *plus ultra,* that is, the land beyond the Pillars of Hercules. Spanish imperialist expansion would be a way of countering the effects of the moral corruption that Gómara attributed to the native inhabitants of the Indies. The foundation of Gómara's imperialist vision is a providentialist conception of history that assigns a conquering mission to Spain in order to enable the evangelization of the native population. Some scholars, however, regard the convergence of conquest and evangelization as a problem in the composition of the *Historia general,* assuming that the two narrative lines contradict each other.[6] The compatibility between Gómara's account of the conquest and Christian tradition does not rest on the immediate ends pursued by the conquistadors, such as wealth or power, but on the creation of a colonial society that would enable the spread of the Catholic religion. We need to look at Gómara's understanding of the New World within the providential design and the legal foundations of Spanish dominion in order to make sense of his way of conceptualizing the ends of imperialism.

TERRITORIALITY AND SACRED HISTORY

Gómara devotes the first twelve chapters of his *Historia general* to constructing a conception of the world based on a comparison of theories and information available at the time. He examines the different theories of authors from both the ancient and Christian traditions, he explains the basic concepts of the geographical discourse of that moment, and he presents what the period's voyages of exploration have revealed. These chapters provide the reader with a summary of all that was known at that time about such geographical topics as the existence of one or several worlds, whether the earth is round or flat, the habitability of different areas, the existence of the antipodes, the possibility of traveling throughout the world, the earth's location in the universe, whether the continents are islands, what degrees are, and who invented the navigator's compass. Chapters 11 and 12, offering a detailed description of each of the territories explored in the New World, complete the basic preparation of the reader in geographical matters and serve as a transition to the narrative section that begins with the account of the first discoveries. The initial section evidently performed a didactic function aimed at establishing a common discursive foundation with readers whose conception of the world did not necessarily correspond with the new information acquired in the voyages of exploration. Along with its didactic dimension, this geographical section sheds light on Gómara's interpretive assumptions as well as his overall treatment of New World history.

Gómara's articulation of what was learned in the voyages of discovery within the theoretical framework of traditional knowledge raises the issue of identifying the discursive economy at work in his writing. Walter Mignolo (1995, 219–313) has suggested that a dialogue between the ancient and Christian traditions and the knowledge acquired through experience created a disassociation between the ethnic and the intellectual perspectives in the European colonial discourse of the Renaissance. This would imply a process of cultural rationalization in which European traditional ideas and social values were bracketed in order to facilitate the activities of colonization. The ethnic perspective hidden in the practices of representation would ultimately be reaffirmed as a function of the authority acquired on the political and economic plane. Thus Mignolo (1995, 301–305, 319) reads Spanish colonialism as a pre-capitalist stage within Western modernity, arguing that technique and reason came to operate as an autonomous sphere in relation to cultural values and traditions. Patricia Seed (2001), however, emphasizes the importance that cultural perspectives have in the formation of European colonizing practices. She convincingly shows that the local traditions, experiences, and cultures of each European nation, far from responding to a common model, led to different modes of appropriating territories and subordinating native populations. Similarly, Ricardo Padrón identifies some principles of rationalization of geographical space in Gómara's *Historia general,* although he characterizes his type of cosmographical discourse as dominated by a "tendency to rationalize the world along ethnically specific values rather than objective geometrical principles" (2002, 51).

Gómara's effort to incorporate new information within the European ethnic perspective allows us to understand how Christian tradition and the knowledge of the ancients could be used to affirm the epistemological privilege of the colonizers. A fundamental point in this respect — evident in the very analysis that he conducts of his sources — is that the tradition did not provide a definitive conception of the world, but rather an opaque outline that we may reconstruct as a wide range of divergent opinions and interpretations.[7] Not only was it possible to assume an ethnic perspective in the incorporation of new information and production of knowledge about the world, it was also necessary as a response to a social system that created the experience of a global reality in which many cultures and ethnic perspectives coexisted. The suppression of the ethnic centers and spatial rationalizations of native cultures in the process of colonization came about from the perspective of the classical tradition and was realized in the name of the exclusivity of the Roman Catholic religion.

An underlying issue here is the debate over the impact of Spanish colonialism in the formation of European culture. John Elliott (1976; 1989, 42–64; 1992; 1995), Michael Ryan (1981), and Anthony Grafton (1995) argue that the impact of the discovery of the New World was diminished in Europe by modes of conceptualization that were based on the assimilation of new knowledge into the framework already established within this intellectual tradition. With respect to the European perception of indigenous cultures, Elliott says that most sixteenth-century authors "felt that the Christian and classical traditions were sufficient to enable them to explore the mysteries of human behavior without any need for recourse to new worlds overseas" (1989, 43). In contrast to the position of those who propose a "blunted impact" of the New World in European culture, other readings emphasize the role of the "invention of America" (O'Gorman 1977) in the formation of Eurocentrism (Zavala 1989; Rabasa 1993, 2000; Mignolo 1995; see also Hulme 1986; Zamora 1993; Padrón 2002). The idea of the invention of America, which Iris Zavala eloquently reformulates as "the New World as an imaginary construct of the conqueror" (1989, 326), supposes the discursive construction of a concept of territorial identity that defines the "colonial subject." These representations of the New World became a key ideological tool within the process of European territorial expansion.[8] Whether they seek to identify a "paradigm shift" or a system articulating relations of power, it seems impossible to avoid looking at early Spanish colonial writing without analyzing its relation to European modernity and its modes of knowledge.

The cultural and religious diversity that the Spaniards encountered in the New World changed European knowledge not by questioning its paradigms, but by making it necessary to seek some sense of certainty amid the great diversity within the world. This was a way to erase differing epistemological perspectives, sources of political legitimacy, and value systems implied within the otherworldliness of the colonized territories. Gómara's geographical discourse subsumed the new information about the world within geocentric theory not simply as a way to rehearse old cosmographic notions within new contexts, but rather to set a foundation of belief in the authority of Christian tradition. The importance of this theory in his interpretation of the world is evident throughout his discussion of geographical categories, but especially in the chapters titled "El mundo es vno, y no muchos como algunos filosofos pensaron" (The world is one, and not many as some philosophers thought) and "El sitio de la tierra" (The location of the earth) (1552, 1:3r–v, 6r). According to Gómara's own explanation of this theory, the earth is situated in the center of the world between two "polos fixos, y quedos, como exes, donde se mueue, y sostiene el cielo" [fixed and stationary poles, like axes, where the sky revolves and is supported] (1552, 1:6r). Not only was the earth at the center of the universe, it was also the place where material reality converged. Gómara offers this definition: "Mundo es todo lo que Dios crio: cielo, tierra: agua, y las cosas visibles, y q[ue], como dize San Agustin contra los Academicos, nos mantiene[n]" [The world is everything that God created: heaven, earth, water, and visible things, which, as Saint Augustine said in opposition to the Academicians, maintain us] (1552, 1:3v). Therefore, his concept of the world supposes an opposition between visible and invisible reality: a space put within the range of human perception where the things that "maintain" human life are found, and another out of range where celestial things exist. This world on earth is fundamentally a space where the relationship between man and the divinity unfolds, thus European understandings of the New World establish the epistemological privilege of Christian knowledge by drawing the invisible beneath the multifarious experience of materiality.

A geocentric world can integrate in a complementary way the geographical concepts that Gómara finds in the classical and Christian traditions with the new information gained from the voyages of exploration, without having to maintain them as parallel and independent perspectives. Margarita Zamora (1993, 102–117) has proposed the concept of "textual cartography" to characterize the complex intersection of symbolic levels in the mapping of the discovery. This texture of cartographic discourse incorporated multiple symbolic codes combining practical instructions for navigation with political, economic, and religious references. José Rabasa (1993, 78) presents a similar opinion when he states that "[n]ovelty and fact, beyond the motivation of the authors, inscribe themselves on the margins of a textualized world." The abandonment of the tripartite figurative scheme of the *mappaemundi* suggests less a process of rationalization in the interpretation of space than one of re-conceptualization. This scheme does not presuppose a "subject of universal knowledge" (Mignolo 1995, 225) in the modern sense, but rather an ecumenical perspective in the sense that is found in Christian tradition beginning with Eusebius. The fundamental distinction is that Christianity is considered an exclusivist religion, but the modern universalist perspective endeavors to achieve absolute validity when situating itself above community affiliations.[9]

In Gómara's account, two of the central aspects that territorially define the New World are the religious practices and customs (especially those morally sanctioned in Christianity) of its native populations. In the process of the Indians' conversion to Christianity, the abandonment of the old beliefs and customs necessarily involved a reconfiguration of the religious symbols that filled the geographic space. A world previously occupied by temples, idols, and customs contrary to Christianity (the most outstanding being idolatry, sodomy, human sacrifice, and polygamy) is transformed into another in which churches, crosses, and the abolition of the earlier practices have left new traces. These common operations in missionary practice came to form an important part of Gómara's accounts of evangelization as well as the interpretation of geographical space in his historiographical discourse.[10] The destruction of the indigenous altars and their replacement by crosses and churches in the New World suggest that the interpretation of space, far from entering into a process of secularization, continued to adhere to the ethnic perspective. The marks that the inhabitants left in the territory acquire a figurative meaning according to the opposition between the *civitas dei* (city of God) and the *civitas terrena* (worldly city, or city of man) characteristic of Augustinian providentialism:

> *Ideoque in illa sapientes eius secundum hominem viventes aut corporis aut animi sui bona aut utriusque sectati sunt* . . . sulti facti sunt et inmutaverunt gloriam incorruptibilis Dei in similitudinem imaginis curruptibilis hominis et volucrum et quadrupedum et serpentium *(ad huiusce modi enim simulacra adoranda vel duces populorum vel sectatores fuerunt),* et coluerunt atque servierunt creaturae potius quam Creatori, qui est benedictus in saecula. *In hac autem nulla est hominis sapientia nisi pietas qua recte colitur verus Deus, id expectans praemium in societate sanctorum non solum hominum verum etiam angelorum,* ut sit Deus omnia in omnibus *(De civitate Dei, book 14, chapter 28).*

> Thus in the earthly city its wise men who live according to man have pursued the goods either of the body or of their own mind or both together . . . "they became fools, and exchanged the glory of the immortal God for images resembling mortal man or birds or beasts or reptiles," for in the adoration of idols of this sort they were either leaders or followers of the populace, "and worshipped and served the creature rather than the creator, who is blessed forever." In the heavenly city, on the other hand, man's only wisdom is the religion that guides him rightly to worship the true God and awaits as its reward in the fellowship of saints, not only human but also angelic, this goal, "that God may be in all" (Augustine 1957–1995, 4:406–407).

From the Augustinian as well as the geocentric perspectives the dominant axes in opposition are earth-heaven and earth-earth. The world of men centered on the cult of worldly things was opposed symbolically, from the Catholic point of view, to Christian regard for the celestial order. The incorporation of new geographical spaces into the image of a geocentric world implied the appearance of new areas of evangelization that enlarged the old map of sacred history.

The Christian interpretation of geographical space from the geocentric perspective focused on the relationship between visible and invisible things within the framework of universal history. When Gómara examines the theories of antiquity with respect to the existence of a multitude of worlds, he is assisted by Christian authors (Origen, Saint Jerome, Saint Augustine, and the New Testament) to support the idea of the oneness or unity of the world. Understood as the result of creation and associated with the plan of making human life possible, the concept of a single world is found directly related to the destiny and the possibilities of man. The unity of the world supposes that all things are governed by divine providence, according to what Gómara establishes from Origen: "no es nauegable el mar Oceano. Y aquellos mundos, que detras del estan, se gobiernan por prouidencia del mesmo Dios" [the Ocean-Sea is not navigable. And those worlds, which are beyond it, are governed by the providence of the same God] (1552, 1:3v). The concept of the multitude of worlds in Origen refers to "orbes, y partes de la tierra"; therefore, the unity of the earth rests on the divine action that governs it. Within these "orbs and parts of the earth," the portion corresponding to the New World is a private and inaccessible geographical space for the ancients, which suggests that the voyages of exploration enlarge the stage of action in which the universal drama of human salvation unfolds. This conception of the world implies a new consciousness of totality in which the histories of peoples dispersed throughout the globe converge, for the unity of the world also assumes the belief in humanity's common descent beginning with Adam and Eve as the first ancestors:

> [U]num ac singulum creavit, non utique solum sine humana societate deserendum, sed ut eo modo vehementius ei commendaretur ipsius societatis unitas vinculumque concordiae . . . quando ne ipsam quidem feminam copulandam viro sicut ipsum creare illi placuit, sed ex ipso ut omnino ex homine uno diffunderetur genus humanum (De civitate Dei, book 12, chapter 22).

> That God created man one and alone did not, however, mean that he was to be left in his solitary state without human fellowship. The purpose was rather to ensure that unity of fellowship itself and ties of harmony might be more strongly impressed on him. . . . For not

even woman herself, who was to be joined to man, did he choose to create as he did that very man, but he created her out of that man in order that the human race might derive entirely from one man (Augustine 1957–1995, 4:110–111).

Gómara's concern for reconciling the providentialist view of human history with the new geographical knowledge is evident in his commentary on the relationship between the different habitable portions of the world. Gómara concludes with respect to the earth:

> *Epicuro . . . tenia por mundos a semejantes orbes y bolas de tierras, apartados de la Tierra-Firme como islas. Y por ventura estos tales pedaços de tierra son el orbe y redo[n]dez que la escritura llama d[e] tierras. Y la que llama de tierra, ser todo el mundo terrenal (1552, 1:3v).*

> Epicurus . . . considered such orbs and balls of earth as worlds, like islands separated from the mainland. And perhaps these pieces of earth are the orb and roundness that scripture calls lands, and what it calls earth is the entire terrestrial world.

The concept of the New World implied the existence of a distinct orb, historically isolated from the world known directly from ancient and Christian traditions, but united in terms of creation. The basic idea is that the parts of the earth correspond to a common plan of creation and share the same nature in the elements, the same human ancestry, and the same historical destiny as defined by Christian universalism. Once it is established that the "orbs and parts of the earth" are governed by the same providence, Gómara examines the theories concerning the habitable world, the antipodes, and whether Europe, Africa, and Asia are islands. The fundamental concern in his analysis of these three topics is the structure of the world in terms of habitable zones, communication between its parts, and its role in the providential plan.

Confronting the Greek and Roman schools of thought that contended that the entire earth could not be inhabited, Gómara responds:

> *No crio el señor . . . la tierra en valde, ni en vazio, sino para que se more, y pueble. Y Zacarias dize al principio de su profeçia, que anduuieron la tierra, y toda ella estaua poblada, y llena de gente. . . . E assi no [h]ay tierra despoblada por mucho calor, ni por mucho frio, sino por falta de agua, y pan. El [h]ombre tambien, alle[n]de de lo sobredicho, que fue hecho de tierra, podra se [sic] q[ue], y sabra viuir en qualquiera parte della, por fria,*

o calorosa, que sea. Especialmente mandando Dios a Adam, y a Eua que criassen, multiplicassen, & [h]inchessen la tierra (1552, 1:4v–5r).

The lord did not create . . . the earth in vain or empty, but rather so that it would move and be populated. And Zechariah says at the beginning of his prophecy that they went about the earth, and all of it was populated and filled with people. . . . And thus there is no land unpopulated for being too hot or too cold, but rather for lack of water and bread. Man also, beyond what is said above, who was made from the earth, will be able and will know how to live in any part of it, as cold or hot as it may be, for God specifically ordered Adam and Eve to be fruitful, multiply, and fill the earth.

In order to come up with an image of the world, Gómara needs to take into account the act of creation when God assigns to the first couple the mission of occupying the terrestrial landscape. The proliferation of humanity is presented in Christian tradition as a dispersion of families through the world who founded communities and even entire peoples. When Gómara discusses the existence of the antipodes, he justifies Saint Augustine's position arguing:

Negolos, segu[n] yo pienso, por no hallar hecha memoria de antipodas en toda la sagrada escritura. Y tambie[n] por quitarse de ruydo, a lo que dizen. Ca si co[n]fesara que los [h]abia, no pudiera prouar que descendia[n] de Adam, y Eua como todos los demas [h]ombres deste nuestro medio mundo, y hemisperio, a quien hazia ciudadanos, y vezinos, de aquella su ciudad de Dios, pues la antigua, y comun opinion de filosofos, y teologos de aquel tiempo era que aunque los [h]auia no se podian comunicar co[n] nosotros (1552, 1:5r).

He denied their existence, I think, because he did not find the antipodes mentioned anywhere in holy scripture, and also to avoid scandal, as they say. For if he admitted that they existed, he could not prove that they descended from Adam and Eve as all the rest of the men in our half of the world and hemisphere, whom he made citizens and residents of that city of God, for the old and common opinion of philosophers and theologians of that time was that although they existed they were unable to communicate with us.

Thus the geographical problem of the possibility of communication between parts of the world implies an interpretation about the larger issue of the division and dispersion of humanity from a common lineage.

The reading that Gómara makes of terrestrial geography from the providentialist perspective of universal history is evident in his discussion of the insularity of Asia, Africa, and Europe. Sacred history provides a foundation for his interpretation of the geographical divisions of the Old World: "el que llaman Beroso dize que Noe puso nombre a Africa, Asia, y Europa. Y las dio a sus tres hijos Cam, Sem, y Jafet. Y que nauego por el mar Mediterraneo diez años" [the one they call Berosus says that Noah named Africa, Asia, and Europe, and gave them to his three sons Ham, Shem, and Japheth. And that he sailed the Mediterranean Sea for ten years] (1552, 1:7r). The parallel between Noah and the explorations of the sixteenth century is evident in the allusion to his Mediterranean navigation and his partitioning of the world (which bring to mind the Alexandrian bull of donation and the treaties between Spain and Portugal). The passage suggests that Noah previously named the continents; therefore, his distribution of world dominion among his sons is framed within the geographical limits of the knowledge of antiquity (based on his Mediterranean navigation). An interpretation of the discovery of the Indies is implied, for Gómara goes on to add: "En fin dezimos agora que las sobredichas tres prouinçias ocupan esta media tierra del mundo" [Finally, we now say that the aforementioned three provinces occupy this half of the world] (1552, 1:7r). The other half of the world corresponds, according to his earlier assertions, to the territory occupied by the New World. From here one could infer that Gómara's conception of the world connects the territorial dominion of the New World with the patriarchal authority of the pope, who as the leader of the church assumes a position equivalent to that of Noah.

Berosus's statement had powerful resonance in the juridical discourse of the sixteenth century. If Noah, as Gómara said, had distributed among his sons the regions of the world corresponding to Africa, Asia, and Europe, then it followed that the New World was not included in the original division. The territorial rights that Spaniards claimed in the New World could find important support in this version of the postdiluvian distribution of the Old World. Noah was recognized among jurists as "lord of the world" because they considered him the "master" or "heir" of the world after the Flood. In juridical tradition this point of sacred history explained the use that man made of the resources of the planet and their distribution among different groups or nations. The Spanish legal scholar Juan López de Palacios

Rubios stated in his *De las islas del Mar Océano* (On the islands of the Ocean-Sea) that God had directly ruled the world up until the Deluge, but then Noah received "el gobierno del Arca" [the governance of the Ark]: he formed communities, divided the world into three parts (Asia, Africa, and Europe), was put in charge of "llevar colonias por todo el orbe" [spreading colonies throughout the globe], "Y así gobernó Noa a todos los pueblos mientras vivió" [and thus Noah governed all the peoples while he lived] (1954, 70–71).

Even Francisco de Vitoria, who did not recognize the authority of the pope to make donations of lands that were not under the power of Christian rulers, understood the origins of property in terms of lineage and succession beginning with Adam and Noah as the original owners. Thus around 1539 he explained in his *Relectio de Indis* (Lecture on the Indies):

> *Adam primo et postea Noe videntur fuisse domini orbis (Gen. 1, 26):* Faciamus hominem ad imaginem et similitudinem nostram, et praesit piscibus maris et volatilibus caeli, *[et bestiis]* universaeque terrae, *etc., et infra (Gen. 1, 28):* Crescite, et multiplicamini, et replete terram, et subicite eam, *etc. Et idem in sententia dictum est Noe (Gen. 8, 17). Sed illi habuerunt succesores (1967, 35).*

> First Adam and then Noah appear to have been owners of the world (Gen. 1:26): "Let us make man in our image and likeness, and let him rule over the fishes of the sea, and the birds of the sky, and the animals, and all of the earth," etc. And further down (Gen. 1:28): "Be fruitful and multiply, replenish the earth and subdue it," etc. And the same dictum was said to Noah (Gen. 8:17). And they had successors.

The basic assumption in sacred history was that God had converted the earth into the property of man and therefore the appropriation of things in the world would have progressively developed according to the multiplication of the human lineage and the gradual occupation of the different regions of the earth. From Vitoria's perspective, the origin of the title and succession of "empires and dominions" in the world could originate either from Noah's partition or the mutual consent of the families when occupying the earth. Vitoria privileges the latter; nevertheless, it is fundamental that the origin of the world's principalities specifically refers back to Noah, whose descendents spread themselves throughout the earth:

[P]*ost Noe orbis fuit divisus in diversas provincias et regna, sive hoc fuerit*
ex ipsius Noe ordinatione, qui . . . in diversas regiones misit colonias, ut
patet apud Berosum Babylonicum, sive quod verisimilius est, ex consensu
mutuo gentium diversae familiae occupaverunt diversas provincias (1967,
38).

After Noah, the world was divided into different provinces and
kingdoms, whether this was by order of Noah himself, who . . . sent
colonies to different regions, as Berosus the Babylonian says, or it
appears more likely that by mutual consent different families of
peoples occupied different provinces.

The concept of the Old World in the *Historia general* presupposes the
act of donation whereby Noah distributed Africa, Asia, and Europe
among his descendents. The story of Noah and the Flood reappears as
a referent in various moments in the *Historia general,* probably because
it serves as a point of departure for interpreting the distribution of
humanity on earth and the relations between the different human groups
that occupy it. Gómara creates a geographical discourse that integrates
new knowledge about the world within the universalist Christian tradition. The ethnic perspective is maintained by privileging the conception of a geocentric world in which sacred history takes place. This new
European conception of the world takes on meaning as part of the process of unifying the spaces on the planet occupied by humans. It is not a
geography understood from a secular perspective, but rather the same
world governed by the same providence. The opposition between the
New and the Old Worlds in the *Historia general* suggests a distinction
between the world known since the period of Noah, who gave spatial
unity to biblical and Christian history, and the world explored by Spaniards, who opened new spaces of action for the expansion of Christianity. This world was new from the European perspective in that it was
not found in the texts of classical and Christian antiquity. Although it
had its own antiquities, it lacked a record that was clearly and directly
linked with universalist constructions of world history recognized in
European tradition.

The New World as a world in which native communities had their
own myths, customs, and religious traditions, however, was incompatible with European conceptions of the world and human history. Inasmuch as the ecumenical tradition of Christianity proposed a universalist perspective concerning the world and humanity, it ultimately led

Europeans to disregard the conceptions that Indians had about their own history and the world around them. Gómara undoubtedly saw this New World as a corroboration of Christian ideas to the extent that Europeans had been able to subject the indigenous populations under their power. The possibility of converting the indigenous population gave a sense of triumph to the providentialist view of history, for it reaffirmed the expansionist model that Eusebius developed when he interpreted the empire as the condition for the diffusion of the Christian religion. The interpretation of the topic of *translatio imperii*, or the transmission of empire, implicit in the *Historia general* reaffirms the notion of a universal dominion based on the displacement of the Indians both in the territorial and cognitive realms. The *Historia general* represents an attempt to give meaning to the Indies within the universalist Christian perspective by defining the modes of their incorporation into the common history of humanity and thus establishing the foundations of the Spaniards' authority over the Indians.

HISTORY, CARTOGRAPHY, AND DOMINION: ESTABLISHING RIGHTS OF CONQUEST

Gómara thought that Castilian rights to the Indies were based on *Inter caetera*, also known as the bull of donation, which Pope Alexander VI issued on May 4, 1493. The bull acknowledged the diplomatic mission the Catholic Monarchs sent to him with news of the lands found on the first Columbian voyage, it asked them to extend the Christian faith to their inhabitants, and it conceded to the monarchs of Castile and León and their heirs an exclusive territorial demarcation for future discoveries. The region granted to them included lands that were not occupied by other Christian rulers and that were found beyond a meridian drawn one hundred leagues west of the Azores and Cape Verde.[11] When Gómara indicated in the dedication of his *Historia general* (1552, 1:[*ii*]v) that the pope granted the conquest and conversion of the Indies to the monarchs of Castile and León, he specifically cited the bull of donation. His choice of the expression "conquest and conversion" suggests that the monarchs would have acquired territorial and evangelization rights through the papal donation. According to this reading of the bull, Spaniards could, with permission from their monarchs, legitimately occupy by force those territories within the area awarded to them in the papal demarcation, impose their forms of government on the native inhabitants they found, and bring in preachers to teach them the Christian faith.[12]

Gómara assumed that the papal donation made Spaniards lords and masters of the Indies and a good part of Asia. The meaning that Gómara attributed to the bull is evident in the chapter entitled "La donacion que hizo el papa a los Reies Catolicos de las Indias" (The donation of the Indies that the pope made to the Catholic Monarchs) (1552, 1:12v–13r). After narrating the Columbian discovery, Gómara transcribes the entire Latin text of *Inter caetera* as proof of Castile's right over the Indies. When introducing his transcription he explains:

> *Y porque las hallaron Españoles, hizo el papa de su propia voluntad, y motiuo, y con acuerdo de los cardenales, donaçio[n], y merced a los reyes de Castilla, y Leon, de todas las islas, y tierra firme, que descubriesen al Ocidente. Con tal que conquistandolas embiassen alla predicadores a conuertir los indios, que idolatrauan (1552, 1:12v).*

> And because Spaniards found them, the pope, of his own will and motive and with the agreement of the cardinals, made to the monarchs of Castile and León the donation and mercy of all the islands and mainland that they may discover to the west, under the condition that after conquering them they would send preachers there to convert the Indians who practiced idolatry.

His use of *Inter caetera* as a territorial title of donation is consistent with the statements made in the text of the bull itself, where it explicitly says: "vobis: h[a]eredibusq[ue] & successoribus vestris (Castell[a]e & Legionis regibus) in perpetuu[m] tenore pr[a]esentium donamus: concedimus: & assignamus" [by the tenor of the present we grant, concede, and assign them in perpetuity to you, your heirs, and successors, the monarchs of Castile and León] (Gómara 1552, 1:13r).

The larger historiographical problem presented by the bull is establishing the nature of the juridical act that the pope employed when issuing it, its legal ramifications, and its validity. Gómara uses it to explain Spain's rights in the Indies and the division of the world between Castilians and Portuguese; therefore, he needs to emphasize the characteristics that presented the bull as a judicially valid act of donation.

A basic requisite for the concession to have the value of a donation was that the donor acted with freedom of will (Zavala 1988, 40). Gómara draws upon the text of the bull itself to construct his account of the donation. When he says that the pope had made the donation of his own "will and motive" (1552, 1:12v), he is paraphrasing the bull's text that indicated that the pope acted by his "[m]otu propio non ad vestram vel alterius pro vobis super hoc nobis oblat[a]e petitionis instantiam, sed de nostra mera liberalitate & ex certa scientia ac de apostolic[a]e potestatis plenitudine" [own will, and not at the instance of your petition, nor any other request on your behalf, but out of our singular kindness and certain knowledge, and out of the plenitude of apostolic power] (1552, 1:13r). Indicating that the Indies had been granted under the pope's own instance, he emphasizes the free will of the donor to make the concession of territorial rights. Gómara (1552, 1:12v) attributes merely an informative function (giving notice of the discovery) to the diplomatic mission the Catholic Monarchs sent to Pope Alexander VI, thereby removing the possibility of interpreting the bull as the result of political negotiation (which undoubtedly would have diminished the force of the donation).

Today the bull is often associated with similar papal documents issued throughout the fifteenth century granting the Portuguese kings rights over lands and slaves in Africa (Gibson 1966, 15; Muldoon 1979, 134–135; Zavala 1988, 31–32). The legal extent of the Alexandrian donation, however, is in dispute, for it is unclear whether it established territorial title or merely the rights to be responsible for preaching in a non-Christian region.[13] Even more problematic is its use to legitimate the conquest because it suggests that the pope possessed the authority to grant dominion over vast territories that were not in the possession of Christian rulers. Anthony Pagden (1990b, 13–14) has said that the territorial claims of the Castilian crown over the Indies had rested on the bull up until 1539, when the argument had already lost force both in the international arena and among Spanish jurists and theologians themselves.[14] Although the argument of the papal donation was not completely accepted by his contemporaries, Gómara used it as the legal basis of the Spanish conquest of the New World, and he referred to the enterprise of converting the Indians simply as a condition under which the pope granted the rights of territorial dominion over the Indies to the monarchs of Castile and León.

The way in which Gómara understood the donation is evident in the chapters following his discussion of the conflict between the Castilians and Portuguese over the Moluccas, especially those titled "Diferencias sobre la espeçieria entre castellanos y portugueses" (Differences between the Castilians and Portuguese over spices), "Reparticion de las Indias y mundo nuevo, entre Castellanos y Portugueses" (Repartition of the Indies and the New World between the Castilians and Portuguese), and "La causa y autoridad por donde partieron las Indias" (The reason and authority whereby they partitioned the Indies) (1552, 1:56r–57v). Among the points that he examines to establish Castilian rights over the Moluccas, Gómara resorted to the Treaty of Tordesillas in which João II finally recognized *Inter caetera* and agreed to change the territorial boundary with Spain to a meridian situated 370 leagues west of the Cape Verde Islands (Gibson 1966, 17; Parry 1971, 45–47). Gómara also argued that the Spaniards had been the first to "find them," that they had taken possession of them in the name of the emperor, and that they had made a contract with Almanzor, a local lord. The weight of his argument, however, fell upon the papal donation, for he added that "dado caso que [h]vuieran ydo primero portugueses alla [h]auian ydo despues de la donacio[n] del papa. Y no adquirieron derecho por esso" [given the case that the Portuguese may have gone there first, they had gone after the pope's donation, therefore they did not acquire the right] (1552, 1:56v). As for the right of discovery, Gómara interpreted that the territorial rights that the bull conceded to the monarchs were for all the lands still undiscovered that would be found within the boundaries fixed by the meridian of partition, that is to say, half of the world.

Gómara cited the bull as a document that granted effective temporal dominion, assuming therefore that the donation was related to the faculties or functions of the pope as an ecclesiastical authority. Gómara treats the donation as recompense to the monarchs of Castile, who had been busy in the war for Granada while the Portuguese were establishing their trading factories in Africa:

> [Fernando] quiso antes guerrear co[n] los moros de Granada, que rescatar
> con los negros de Guinea. Y assi q[ue]daron los portugueses con la
> conquista de Africa del estrecho afuera, que començo, o estendio, el infante
> de Portugal don Enrique: hijo del rey don Juan el bastardo, y maestre de
> Auis. Sabiendo pues esto el papa Alexandre sexto, que valenciano era, quiso
> dar las Indias a los reies d[e] Castilla sin perjudicar a los de Portugal que
> conquistauan las tierras marinas de Africa (1552, 1:57r).

Ferdinand wished rather to wage war with the Moors of Granada than to trade with the blacks of Guinea. And thus the Portuguese

were left with the conquest of Africa beyond the strait, which was
begun, or extended, by the *infante* of Portugal *dom* Henrique, son of
the king *dom* João, the bastard, and master of Avis. Knowing this,
then, Pope Alexander VI, who was Valencian, wanted to give the
Indies to the monarchs of Castile without prejudicing those of
Portugal who were conquering the coastal lands of Africa.

The argument that the Catholic Monarchs had postponed their projects
of discovery in order to tend to the war in Granada posed a probable
motive for the donation, particularly seeing that this explanation is
mentioned in the bull itself.[15] Gómara's account made the donation credible as a valid juridical act, attributing to it the sense of rewarding the
Catholic Monarchs for their services to Christianity. The condition that
the monarchs would take charge of the conversion effort makes it consistent with the principle of promoting the diffusion of Christianity in
hitherto unknown lands.

Gómara does not explain the source of the authority that he attributes to the pope for making the "donation and mercy" of the previously and soon to be discovered lands to the Catholic Monarchs, but
the *Historia general* holds this as a central assumption concerning the
legitimacy of the Spanish empire in the Indies. The support for this
interpretation of the bull was in the tradition of the conquest itself, in
which reading a document called the Requirement was employed to
summon the Indians to recognize the authority of the Catholic Church,
the pope, and the monarchs and to consent to the entry of missionaries
to preach the Christian faith.[16] The legal foundation of these summons
rested in the doctrine of the pope's universal dominion. In fact, the
Requirement itself cited the bull of papal donation in order to justify
the conquistadors' demands of authority. Although it was employed to
justify the use of force in the subjection of indigenous communities, it
also served to regulate the conduct of the conquistadors within a formal procedure to initiate war.[17] The document had been composed by
Palacios Rubios to create a protocol of conquest establishing that the
war waged against the Indians satisfied the requirements of a just war
according to the Spanish legal principles of the day.[18] Gómara undoubtedly ascribed to the theory of the pope's temporal dominion and incorporated it into his geographical discourse (when explaining the geographical category of the New World in relation to sacred history) and
his narrative of conquest (where the conquistadors acted under the

assumption of the king's legitimate dominion over the invaded territories and proceeded according to the principles of the Requirement).

Although juridical positions like those expressed by Vitoria (1967, 43–54) absolutely rejected the temporal authority of the pope, the use of the Requirement occupied a prominent place in the conquest narrative.[19] The legitimacy of the papal donation as a title of dominion, however, continued to be accepted among those who justified the conquest. Juan Ginés de Sepúlveda stated in his *Democrates secundus* that the Indies legitimately belonged to the Spaniards:

> *Non igitur, quod regiones illae nullius essent, sed quoniam ipsi mortales, qui regiones tenebant vacui erant ab imperio christianorum, et humanarum gentium. Idcirco in Hispanorum occupantium ditionem iure gentium concessere atque item propter decretum, de quo supra memoravimus summi Sacerdotis et Christi vicari, cuius et potestatis est et officii quae pertinent ad tollendas dissensiones inter principes christianos, occasiones providere et officio religionem christianam, si qua se ostendat via ratione ac jure, dilatandi, quem oportere visum fuerit, praeficere (1997, 101).*

> Therefore, not because those regions did not belong to anyone, but because those mortals who held the regions were devoid of the empire of Christian and civilized peoples, they had relinquished dominion to the Spanish occupants according to the law of nations and because of the previously cited decree of the supreme priest and vicar of Christ, who has the authority and the duty to provide opportunities to eliminate conflicts among Christian princes and to appoint one who seems appropriate to extend the Christian religion, if a reasonable and just occasion should arise.

Although Sepúlveda emphasized the role of the pope as mediator for maintaining peace among Christian rulers, the pontiff ultimately made the act of donation of "empire," that is to say, a transmission of territorial sovereignty.

Gómara created various scenes in which the conquistadors demanded the Indians' obedience through sermons that invoked the papal donation as the title of dominion. Gómara's position is even more extreme than Sepúlveda's because he postulates that the emperor is lord of the world, a title that is also refuted in Vitoria's *Relectio de Indis* (1967, 36–42).[20] Several passages in the *Historia general* suggest that Gómara not only considered the papal donation as a valid juridical act, but also thought that Charles had acquired temporal authority equivalent to that of the pope in the spiritual realm. Various passages in the *Historia general* and in the *Conquista de México* describe the conquistadors presenting themselves before native lords as ambassadors of the world monarch. In Gómara's account of the conquest of Peru, Francisco Pizarro introduced himself to Atahualpa as an ambassador "del papa, y del Emperador, señores del mu[n]do" [of the pope and of the emperor, the lords of the world] (1552, 1:63r), and *fray* Vicente de Valverde told the Inca ruler that Pizarro came to "rogaros, seays amigo, y tributario del rey de España, Emperador de Romanos, Monarca del Mundo" [ask that you be a friend and tributary of the king of Spain, emperor of the Romans, monarch of the world] (1552, 1:64r). In a similar manner, the conquistador Gil González Dávila explains to the *cacique* Nicoyan in Nicaragua that he came to make him a "Seruidor del Emperador que monarca del mundo era" [servant of the emperor who was the monarch of the world] (1552, 1:109v). Gómara also explicitly puts the expression in Cortés's mouth in the chapters titled "Combate y toma de Potonchan" (Battle and taking of Potonchan) (1552, 2:10v–12r), "Como los de Potonchan quebraro[n] sus idolos, y adoraron la cruz" (How those of Potonchan destroyed their idols and worshiped the cross) (1552, 2:14v–15r), and "Lo que hablo Cortes a Teudilli criado de Motecçuma" (What Cortés said to Teudilli, Motecuhzoma's servant) (1552, 2:16r–v). Gómara included the epithet "monarch of the world" in the emperor's title as the basis for demanding the Indians' submission.

All these cases of conquistadors alluding to Charles as "lord of the world" are related to the presentation of the Requirement to the Indians. These allusions to the emperor and the pope as lords of the world only have meaning in reference to the partition of the world between the Spaniards and the Portuguese, or within the notion of universal dominion shared between the pope and the emperor. The justification of the dominion that the conquistadors claimed in the Requirement rested on the universalist perspective of sacred history. Gómara's geographical theory implied a providentialist interpretation, which brought the application of law in the conquest into dialogue with sacred history. In his version of *fray* Vicente de Valverde's sermon to Atahualpa, Gómara takes from the Requirement the brief explanation of human history from the original sin of Adam and Eve to the papal donation that awarded the Indies to the monarchs of Castile (1552, 1:64r).

The type of dominion claimed by the Spaniards required situating the history of the Indies in the context of universal history, according to how it was understood in Christian tradition. Gómara also incorporated this universalist perspective into the formulation of geographical knowledge that resulted in establishing territorial dominion. His citation of Berosus on the exploration of the Mediterranean by Noah emphasizes the cognitive basis of the distribution of Africa, Asia, and Europe to his three sons. His analysis of geographical matters is directly related to issues of dominion. When he discusses the problem of either the unity or plurality of worlds, he mentions the case of Alexander the Great's reaction to Anaxarch's words about the plurality of worlds. Gómara says that listening to Anaxarch made Alexander cry because "[h]auie[n]do tantos mundos, como Anaxarco dezia, no era el aun señor de ninguno. Y assi despues, quando emprendio la conquista deste nuestro mundo, imaginaba otros muchos. Y prete[n]dia señorearlos todos" [there being as many worlds as Anaxarch said, he was not even lord of one. And thus later, when he embarked on the conquest of this world of ours, he imagined many other worlds. And he intended to be lord of all of them] (1552, 1:3r). Gómara reads the case of Alexander as a lesson on the relationship between knowledge of the world and the construction of a universal empire. Christian universalism constitutes the foundation of interpretations of territorial dominion in the historical and geographical discourse of Gómara.

The only practical way of establishing a claim of dominion over the Indies was through a record of territories explored. After the introductory chapters on geography, Gómara wrote about the discovery of the New World and the Columbian voyages. He closed this section with various specifics related to Hispaniola. The transitional chapter presenting the rest of the first part is titled "Que todas las Indias [h]an descubierto Españoles" (That Spaniards have discovered all the Indies) (1552, 1:20r). This section is dedicated to the exploration and conquest of the Indies, region by region, following the same order that had been used in the chapter "El sitio de las Indias" (The location of the Indies). He began with Gaspar de Corte Real's exploration of Labrador (1500) and culminated with Francisco Vázquez de Coronado's expedition to Quivira (1540–1542). He ends the first part with a series of complementary chapters on indigenous themes, the Council of the Indies, Seneca's prophecy, Atlantis, the route to the Indies, the history of the Canaries, and finally "Praise of Spaniards."

Because the crown of Castile claimed the rights of dominion over the Indies, it was also necessary to demarcate the territory on the basis of what was revealed in the navigation and voyages of discovery. Gómara defines the correlation between dominion and naming territory when organizing the first part of the *Historia general* under a narrative scheme of accounts of discovery. In chapter 38 Gómara explains his arrangement of the chapters:

> *Comienço a contar los descubrimie[n]tos de las Indias en el cabo del Labrador por seguyr la orden que lleue, en poner su sitio, pareciendome que seria mejor assi, y mas claro de contar, y au[n] de ente[n]der (1552, 1:20r).*

> I begin by discussing the discoveries of the Indies on the cape of Labrador to follow the order I set in establishing their location, for it seemed that it would be better this way, and clearer for narrating and even understanding.

The narrative portions that Gómara treats apart from the proposed order are the accounts of the discovery of the Indies (including the Columbian voyages and colonization of Hispaniola) and the conquest of Mexico. Both the discovery and the conquest of Mexico are prominent in the organization of the narrative because they provide the foundations of the *Historia general*'s imperialist stance. Gómara chooses to present the rest as part of the account of "the discoveries of the Indies," emphasizing the aspect of exploration and the production of geographical knowledge.

Discovering a territory meant incorporating it within the dominion of the Spanish monarchs, thus recounting the histories of particular voyages of exploration constitutes a more general account of the construction of empire. This becomes a narrative issue to the extent that Gómara, after discussing the colonization of Hispaniola, is confronted with the problem of how to continue his account with the many expeditions that do not conform to a central axis of meaning. He resolves this with the following explanation:

> *Entendiendo qua[n] grandissimas tierras era[n] las q[ue] Christoual Colo[n] descubria, fuero[n] muchos a continuar el descubrimie[n]to de todas. Unos a su costa, otros a la del rey. Y todos pe[n]sando enriquecer, ganar fama, y medrar co[n] los reyes. Pero como los mas dellos no hicieron sino descubrir, y gastarse, no quedo memoria d[e] todos, q[ue] yo sepa (1552, 1:20r).*

> Understanding how enormous the lands were that Christopher Columbus discovered, many went to continue the discovery of them

all; some at their own expense, others at that of the king. And everyone thought of getting rich, achieving fame, and prospering with the monarchs. But as most of them did no more than discover and exhaust themselves, no record of all of them, that I know of, remains.

Narrating the deeds of those who "did no more than discover and exhaust themselves" is a somewhat unpleasant task when one is more interested in praising the achievements of the conquest. Gómara suggestively entitles the chapter "That Spaniards have discovered all the Indies," linking the narrative problem of recounting voyages of discovery with the claim of Spanish territorial rights to the Indies. He resolves this issue with a declaration that reaffirms the Spaniards' political and cognitive authority over the New World:

> *Porne los q[ue] supiere sin conte[m]placion de ninguno, certifica[n]do que todas las Indias han sido descubiertas, y costeadas por españoles, saluo lo q[ue] Colon descubrio. Ca luego procuraro[n] los reyes catholicos de las saber y señalar por suyas, tomando possession de todas ellas, con la gracia del Papa (1552, 1:20r).*

I will set down those that I know without any partiality, certifying that all of the Indies have been discovered and its coasts sailed by Spaniards, except for what Columbus discovered. For the Catholic Monarchs then endeavored to learn about them and claim them as their own, taking possession of all of them, with the grace of the pope.

When Gómara describes the Indies in chapter 12, he lists the name of each region and its location in degrees and leagues of distance from one territory to another. His description of the territories incorporated into the empire is based on the dominion that the crown of Castile claimed over them. Gómara states at the end of his description of the Indies: "La cuenta que yo lleuo en las leguas, y grados, va segun las cartas de los cosmografos del rei. Y ellos no reçiben, ni asientan relaçion de ningu[n] piloto, sin juramento, y testigos" [The count that I follow in leagues and degrees goes by the charts of the king's cosmographers. And they did not accept or record any information from any pilot without a sworn statement and witnesses] (1552, 1:9v). The legal foundation of the construction of the cartographical record is at the same time a guarantee of exactitude with respect to the process of gathering information and the effective incorporation of land into the dominions of the empire.

The *Historia general* emphasizes the role of Spain in enabling the knowledge of the world it had been achieving at this time. Discovery and conquest imply removing diverse regions of the world from their isolation and bringing them to the knowledge of Europeans:

> *[S]abemos como es habitable toda la tierra: y como esta habitada, y llena de gente. Gloria sea de Dios, y honra de españoles, que [h]an descubierto las Indias, tierra de los Antipodas. Los quales, descubriendo, y conquistandolas corren el gran mar oçeano, atrauiessan la torrida, y passan del circulo Arctico espantajos de los antiguos (1552, 1:5r).*

> We know how the entire earth is inhabitable, and how it is inhabited and full of people. Glory be to God, and honor to Spaniards, who have discovered the Indies, the land of the Antipodes. The ones who, discovering and conquering them, travel the great ocean-sea, cross the torrid zone, and go beyond the Arctic Circle, all feared by the ancients.

The information of the habitability of the planet obtained in the voyages of discovery situated the Spaniards in a privileged position for articulating a global geography, both in terms of knowledge and dominion. When transforming the conception of the world known by the ancients, the Spaniards take over a new geography while developing the practical tools for connecting its diverse territories. Gómara revises antiquity and Christian tradition by means of what is revealed by experience in the voyages of navigation:

> *Empero esta ya tan andado, y sabido, que cada dia van alla nuestros españoles, a ojos, como dize[n] çerrados. Y assi esta la esperiençia en contrario de la filosofia. Quiero dexar las muchas naos que ordinariame[n]te van de España a las Indias. Y dezir de vna sola, dicha la Victoria, que dio buelta redonda a toda la redondez de la tierra. Y, tocando en tierras de vnos, y otros antipodas, declaro la ignora[n]çia de la sabia antiguedad y se torno a España, dentro de tres años que partio, segun que muy largamente diremos cuando tratemos del estrecho de Magallanes (1552, 1:6r).*

> Nevertheless it is now so trodden and well-known, that every day our Spaniards go there, with their eyes, as they say, closed. And in this manner experience is contrary to philosophy. I wish to omit the

many ships that ordinarily go from Spain to the Indies, and tell of only one, called *Victoria,* that made a round-trip voyage completely around the world. And, landing on one and other antipodes, it exposed the ignorance of wise antiquity and returned to Spain, within three years of leaving, according to what we will more fully say when we deal with the Strait of Magellan.

Gómara conveys the construction of the empire through an account of the acquisition and production of geographical knowledge. In a similar way, the writing of history becomes a stage within the narrative sequence by compiling and presenting the sum of the knowledge acquired in the conquest. This economy of historiographical discourse can be read in relation to the concept of the New World by which Gómara constructed the territorial identity of the spaces incorporated into the empire. The clash between knowledge inherited from antiquity and knowledge gained from experience and navigation posed a challenge for creating a new conception of the world. Monique Mustapha (1979) has analyzed the geographical plan utilized by Gómara and emphasizes its functionality in relation to the construction of a composite view in the *Historia.* She reads in the geographical plan "an instrument of critical reflection" that allows Gómara to present "a providentialist view of the events, the mechanisms of conquest, the lines of force of expansion, and the motivations and ideologies of the conquistadors" and concludes that "the choice of the geographical plan is the product of a concern for coherence."[21] As Mustapha persuasively demonstrates, Gómara's *Historia general,* all things considered, presents the construction of the Indies as a space of imperial power. This power is acquired in the production of a knowledge that allows the colonizing subject to establish modes of relation within the diversity he encounters in the world.

THE INDIES AND HUMAN DIVERSITY

Toward the end of the *Historia general* Gómara includes a chapter titled, "Del color de los indios" (On the color of the Indians), where he comments on the variety of colors existing in the human race. He referred to color as "una de las marauillas que dios vso en la composicion del [h]ombre" [one of the marvels that God used in the composition of man] (1552, 1:117r), principally for the contrasts and gradations that exist in the physical appearance of humans. The observation permitted him to reflect on human diversity, because although he saw "contrarios colores" [opposite colors] in the extremes of white and black, in the intermediate tonalities the differences were only of "degree." Gómara did not employ skin color to define racial categories (that is, color does not suggest difference in human types), but it allowed him to characterize in a general manner the native inhabitants of the Indies "como leonados, o membrillos cochos, o tiriciados, o castaños" [as tawny, cooked quince, jaundiced, or chestnut] (1552, 1:117v). This division of colors is also presented as a territorial distribution of human groups: "assi como en Europa son comunmente blancos, y en Africa negros, assi tambien son leonados en nuestras indias" [just as in Europe they are commonly white, and in Africa, black, likewise they are tawny in our Indies] (1552, 1:117v). Gómara attributes these differences to nature, abandoning the interpretations of skin color common in his time, which explained it as the result of exposure to the sun (Hodgen 1971, 214; Elliott 1989, 48). If it is not latitude that determines differences in color, then it would be appropriate to assume that this distribution by regions is associated with groups or branches of human descent from a common ancestor because skin color, as Gómara tells us, "va en los [h]ombres, y no en la tierra, que bien puede ser, aunque todos seamos nascidos de adam, y Eua" [runs in humans and not in the land, which may well be, although we are all descended from Adam and Eve] (1552, 1:117v).

Gómara does not think that skin color is an indication of any other type of distinction among human beings; on the contrary he rejects the possibility, explaining it by reference to humans themselves to present it as an expression of divine power and wisdom: "Bien que no sabemos la causa porque dios lo ordeno, y diferencio, mas de pensar que por mostrar su omnipotencia, & sabiduria en tan diuersa variedad d[e] colores, que tienen los [h]ombres" [Although we do not know the reason why God ordained and differentiated it, beyond thinking it was to show his omnipotence and wisdom in such a diverse variety of colors that humans have] (1552, 1:117v). One could infer from the text that color makes visible the differences between the members of each human group associated with three great regions of the world and, therefore, could function as a barrier against the assimilation and confusion of identities. According to the biblical account attributed to Moses, the diverse peoples who had populated the planet originally belonged to Noah's three sons Japheth, Ham, and Shem. If the account in Genesis affirmed the monogenetic origin of humanity after Noah, the interpretation that Gómara proposes for skin color establishes a territorial distribution that could be explained as a delimitation of descent groups. Although the traditional accounts identified the directions taken by Noah's sons in the tripartite division of the world among Africa, Asia, and Europe, Gómara offers in skin color an external indicator of the differences that separated these groups in the course of their gradual occupation of the planet.

Anthony Pagden (1990a) explains that the descriptions of human groups are constructed fundamentally in terms of an idea concerning human nature that is considered universal, which tended to obliterate the differences and discontinuities in diverse societies. In the passage of the dedication where Gómara lays out the differences between the inhabitants of the New World and those he calls *nosotros* (us, that is, Spaniards and presumably Europeans in general), the two outstanding criteria of distinction are "civility and livelihood" and their "greatest sins of idolatry, live human sacrifice, eating human flesh, speaking with the devil, sodomy, herding women, and the like" (1552, 1:[*ii*]v). This typology of traits of civility and religion circumscribes a system of opinions that establish a contrast en bloc between natives and Europeans. In this way social and cultural particularities that take place outside the basic binary of either possessing or lacking the things necessary for civil life are erased and reduced to either being Christian or living in the greatest sin. This renders the differences existing among the different indigenous communities irrelevant in order to subsume them under the regional category of *"indios,"* which groups all native inhabitants of the New World.

J. Jorge Klor de Alva (1995, 248–249) explains the imposition of the collective term "Indians" as a consequence of the colonizers thinking that differences among indigenous groups were irrelevant for their plans. Undoubtedly, this is in part Gómara's attitude when he assumed that indigenous cultures could be reduced to a common denominator; however, it is equally important that when considering them as a collectivity he presumed that their links were real and not imposed. Peter Hulme suggests that the dichotomy that Christian discourse establishes between the saved and the condemned appeared in "several of the key stories in Genesis," which could be interpreted as "allegories of political and cultural . . . distinctions, providing a repertoire of explanatory genealogical narratives in which the development of religious, cultural, ethnic, and eventually colonial distinctions could be inscribed" (1994,

176). With some qualifications, Gómara's distinctions between Indians and Spaniards operate in a very similar way to what Hulme describes.

Sixteenth-century notions of European territoriality were closely tied to the boundaries of Christendom (Hay 1968, 61; Hulme 1994, 193–194); however, Gómara also ascribes to a tradition that postulates along general lines that Europeans, Asians, and Africans descended respectively from Japheth, Shem, and Ham.[22] By analogy he likely assumed that the Indians had a common origin (a first ancestor who populated the region) and shared common characteristics.[23] Considering that each of Noah's sons received one part of the world in the partition, Gómara assumed that the inhabitants of the New World could be characterized as a unique group that shared similar characteristics and customs. This way of thinking about human diversity was supported in biblical and Christian tradition. Saint Augustine understood that the genealogical discourse in the Bible was a means of establishing a chain of succession from fathers to sons, which allegorically signified the opposition between the *civitas dei* and the *civitas terrena*. He grouped the biblical genealogies into three chains of descent: that of Cain to Lamec in the eighth generation, that of Seth to Noah, and that of Shem to Jesus Christ.[24] Saint Augustine observes that the "spirit of God" chose not to complete the lineage of Cain up until the Flood and fully constructed the lineage from Seth to Christ, while leaving many other descendents of Adam unnamed. This genealogical scheme would have an allegorical explanation:

> *Cum itaque istae duae series generationum, una de Seth, altera de Cain, has duas, de quibus agimus, distinctis ordinibus insinuent civitates, unam caelestem in terris peregrinantem, alteram terrenam terrenis, tanquam sola sint, gaudiis inhiantem vel inhaerentem* (De civitate Dei, book 15, chapter 15).

> Thus there are these two lineages, one descending from Seth, the other from Cain, and they suggest by their separate genealogies these two cities which we are discussing, one the heavenly city sojourning on earth, the other the earthly city craving for or clinging to earthly joys as though they were the only ones (Augustine 1957–1995, 4:494–497).

These allegorical genealogies could be interpreted under a criterion of both spiritual and familial continuity. In the descendents of Seth,

Augustine saw a familial lineage that permitted the arrival of the two personages—Noah and Christ—who occupied pivotal positions in sacred history. The lineage of Cain was composed of men inclined toward sin, but the lineage of the patriarchs and prophets mainly included just men who fulfilled a role in the divine plan for the salvation of humanity. In this way, Augustine established a direct association between the groups of descent and the moral traits that identify them.

The generalizations that Gómara made concerning the natives are better understood within the Augustinian interpretation of biblical genealogies. Toward the end of the *Historia general* Gómara alleges that the New World was the ancient Atlantis mentioned by Plato in his *Timaeus* and *Critias*. Referring his readers to the authority of Marsilio Ficino to confirm the veracity of the myth narrated by Plato, Gómara stated that the origin of the inhabitants of the New World had been established, thus they remained intertwined with the ancient past of Europe and Africa.[25] George Hoffman (2002, 212) explains that Montaigne in his essay "Des Cannibales" rejected the identification of the Indies with Atlantis or with a Carthaginian colony in order to adopt a polygenetic perspective with respect to the origin of the Indians (that is to say, he preferred to speak about them as if they were not descendents of Adam and therefore born outside of original sin). Montaigne's refutation of Gómara's identification of the New World with Atlantis would suggest, as Hoffmann persuasively demonstrates, that the assumptions concerning the genealogical descent of the indigenous inhabitants had serious consequences when interpreting their moral characteristics, religion, and culture. Gómara viewed their religion and customs as the product of men who shared a common lineage, whose internal differences as in the case of color were only a matter of degree compared to those that separated them from Europeans and Africans. Treating them as descendents of Noah, therefore, left no other option than to consider them a human group that had been separated from the biblical God after the Flood. The tradition of sacred history made it seem natural to speak of them as if they were one people and to imagine that the Christian divinity dealt with them in that way.

The monogenetic stance concerning the origin of the Indians also allows Gómara to perceive the differences and peculiarities that distinguished communities and individuals. The *Historia general*'s varied descriptions of native customs in different territories of the New World do not completely conform to the general characterization made in the dedication; rather they tend to establish a pattern that permits him to recognize a list of sins as a general tendency. For example, Gómara attributes sodomy, human sacrifice, and idolatry to them in Panuco (1552, 1:25r); sodomy and indifference toward virginity and matrimonial bonds in Cuba (1552, 1:26v); idolatry and human sacrifice in Yucatán (1552, 1:28r); lust in Honduras (1552, 1:28r–v); sodomy and idolatry in Darién (1552, 1:30r); carnality and sodomy in Castilla de Oro (1552, 1:36r–v); sodomy and eating human flesh in Santa Marta (1552, 1:40r–v); and sodomy, idolatry, and speaking with the devil in Venezuela (1552, 1:41v). Other cases suggest that not all Indians shared the same customs such as the case of those in Darién who Gómara says were pleased with Balboa's torture and massacre of sodomites (1552, 1:35r–36r), or those of Yucatán where he explains sodomy was a practice accustomed by few (1552, 1:28r), or the Chibchas, who "Castigan rezio los pecados publicos. Hurtar, matar, y sodomia" [severely punish the public sins theft, murder, and sodomy] (1552, 1:40v). Moreover, his characterization of the customs of the Mexicans enters into details that allow the reader to form a more complex idea of their culture than what is suggested in the dedication. The text presented a dominant pattern, without excluding the existence of variations and differences among or within communities.

The characterization of the Indians through what Gómara called the "grandissimos pecados" [greatest sins] has less to do with not knowing the particularities and diversity of indigenous communities than with assuming an underlying unity among the inhabitants of the New World as a lineage or group of common descent. Undoubtedly, the assumption in part derived from the fact that they occupied the territories that the Spaniards called the "Indies" and were conceived as a unit for the purpose of claiming them as a territorial possession of their monarchs. It is also important to note, however, that the common characteristics Gómara attributes to them (skin color, lacking in civility, and sins) assumes the monogenetic origin of humanity beginning with the various nations that descended from each of Noah's three sons.[26] This kind of ethnic typology was applied in a general manner to the inhabitants of the New World at the same time that the colonizers created and added new distinctions that would serve to explain the implementation of colonial institutions and practices such as slavery.

The problem of interpreting the diversity among indigenous communities was closely linked to imperial politics, especially the debates

concerning the liberty of the Indians. The first distinction made between native groups appeared in Columbus's March 1493 letter to the
monarchs in which he announced the success of his first voyage of discovery. He told them that he had encountered communities of gentle
and docile Indians in Cuba and Hispaniola who were attacked by the
Caribs, whom he characterized as violent and bellicose. Michael Palencia-
Roth (1993) explains that this initial distinction established by Columbus had a fundamental impact on the issue of laws about Indian slavery
beginning in 1503, when Queen Isabel authorized the capture of those
in the Caribbean who were considered "cannibals." The legal basis of
this decision rested on the right to enslave captives in just war; therefore, it affected those Indians who were perceived as a threat to the
colonization effort.[27] Given the scant knowledge they had of the Spaniards, it was not reasonable to expect them to be disposed to subjugation, thus the laws supported the application of the right of capture
only in special cases of resistance. In the case of the Caribs, the association between the habit of eating human flesh and their sustained resistance to the Spanish invaders served as the basis for the decision to
declare them slaves (Palencia-Roth 1993, 41).

In the *Historia general*, Gómara associates the law sanctioning the
enslavement of the Caribs with a list of their alleged sins and offers his
own explanation for its promulgation in his account of the conquest of
Darién:

> A los quales llaman Caribes de Caribana, o porque son brauos, y ferozes,
> conforme al vocablo. Y por ser tan inhumanos, crueles, sodomitas,
> idolatras, fueron dados por esclauos, y rebeldes, para que los pudiessen
> matar, catiuar, y robar, si no quisiessen dexar aquellos grandes pecados, y
> tomar amistad con los españoles, y la fe de Jesu Christo. Este decreto, y ley
> hizo el rei catolico don Fernando con acuerdo de su consejo, y de otros
> letrados, theologos, y canonistas (1552, 1:30r).

> They call those from Caribana Caribs, or because they are brave and
> ferocious as the term suggests. And for being so inhuman, cruel,
> sodomitic, idolatrous, they were considered slaves and rebels, so
> that they could be killed, captured, and robbed, if they did not wish
> to quit those great sins and make friends with the Spaniards and the
> faith of Jesus Christ. This decree and law the Catholic king *don*
> Ferdinand made with the concurrence of his council, and other
> lawyers, theologians, and canonists.

When discussing "la libertad de los indios" [the liberty of the Indians] (1552, 1:117v–18r) Gómara explicitly indicated that this provision did not apply to all the Indians, but only to the Caribs. The characterization of moral traits of the communities designated Carib in the *Historia general* has the central function of explaining the courses of action taken in the conquest, recommending in some cases the application of sanctions such as slavery. The enslavement of the Caribs was based on criteria of inclusion and exclusion that specifically determined the ones who were subject to capture. Gómara identified the area of Tierra Firme occupied by the Caribs as the entire coast from the Paria Peninsula to Cape Vela (approximately from the mouth of the Orinoco River to Lake Maracaibo) and also the coast of Darién (at the mouth of the Atrato River). This territorial demarcation grouped the indigenous communities of the region under the Carib collective as one ethnic unit. There was no social basis to define them as a single people, but the basic criterion Gómara employed was the practice of eating human flesh. The possibility of making generalizations about the native population and classifying groups of indigenous communities (that is to say, creating ethnic categories) rested on basic moral traits that determined the greater or lesser difficulty of their subjugation by the colonizers and their assimilation to Christianity. It was a discourse that identified inclinations or tendencies that established their distance with respect to the Christian world, or rather, their potential resistance to the colonial project.

The inclination toward the sins of idolatry, sodomy, eating human flesh, and so on promoted an interpretation of the Indians of the New World as persons incapable of living on their own. The practice of placing the Indians under the direct tutelage of Spanish colonizers had originated in the institution of the *encomienda*, which provided Indian manual labor for mining, agricultural work, and domestic service for the conquistadors.[28] Its importance as a tool of colonization had become evident when Queen Isabel ordered the abolition of the *encomienda* in 1502, for the Indians refused to work and abandoned the Spaniards, resulting in a decrease in tribute, a shortage of manual labor, and stagnation in the evangelization process. In 1503 Governor Nicolás de Ovando recommended to maintain the system of forced labor, conditioning the Indian's freedom on their collaboration with the colonial order. Their forced labor in agriculture and mining provided food for the Spanish settlers and enabled the economic survival of the colony.

The controversies concerning the capacity of the native population stemmed from the *encomienda* and the wider problem of developing mechanisms for their integration into the colonial order. According to the so-called Clarification of the Laws of Burgos of 1513 (Las Casas 1988–1998, 5:1826), the declared purpose of the law was to facilitate the Indians' gradual integration into a system of wage labor and their conversion to Christianity until they became free of the *encomenderos'* tutelage. The Indians, however, were already considered free vassals of the crown, therefore a legal mechanism was employed that treated them as rustics or minors and declared them incapable of living on their own without the tutelage of a Spaniard (Ots y Capdequí 1982, 24–25). Beginning in 1515, Las Casas sought liberty for the Indians as a means of remedying the situation of abuse they experienced in the *encomiendas* (1988–1998, 5:2108). The greatest obstacles that he faced were testimonies against their capacity raised by the Spanish colonists' solicitors before the Royal Council (1988–1998, 5:2132). Thus the debate over the legal condition and treatment of the Indians began to be formulated in terms of the characteristics that defined their nature. The public image of the native inhabitants was not debated simply as a legal and administrative problem; it came to take on a more profound philosophical importance. On the one hand, a figure like Las Casas, who supported Indian liberty, accused the colonists of defamation, while on the other, those who defended the *encomienda* sought proof to show that the Indians were not freely disposed to receive the faith and submit themselves to the authority of the Spaniards. Proving a point such as this relied on showing that their inclinations were contrary to the ways of civil life and Christian religiosity.

Gómara recognized that the *encomienda* was in conflict with the Indians' status as free vassals. At least he implies this when he states that the Catholic Monarchs initially had declared them free, although the soldiers and settlers used them in the mines, agriculture, transportation, and war (1552, 1:117v). The defamation of the native population played a preponderant role with respect to the issue of slavery. Gómara not only attributed the 1503 law to enslave the Caribs to their "inhuman, cruel, sodomitic, idolatrous" character, he also used similar criteria to explain Loaysa's decision to authorize slavery in 1525. Specifically, he ascribed it to the impact of *fray* Tomás Ortiz's report to the Council of the Indies on the destruction of the Santa Fe monastery at Chiribichí in September 1520. Ortiz had participated in the mission led by *fray* Pedro de Córdoba to evangelize and educate the sons of native *caciques* outside the political and legal structures of the Spanish occupation. The mission had been founded in 1517, but various indigenous communities of Tierra Firme began to rebel against the Spaniards who depended on Indian slaves to fish for pearls at the island of Cubagua. Two of the boys educated by the missionaries in Chiribichí organized the surrounding communities to attack the Santa Fe monastery and kill the friars. Ortiz, who was one of two Dominicans who managed to escape to Cubagua, testified before the council and presented a long list of customs and negative moral traits of the Indians. Bestiality, an inclination toward filthy sins, and an incapacity for instruction were the central characteristics that Ortiz employed to define their nature. His report fundamentally suggested that they were incapable of acquiring the faith and living outside the tutelage of the Spaniards without placing the colonial order in danger.

Ortiz's testimony was communicated by way of Peter Martyr, then a member of the council, who cited it in his *Decades* as proof of the inappropriateness of granting liberty to the Indians. He explained that "An vt liberi esse debeant, nec ab inuitis labor vllus, aut sine precio exigatur, haesitam[us]" [We vacillate on whether they should be free and not be required to work against their will or without pay] (1966, 222). The question of Indian liberty in the end led to an examination of their moral condition based on their resistance to submit themselves to the colonial order:

> Q[uo]d nusqua[m] potuisse Christianis barbaros illos internici[on]em machinari, quin sua fuerint executi cogitata, & quu[m] saepe tentatu[r], an libertas esset p[ro]futura, pernicie[m] illis peperisse co[m]pertu[m] fuit. Vaga[n]tur c[u]m desides & ignaui, ad veteresq[ue] suos ritus & foeda facinora reuertu[n]tur (1966, 222).

> As those barbarians could never plot the massacre of Christians without carrying it out, and having been tested many times whether freedom was suitable for them, it was observed that it brought forth their ruin. They roam about in idleness and sloth, and return to their ancient rites and filthy iniquities.

Martyr's generalizations are focused on the issues of their submission, their labor in the colonists' service, and their conversion. Inasmuch as they attempted to abandon the yoke of the Spaniards, refused to work for them, and would not miss any opportunity to return to their old religion, Martyr concurred with judgments that denied their capacity to live on their own. Martyr's commentary sets a discursive precedent for Gómara's treatment of the subject, so it comes as no surprise for him to explain Indian slavery as a consequence of their sins.

Gómara reproduces Ortiz's testimony and says that Loaysa "dio grandissimo credito" [gave the utmost credit] to Ortiz, so "el emperador con acuerdo del consejo de indias declaro que fuessen esclauos" [the emperor with the agreement of the Council of the Indies declared that they would be slaves] (1552, 1:118r). Ortiz's testimony served as a justification of the crown's political decisions based on the Indians' resistance to colonization, which is why Gómara worked so hard to discredit them before his readers. At the same time, Gómara attributes the laws prohibiting the enslavement of Indians to the Dominican friars, especially Minaya and Las Casas. He even praises the emperor, whose decision to promulgate them was considered appropriate for an "emperador cleme[n]tissimo" [a most clement emperor] (1552, 1:118r). While exalting the justice of these laws, however, he still provides space for his readers to think that slavery and the destruction of indigenous communities was justified:

> *Justo es que los [h]ombres que nacen libres no sea[n] esclauos de otros [h]ombres, especialmente saliendo de la seruidu[m]bre del diablo por el santo bautismo. Y au[n]que la seruidumbre, y catiuerio, por culpa y por pena, es del pecado, segun declaran los santos doctores Agustin y Chrisostomo. Y dios, quiça, permitio la seruidumbre, y trabajo, destas gentes de pecados para su castigo. Ca menos peco Cam contra su padre Noe que estos indios co[n]tra dios. Y fueron sus hijos, y descendientes esclauos por maldicion (1552, 1:118r).*

> It is just that men who are born free not be slaves of other men, especially after leaving the devil's servitude through holy baptism, although slavery and captivity, as punishment for guilt, stem from sin, according to what the holy doctors Augustine and Chrysostom state. And God, perhaps, permitted the servitude and work of these peoples of sins for their punishment. For Ham sinned less against his father Noah than these Indians [do] against God. And his sons and descendants were slaves by curse.

Although Gómara recognized that the Indians were born free, he contemplated the possibility of their servitude being explained by their sins. The reference to Ham linked slavery with the punishment for the sin that befell the entire lineage. In this sense, the concept of descent that Gómara takes from the Bible offers him a method for making generalizations about human groups to determine sins and punishments. The Indians' deficiencies in civility and religion were the fundamental arguments that Gómara utilized to explain the decisions taken by the crown with respect to slavery. Therefore, the subordination of the native population was associated with the efforts of the colonizers to establish order in a world where crass violations of Christian principles were the rule. Because Gómara presented the inclination toward sin as a general deficiency in the native communities of the New World, slavery and the *encomienda* appeared to be acceptable solutions to him for maintaining their subordination and rewarding the colonizers for their services to the king.

TO INHERIT THE WORLD:
HUMAN INTELLECT AND DOMINION

The problem of the Indians' capacity also was posed in terms of prudence (understood by the colonizers as discernment, good judgment, or the disposition to distinguish good from evil within a system of Roman Catholic values). Along with affirming that the Indians lacked the capacity to live on their own, some Spaniards argued that they were slaves by nature and therefore it was justified to capture and enslave them. The concept of natural slavery was based on Aristotle's *Politics*, which stated that there were men who had not been endowed with the capacity to make their own decisions and should be subjected to the condition of slaves.[29] The bishop of Tierra Firme Juan de Quevedo seems to have first employed Aristotle's theory to justify Indian slavery in his debate with Las Casas before Charles V and the Royal Council in 1519 (Las Casas 1988–1998, 5:2410–2426). Quevedo stated that the Indians were slaves in the Aristotelian sense. Las Casas refuted his position arguing that "son gentes capacísimas de la fe cristiana y a toda virtud y buenas costumbres y por razón y doctrina traíbles, y de su *natura* son libres, y tienen sus reyes y señores naturales que gobiernan sus policías" [they are peoples most capable of the Christian faith and all virtues and good customs, and able to be guided through reason and doctrine, and concerning their *nature* they are free, and they have their own kings and natural lords who govern their affairs] (1988–1998, 5:2412).

The intellectual limitations of the discourse used to deny the Indians' capacity mainly arose from the problem of dominion. Vitoria makes this very clear in his lectures of 1535 at the University of Salamanca. Although he thought that the Indians were completely incapable of governance and considered them comparable to *brutis animantibus* (brutish creatures), he did not believe that the presumption of their incapacity would justify their loss of dominion, for dominion was merely the "ius utendi re in usum suum" [right to make use of something for one's own utility] (1967, 26). The natives retained their dominion to the extent that they were susceptible to injustice and they did not exist for anybody else's sake. From a theological perspective, the foundation of dominion was being the "imago Dei" [image of God] (1967, 18) and "Deus et natura non deficiunt in necessariis pro magna parte speciei" [God and nature do not fail in endowing the essentials to most members of a species] (1967, 30). For this reason he concludes that the fact "quod videantur tam insensati et hebetes, puto maxima ex parte venire ex mala et barbara educatione, cum etiam apud nos videamus multos rusticorum parum differentes a brutis animantibus" [that they appear so irrational and stupid, I think, for the most part comes from a poor and barbarous upbringing, for even among us we see peasants not so different from brutish creatures] (1967, 30). From Vitoria's point of view, the bestial quality of the Indians could not be treated as a matter of nature, but rather something that could be corrected through education and evangelization. This position began to be consolidated in 1537, when *fray* Bernardino de Minaya solicited the intervention of Pope Paul III, who condemned Indian slavery and classified as heretical the opinions that claimed they were irrational and incapable of receiving the faith.

After the bulls of Paul III, the defenders of the *encomiendas* lacked a theory about human difference that allowed them to legitimate the subordination of the Indians to the colonizers. Sepúlveda was the first to put forward a reinterpretation of the theory of natural slavery to serve as a justification of the conquest and the *encomienda*. Two moves are fundamental to his argument: first, he redefined the criteria of natural slavery as "tarditatem insitam et mores inhumanos ac barbaros" [innate retardation and inhuman and barbarous customs] (1997, 54); then, he tried to relativize the concept of dominion, to which he attributed different qualifications according to the degree of prudence and ingenuity of the one holding it. Now that the incapacity of the Indians could no longer be sustained in the natural realm, the argument moved to their civility and moral disposition. Sepúlveda evaluated human intellect as a function of customs, ways of life, government, material production, and thought. It was possible for him to consider them slaves by nature as a function of their culture rather than their condition as human beings. In fact, he recognized their capacity in terms of their potential when only provisionally subjecting them to the tutelage of the Spaniards. Attempting to justify their servitude, Sepúlveda focused on evaluating their social and cultural achievements.

Gómara employs a similar concept when he begins his *Historia general* with a reflection on man's desire to know the secrets of the world because of its diversity. Not only is this desire a way of relating to the diversity of things in the world, it also implies a way of understanding human history. The passage serves as an epigraph in the text, for it prepares the reader to think about the kind of intellectual appeal the history of the Indies could have. Gómara thought that man's natural inclination to discover the secrets of the world would lead him to contemplate its extraordinary nature: its size, its beauty, and the diversity of its things. Under the assumption that the desire to ponder the wonders of the world is something typically human, Gómara will make the topic of knowledge the central theme of his reflection:

> *Pocos [h]ombres [h]ay, si ya no biuen como brutos animales, que no se pongan alguna vez a considerar sus marauillas. Porque natural es a cada vno el desseo d[e] saber. Empero vnos tienen este desseo maior que otros, a causa de [h]auer juntado industria, y arte a la inclinaçion natural. Y estos tales alcançan muy mejor los secretos, y causas d[e] las cosas que naturaleza obra (1552, 1:3r).*

> Few men, if they no longer live like brutish creatures, would not at some time set about to consider its wonders, for the desire to know is natural in everyone. But some have this desire more than others, because they have joined industry and art to natural inclination. And these kinds of people grasp much better the secrets and causes of the things that nature works.

When he says that those who have "joined industry and art to natural inclination" not only have a greater desire, but they better grasp "the secrets and causes of the things that nature works," he establishes a distinction between communities (as cognitive subjects) on the basis of their conceptual frameworks and social practices of intellectual production.

Gómara's reference to art and industry here is related to Sepúlveda's notion of prudence, for it implies the existence of a cultural hierarchy.

Gómara understood cultural diversity as part of a wider historical process where human groups are found in a confrontation of power, which he explains in the following terms:

> *Dios crio el mundo por causa del [h]ombre. Y se lo entrego en su poder. . . . Y como Ezras dize, los que moran en la tierra pueden entender lo que [h]ay en ella. Assi que pues dios puso el mundo en nuestra disputa: y nos hizo capazes & merecedores de lo poder entender, y nos dio inclinaçion voluntaria, y natural de saber: no perdamos nuestros preuilegios, y merçedes (1552, 1:3r).*

> God created the world because of man. And it was delivered into his power. . . . And as Ezra says, those who dwell on the earth are able to understand what is on it. Therefore, because God put the world in our dispute and made us capable and deserving of the power to understand it and gave us a voluntary and natural inclination to know, let us not lose our privileges and mercies.

Human diversity in this case implies a differentiation of subjects of knowledge. What is commonly human is the inclination to know, but differences are found in the "art and industry" that each culture employs to reach an understanding of the world. The cognitive incompatibilities of conceptual frameworks and social practices of intellectual production from one community to another suggests that the "privileges and mercies" of knowledge could not be shared equally by humanity. Privileges and mercies are graces that a king grants to his vassals, normally as recompense for some service. The *Historia general* and the *Conquista de México* give a prominent place to the privileges and mercies that kings award to discoverers and conquistadors in the form of vassals (*encomiendas*) or some other type of recognition.

The general suggestion for the reader is that the capacity to know things in the world is part of the legacy that God has given man and therefore the acquisition of knowledge should be considered an expression of divine favor. The clash of intellectual ways of life and understanding would determine the place that each group occupies in the broader picture of human history, ultimately leading to colonial relationships. Gómara's reflection that the world is under dispute among men so that no one may discover God's works is based on two verses from the book of Ecclesiastes.[30] Gómara uses the word "*disputa*" to translate the Latin "*disputatio*," which means "argument," "consideration," "controversy," "debate," "discussion." This *disputa* is a challenge for humanity, because in the quest for knowledge man exercises the dominion that God has given him over the world. If the book of Ecclesiastes indicated that humanity had been denied the possibility of knowing or understanding the works of God, Gómara in contrast cited the fourth book of Esdras,[31] in which it is suggested that the things on the earth constitute the cognitive realm assigned to man. The possibility of knowing is directly related to exercising dominion over things, as is evident in the prophet Ezra's passage:

> *Quemadmodum enim terra silvae data est et mare fluctibus suis, et qui super terram inhabitant quae sunt super terram intellegere solummodo possunt, et qui super caelos super altitudinem caelorum (2 Esd. 4:21).*

> For just as the land is given over to the forest and the sea to its waves, so also those who inhabit the earth can understand only the things on earth, and only those above the heavens can understand the things above the heavens.

The verse quotes the words of the angel Uriel who explains to the prophet why he cannot hope to fully comprehend the way of God (*viam Altissimi*). Ezra had just finished examining human history since the creation of the world, observing that the proliferation of peoples had always brought impiety among men. God had chosen just men like Noah, Abraham, and Jacob, but their descendants had always betrayed his commands and fallen into error. He concludes: "Homines quidem per nomina invenies servasse mandata tua, gentes autem non invenies" [You will find extraordinary men who have kept your commandments, but not nations] (2 Esd. 3:36). Ezra did not understand the place that the chosen people occupied in the divine plan for human history because in the proliferation of man he observed the propagation of evil.

When the angel tells Ezra that he can only understand things that are on the earth, as much as limiting his sphere of incumbency, he is defining the space of power granted by God to man in the history of redemption. In this sense, the "privileges and mercies" that Gómara mentions have their background in a way of thinking about the divine plan for human history beginning with Adam, "quem constituisti ducem super omnibus factis quae fecisti, et ex eo educimur nos omnes quem elegisti populum" [whom you have put in charge of all the works you have created, and from him are descended all of us people you have chosen] (2 Esd. 6:54). Although Gómara does not directly cite sacred history in his text, the context of the citation cannot be ignored. Ezra employed it to explain the people of Israel's dominion over a land in which many other peoples grew and multiplied. Ezra indicated that the exercise of this power over the world had been inherited by Israel, "Residuas autem gentes ab Adam natas dixisti eas nihil esse" [but you have said that the rest of the people descended from Adam will get nothing] (2 Esd. 6:56).

This passage from sacred history quoted by Gómara would suggest that cultural diversity was the result of humanity straying from the path set by the divinity. The fundamental perspective was genealogical. From a common line with Adam and Eve at its base, humanity had begun to multiply, resulting in a variety of peoples. One of these groups had maintained a bond with the creator god, but the other peoples had been removed from the line. In the same way that these genealogical ramifications explained the variety of peoples and religions, they also determined who would be the inheritors of the world. In other words, those who had been removed from the main line had lost the dominion that God had given to Adam over the world. For within the divine plan, the knowledge of the world produced in the process of European colonial expansion was presented as a privilege or a mercy that Providence granted a chosen people, in a manner analogous to Noah's repartition after his exploration of the Mediterranean mentioned by Berosus.

Gómara's representations of native communities and the territories they inhabit tend to reaffirm the idea that the Indians lacked the conditions necessary for holding the sovereignty of their territories. Employing the discourse of defamation in order to criticize the Indians' ways of life, however, Gómara not only dispossessed them of public property, he was also able to propose, as Oviedo had previously done, that the evils that Spanish imperialism had brought to the Indians were a divine punishment. It is difficult to determine the degree of force that these arguments may have had on Gómara's readers, but there is little doubt that his contemporaries would have given serious consideration to the histories of Noah and the people of Israel. On the other hand, it is necessary to note that geocentric, providentialist Christian discourse only allowed him to justify the conquest and the *encomienda* in relative terms. Vitoria and Las Casas had already constructed a discourse that rendered slandering Indians ineffective. Vitoria, stating that the foundation of dominion was being "the image of God," necessarily extended this right to anyone considered to be a descendant of Adam. Las Casas, refuting criticism against the nature of the Indians, had eliminated vital conceptual ground for the theory of natural slavery, which then would be reformulated by Sepúlveda and Gómara upon a significantly more fragile base.

NOTES

1. Gattinara's reformulation of Charles's imperial title is discussed by Hayward Keniston (1958, 56); see also Alonso de Santa Cruz, *Crónica del emperador Carlos V* (1920, 204). The form used in official documents is "Don Carlos por la gracia de Dios, Rey de romanos e Emperador semper augusto; doña Juana, su madre, y el mismo don Carlos por la misma gracia, Reyes de Castilla, de León, de Aragón, de las dos Secilias, etc." [*Don* Carlos by the grace of God, king of the Romans and forever august emperor; *doña* Juana, his mother, and the same *don* Carlos by the same grace, monarchs of Castile, León, Aragón, the two Sicilies, etc.]. With respect to Gómara, everything suggests that he assigned more than a purely formal significance to the question of Charles's imperial title. In the *Conquista de México,* he says that Cortés "escriuio vna muy larga carta al Emperador. Llamolo assi aunque alla no sabian" [wrote a very long letter to the emperor. He called him such even though they did not know [he had received the title] there] (1552, 2:25r–v).

2. Anthony Pagden (1990b, 3) explains that although the administration of the Habsburg territories functioned as an empire, there was never a Spanish empire from the legal point of view. Territories such as Naples, Milan, or the Indies operated more like a confederation of kingdoms. The patrimonial concept that Charles V applied to govern his territories suggested the existence of independent traditions in which each one retained its liberties and exceptions (Elliott 1990, 166).

3. Similar judgments also appear in other sixteenth-century Spanish texts. *Fray* Bernardino de Sahagún emphasized in the prologue of his *Coloquios y doctrina cristiana* that "después de la primitiva yglesia acá no ha hecho en el mundo nuestro Señor Dios cosa tan señalada como es la conuersión de los gentiles que ha hecho en nuestros tiempos en estas yndias" [after the primitive church until now, there is nothing our Lord God has done as outstanding as the conversion of the gentiles that he has done in our times in these Indies] (Sahagún 1986, 72).

4. Foresti explicitly links Columbus's first voyage to the capture of Granada, stating that Ferdinand ordered him to set sail to keep his soldiers occupied after the siege had ended (1513, 328r). Sabellico (1498–1504, 2:121) likewise includes the wars against the Moors in Granada in his account of the Columbian discovery.

5. Eusebius's *Chronicle* divided history into five ages, with the last one covering the period between the death of Christ and the twentieth year of Constantine's reign. His *Ecclesiastical History* is also significant, but it was not translated until the sixth century CE by Cassiodorus. In addition to the importance of Eusebius's works in the development of Christian historiography, it is fundamental to add that the problem of the relationship between sacred and profane history will end up acquiring a theological dimension in Saint Augustine's *City of God*, which interprets human history in terms of the struggle between the *civitas dei* (city of God) and the *civitas terrena* (worldly city, or city of man). See Barnes (1962, 44–54), Dannenfeldt (1954, 11–14), and Breisach (1994, 80–88); for a wider examination of the significance of Christian historians, see Momigliano (1963, 79–99).

6. There is no agreement in recent studies of the *Historia general* with respect to the internal coherence of the work. On the one hand, Monique Mustapha (1979) and Jonathan Loesberg (1983) have detected the coexistence of contradictory views in the text. On the other hand, Glen Carman (1992, 1993) finds unity in Gómara's effort to interpret the empire. Although Mustapha reduces the balance that Gómara achieves between the history of the discovery and the conquest to the mere acquisition of gold and Loesberg reads in the *Conquista de México* the juxtaposition of contradictory narrative lines (one secular and the other divine), Carman emphasizes the internal coherence and pragmatics of the work to the service of the empire. His analysis of the *Conquista de México* relates Cortés's explanation of the conquest to the unfolding of events and Gómara's own political position (1992, 230–235; 1993, 139, 152, 175–176). Another interesting aspect of his study calls attention to a mixture of voices found in the work, suggesting that they incorporated elements of the debate over the conquest (1992, 226; 1993, 103). When presenting the *Conquista de México* as a text of debate, eloquence, and argumentation, Carman shows the complexity of Gómara's historiographical plot and the range of his interpretive effort.

7. One could argue that Gómara presented the theories of antiquity as a group of divergent opinions because he was writing from a post-discovery interpretive point of view. This problem, however, is also evident in the work of Pius II (Eneas Silvio Piccolomini, 1405–1464), who juxtaposed different authors' opinions about the world instead of offering a definitive representation (1992, 5–17). In addition, it has not been possible to ascertain with total certainty the cosmological foundations that led to the conception of the world upon which Columbus based his project of discovery. Jacques Heers (1986) has managed to construct the calculations employed by Columbus through a difficult process

of biographical contextualization and contrasting sources, but the task is plagued with uncertainties.

8. When Edmundo O'Gorman (1977) spoke of the "invention of America," he emphasized the constructed character of the concept of America and the idea of a discovery. His thesis is that "la clave para resolver el problema de la aparición histórica de América estaba en considerar ese suceso como el resultado de una invención del pensamiento occidental y no ya como el de un descubrimiento meramente físico, realizado, además, por casualidad" [the key to resolving the problem of the historical appearance of America was in considering this event as the result of an invention in Western thought and no longer merely as a physical discovery, moreover, realized by accident] (1977, 9). O'Gorman linked this notion of "invention" with widely circulated statements concerning the destiny of America. José Rabasa (1993) has reinterpreted the "invention of America" as a form of Orientalism, that is to say, the creation of forms of cultural authority that support the construction of the colonial subject based on a concept of territorial identity. Previously, Edward Said (1979, 20) employed the concept of strategic formation to describe the relations that are established between texts, allowing them to acquire a certain authority including a "referential power" in culture. His Orientalism implies a system of rules for producing statements about the Orient in the same sense that a "discursive formation" (Foucault 1972, 31–39) regulates the construction of objects, types of statements, concepts, and thematic choices.

9. In this sense, the idea of a "subject of universal knowledge" implies, among other things, the concept of freedom of conscience and, therefore, freedom of religion. Only then does it involve a separation between knowledge (acquired through reason and experience) and the ethnic perspective (defined in relation to cultural and religious traditions).

10. This replacement of indigenous temples and idols with crosses and churches is one of the processes mentioned by Motolinía (*fray* Toribio de Benavente) in his narrative on converting the Mexicans (1985, 74–86). Gómara, in turn, calls attention to this in various places in his *Historia general,* but it will take on a particular relevance in his account of the conquest of Mexico, where he emphasizes the role of the Spaniards in the destruction of indigenous temples and idols. This symbolic occupation of space is reiterated regularly in the narrative progression until becoming the thematic axis in the titles of various chapters. Clear examples include "Como derribo Cortes los idolos en Acuçamil" [How Cortés cast down the idols in Acuzamil] (1552, 2:[9]r–v), "Como los de Potonchan quebraron sus idolos, y adoraron la cruz" [How those of Potonchan smashed their idols, and worshiped the cross] (1552, 2:14v–15r), "Que los de [Cempoallan] derocaron sus idolos por amonestacion de Cortes" [That those of Zempoala destroyed their idols at the admonition of Cortés] (1552, 2:26v–27r), "La respuesta que dieron a Cortes los de Tlaxcallan sobre dexar sus

idolos" [The reply that those of Tlaxcala gave Cortés about abandoning their idols] (1552, 2:35r–v), "Como Cortes començo a derrocar los idolos de Mexico" [How Cortés began to destroy the idols of Mexico] (1552, 2:50v), "La platica que hizo Cortes a los de Mexico sobre los idolos" [The conversation that Cortés had with those of Mexico about the idols] (1552, 2:50v–[51]v), "De como trato Cortes la conuersion de los Indios" [How Cortés dealt with the conversion of the Indians] (1552, 2:96v), "De como Canec quemo los idolos" [How Canek burned the idols] (1552, 2:104r–105r), and "De la conuersion" [On the conversion] (1552, 2:135r–v). In Zacotlan, Gómara says Cortés "[p]uso muchas cruzes en los templos derrocando los idolos como lo hazia en cada lugar que llegaua. Y por los caminos" [set up many crosses on the temples and cast down idols as he did in each place he arrived and along the way] (1552, 2:28r). The recurring activity of destroying idols thus appears as one of the immediate objects pursued by Cortés in his advance toward Tenochtitlan.

11. João II of Portugal did not accept *Inter caetera* until 1494 when the Catholic Monarchs agreed to change the line of demarcation to a meridian located 370 leagues from the Azores in the Treaty of Tordesillas (Gibson 1966, 15–17; Parry 1971, 45–47; Muldoon 1979, 139; Elliott 1984a). The correction of the original demarcation did not require papal authority because Spanish territorial claims continued to rest on the bull.

12. Gómara is consistent in treating the bull primarily as a concession of rights of conquest. James Muldoon (1979, 137–138) has contended that bulls were fundamentally addressed to grant ecclesiastical jurisdiction in the lands in question, whereas war would be based on the indisposition of the natives to receive the missionaries.

13. Silvio Zavala (1988, 30–43) explains that although the promulgation of *Inter caetera* in 1493 continued medieval practice, it differed from its antecedents in that it led to disputes that previously had not occurred. He thinks that the bull lacked arbitral value and therefore could not be used to establish territorial rights of lands but could only authenticate the claims made by a king. The rights would come from the discoveries of which the bulls would serve as formal proof. On the other hand, Zavala recognizes that the bulls were interpreted as arbitral decisions that effectively granted territorial rights during the period of the discoveries. Some authors suggest that the bulls granted territorial rights, but others only recognize the rights of exclusivity for carrying out the evangelization of the native populations. James Muldoon (1979, 152) argues that the legal tradition incorporated a hierarchy of principles among which there was no obvious way of determining which had precedence. The conquest of the Indies, however, had led to conflicts of interest that forced one to take a definite position among the available options. On Spain's territorial rights in the New World, see also Parry (1940; 1971, 45–47), Pagden (1990b, 13–36), and Seed (1992; 1995).

14. Palacios Rubios and the canonist *fray* Matías de Paz were the first to employ the bull of donation to explain the monarchs of Spain's dominion over the New World (1954, 36, 223). The theologian Francisco de Vitoria, however, later negated the validity of the papal donation as a title of dominion over the Indies because the pope lacked "plenam jurisdictionem in temporalibus in toto orbe terrarum" [absolute temporal jurisdiction over the entire world] (1967, 43–54). Domingo de Soto likewise denied that the pope had temporal dominion over the world (Zavala 1988, 316).

15. "Sane accepimus quod vos qui dudum animu[m] proposueratis aliquas insulas & terras firmas remotas & incognitas ac per alios hactenus non repertas qu[a]erere & inuenire vt illarum incolas & habitatores ad colendum Redemptorem nostrum: & fidem catholicam profirendum: reduceretis: hactenus in expugnatione & recuperatione ipsius regni Granat[a]e plurimum occupati huiusmodi sanctum & laudabile propositum vestrum ad optatum finem perducere nequiuistis" [We understand that earlier you had planned in your soul to seek and discover some distant and unknown islands and continents not found by others until now in order to reduce the inhabitants and natives there to the service of our Redeemer and to profess the Catholic faith, and that for having been very busy with the recovery of the said kingdom of Granada, you could not until now bring your holy and laudable plan to the desired end] (Gómara 1552, 1:12v–13r). James Muldoon (1979, 137) states that the papal bulls of donation granted to the Portuguese and Castilians contained a brief summary and a conclusion concerning the facts presented by the ambassadors before the papal court. This pattern in *Inter caetera* (1493) is already found in *Romanus Pontifex* (1454), which mentioned the history of the Portuguese in Africa and then concluded by granting them the Canaries with the rights to invade, capture, take slaves, and so on.

16. The Requirement was the basic legal mechanism employed in the most important conquests conducted in the continental regions of the Americas. Before initiating an attack, the conquerors read a document to the Indians requesting them to submit to the Castilian monarchs' authority and to allow preachers into their communities to teach them the Christian faith. If they ignored these demands, the Spaniards would wage war against them, confiscate their property, and enslave them. The basis for this "request" was explained to the Indians through a short account of the creation of the world and the first human couple, the settlement of the earth, Saint Peter's appointment as head of the church, and Pope Alexander VI's donation of the Indies to the monarchs of Spain. The Indians were given some time for deliberation, but if they ignored or rejected the request, then war would ensue on the grounds of native resistance to legitimate claims of sovereignty. James Muldoon (1979, 142) affirms that the Requirement had the purpose of demonstrating that the natives had refused to admit the missionaries, thus providing the grounds for the Spanish military invasion.

17. Both Patricia Seed (1995, 72) and José Rabasa (2000, 10–11, 84–96) emphasize the Requirement's importance as a codifying tool of violence in the Spanish conquest of the Indies, although Rabasa thinks that the Ordinances of 1526 came to form the dominant ideology. The language of peaceful conquest in the ordinances, Rabasa argues, lent itself more to the kind of Christianity that the Spanish crown tried to impose in the Indies. On the Requirement in the more general context of Spanish colonialism, see Charles Gibson (1966, 38–40), John H. Parry (1971, 137–139), Lewis Hanke (1974, 35–38), and Silvio Zavala (1988, 78–81).

18. Patricia Seed (1992) attributes the composition of the Requirement to the crisis brought on by the sermon of *fray* Antonio de Montesinos in 1511 denouncing the abuses that Spaniards were committing against the Indians. King Ferdinand's response was to name a commission composed of Juan López de Palacios Rubios and Matías de Paz to examine the matter. Both wrote treatises that based the authority of the monarchs over the Indies in the papal donation of 1493. Palacios Rubios appealed specifically to the doctrine of the pope's temporal dominion to adduce the legitimacy of the war against the Indians in terms very similar to those set in the Requirement: "[E]l cuidado del mundo entero y la potestad sobre él residen en el Papa, el cual hizo donación y concesión de la provincia en que viven a Vuestra majestad, a la cual tienen que obedecer como a divino depositario de la Iglesia, así como están obligados a admitir a los predicadores de nuestra fe para que les expliquen detalladamente todos sus misterios. Y si después de un plazo prudencial para decidirse no quisieren hacerlo, pueden ser invadidos y expugnados por medio de la guerra, la fuerza y las armas, aprehendidos sus bienes, y reducidas a esclavitud sus personas, porque la guerra de parte de los Cristianos está justificada" [The care of the entire world and the jurisdiction over it reside in the pope, who made the donation and concession of the province in which they live to Your Majesty, whom they have to obey as a divine depository of the Church, just as they are obligated to admit preachers of our faith so that they may explain in detail its mysteries to them. And if after a prudent period for deciding they do not wish to do it, they may be invaded and taken by means of war, force, and arms, apprehending their goods, and reducing their persons to slavery, because war on the part of Christians is justified] (Palacios Rubios 1954, 36). Paz, in turn, clearly agreed with Palacios Rubios in posing the pope's authority as the foundation of the king's dominion: "Por la autoridad del Sumo Pontífice, y no de otra manera, le será permitido a nuestro católico e invictísimo monarca gobernar a los sobredichos indios con imperio real, mas no despótico, y retenerlos así perpetuamente debajo de su dominación" [By the authority of the Supreme Pontiff, and in no other manner, our Catholic and most triumphant monarch is permitted to govern the aforementioned Indians with royal but not despotic empire, and thus perpetually keep them under his domination] (Paz 1954, 223).

19. Rolena Adorno (1994) has shown that Álvar Núñez Cabeza de Vaca's narrative in his *Relación* acquired particular significance based on the Ordinances of 1526. Her suggestion of reading conquest accounts in light of the legal discourse proposes a fundamental methodological premise for reading colonial texts. José Rabasa (2000), although with a different objective, follows this same premise in his analysis of the way in which Althusserian acts of interpellation involved in the Requirement and the Ordinances of 1526 determine the dominant features in sixteenth-century Spanish colonial discourse.

20. James Muldoon (1999, 87–93) explains that the concept of the emperor as *dominus mundi* emerges in the twelfth century when Roman law reappeared, but it would not become a theory of universal empire until Dante's *De monarchia*. Ramón Menéndez Pidal (1963, 1966), however, argued that the concept of universal empire sustained by Mercurino Gattinara, Charles V's chancellor, ultimately led to *universitas christiana*.

21. "Tour à tour utilisé pour traduire une vision providencialiste des faits, les mécanismes de la conquête, les lignes de force de l'expansion, les motivations et l'idéologie des conquistadores, le plan géographique apparaît comme un instrument de réflexion critique propre à mettre en lumière les caractéristiques profondes d'une époque . . . Le choix de l'ordre géographique relève ainsi d'un souci de cohérence" (Mustapha 1979, 439).

22. Denys Hay (1968, 8–14, 107–109) states that Josephus was the first to relate the tripartite division of the world with the dispersion of the descendents of Noah's three sons; this theory would then be recycled by the authorities of Christian tradition (Saint Augustine, Lactantius, Saint Jerome, and Saint Isidore) and still had currency among sixteenth-century historians.

23. On Noah and the monogenetic theory of the origin of humanity, see Hodgen (1971, 207–251).

24. See books 15 and 16 of *City of God.*

25. Gómara cites the edition of Plato's works prepared by Marsilio Ficino (1546, 734), who stated in an introductory note to *Critias* that the history of Atlantis was true because it had been established as fact through a chain of sources that led from the Athenian poet-philosopher Critias (ca. 460–403 BCE) to someone named Proclus Marcelli.

26. Walter Mignolo (1995) and Gustavo Verdesio (1999) question the uncritical use of territorial categories created in the process of colonization and make an effort to recover the spatial conceptions employed by diverse indigenous communities before their contact with European invaders. Although I recognize the importance of revising the categories of geographical discourse that we have accepted, my main interest here is to emphasize that their assumptions came from the tradition of sacred history.

27. Sepúlveda (1997, 108–110) explained that the laws of slavery had the purpose of saving the lives of the vanquished and therefore a just war was just

cause for enslavement. This principle was adapted to the specific circumstances of the Indies where, even assuming that Spaniards had cause for a just war, slavery was reserved for cases of "crudelitatem et pertinaciam aut perfidiam et rebellionem" [cruelty, obstinacy, treachery, and rebellion] (1997, 129). The differences in this respect were in what could be considered just war; for as Rolena Adorno (1992d) emphasizes, the right of capture in just war was also accepted by Las Casas, who defended the Indians' liberty. On the right of capture, see Zavala (1988, 182–196).

28. On the *encomienda,* see Chapter 1, note 23.

29. Aristotle (1995, 1999) differentiates between the master, the wife, children, and the slave. The first three possess the faculty to make decisions and are differentiated only in authority and maturity, but the slave completely lacks this ability.

30. The first verse Gómara uses from the book of Ecclesiastes is "puso dios al mundo en disputa de los [h]ombres con que ninguno dellos pueda hallar las obras q[ue] el mismo obro y obra" [God put the world in men's dispute so that none of them may discover the works that he himself worked and works]. It is a fairly appropriate translation of Eccles. 3:11, which says: "cuncta fecit bona in tempore suo et mundum tradidit disputationi eorum ut non inveniat homo opus quod operatus est Deus ab initio usque ad finem" [He has made everything good in its time and has delivered the world to their consideration, so that man cannot discover the work that God has done from the beginning to the end]. The second verse is probably paraphrased from Eccles. 8:17, which says: "et intellexi quod omnium operum Dei nullam possit homo invenire rationem eorum quae fiunt sub sole et quanto plus laboraverit ad quaerendum tantus minus inveniat etiam si dixerit sapiens se nosse non poterit repperire" [And I realized that man can find no reason for all the works God does under sun; and the more one endeavors to seek, the less one will discover; and although the wise man says he knows, he can never find out].

31. The third and fourth books of Esdras have been removed from many editions of the Bible because they have not been found in Hebrew manuscripts. Saint Jerome included them in the Vulgate, which was derived from the Septuagint, the third-century BCE Greek version of the Hebrew Scriptures along with additional material. In the subsequent Clementine edition of the Vulgate, they appear after the book of Revelation. In most English-language texts, the Vulgate's first and second books of Esdras are known respectively as Ezra and Nehemiah, and the third and fourth are recognized and cited as 1 and 2 Esdras (Esd.) of the Apocrypha, which will be the citation format followed here to facilitate locating the passages.

CHAPTER 3

Exchange as a Narrative of Imperial Expansion

CHRISTIAN RHETORIC, ECONOMIC ENDS

In order to articulate and promote an imperial mission for Spain in the Indies, Gómara needed to explain how the conquest had benefited the crown, the conquistadors, and the native inhabitants. As goals for imperial expansion he proposed things such as increasing royal rents, converting the Indians, creating businesses and enterprises, producing wealth, bringing the native population to the service and obedience of the emperor, gaining honor and recompense, and achieving social and economic status. The subjects of these actions were the conquistadors, settlers, missionaries, and officials who served the emperor in the New World, but their services purportedly brought improvements in religion, prosperity, and royal rule to everyone in the empire. The different activities of colonization and their consequences can be understood individually as beneficial within Spanish colonial discourse, but proposing a way to articulate these various colonial ends as a well-defined set of guiding principles still presented enormous difficulties on ethical and political grounds. The fundamental problem in political terms was to construe an overarching notion of common good that accounted for Spain's imperial rule, and the main ethical issue was to determine what ends should be prioritized and which should be postponed.

Conflicting views about how to conduct the affairs of the Indies had plagued the historical experience of Spanish imperialism. When Gómara wrote the *Historia general,* fifty years of colonization had not resolved the contradictions that emerged among the different objectives organizing the Spaniards' activities in the New World. The debates over the treatment of the Indians, authorizations for conquest, and perpetual rights to *encomiendas* were some of the areas where incompatible agendas within the enterprise manifested. This scenario of contested policies and heterogeneous views made it impossible to rely on a dominant ideology in support of the conquistadors' aspirations for hegemony. Facing the task of conceptualizing Spain's imperial mission in the Indies, Gómara encountered a set of stories fraught with incongruities, lacking unity and clear purpose. Without a solid discursive base, he could only avail himself of his own narrative skill as he endeavored to praise the Spanish conquest of the New World. The major difficulty for constructing a coherent account of the colonization process rested in the limitations of the available ideologies to talk about processes of globalization in which human agency operated within conditions fixed by economic forces.[1]

James Muldoon (1979, 132–157), for example, has observed an inconsistency between the activities of colonization dominated by temporal interests and the rhetoric employed in legal documents, which was focused on spiritual ends. From Muldoon's point of view, the juridical foundations of fifteenth- and sixteenth-century Portuguese and Spanish colonial expansion created dislocations that made irrelevant the arguments criticizing the conquest developed by Vitoria and Las Casas. Muldoon's insightful observation reveals the inadequacy of the discourse to account for the actions of Spanish settlers and conquistadors. Ideologies of colonization worked rather precariously during the period of Spanish expansion. The theories created by the Spaniards concerning empire, just war, and the crown's dominion over the native inhabitants were ineffective as a justification for the conquests if we follow most of the reports written by the conquistadors themselves. Las Casas's criticisms concerning the conquest were disturbing because they denounced open violations of the "judicial infrastructure," which the Spaniards themselves had designed for the subjugation of the native population. The creation of new prototypes of power appears more conspicuously in the development of the international anti-Spanish criticism associated with the revolt of the Low Countries and the strengthening of expansionist interests in Elizabethan England (see Maltby 1971).

Gómara's reflection on the empire's objectives in his *Historia general* attempted to construct such a prototype by solving the inconsistencies that the colonization of the Indies posed from a historiographical perspective. The main difficulty with composing his historical narrative was conveying a sense of continuity in the sequence of discoveries, explorations, and conquests that had occurred during the most active periods of Spain's invasion of the New World. Gómara resolved this problem by writing an account of the origins of the empire that provided purpose and meaning to the colonial enterprise. He also placed the diverse narrative sequences within a signifying structure able to encompass the goals of colonization. Finally, he had to assess the concrete results that the Spaniards had achieved in the conquests and territorial occupation of the Indies. Gómara needed to show what they had accomplished after more than fifty years of colonial expansion.

The *Historia general* presents the account of the explorations and conquests in a simple geographical order, treating them as isolated units instead of incorporating them within a wider progression of events. Gómara, however, set apart both the discovery (including the Columbian voyages and the colonization of Hispaniola) and the conquest of Mexico from the rest of the narrative. This organization suggests that Gómara used these accounts as some sort of framing device to give structure to the history of the Indies and create the impression of continuity throughout the text. In fact, his discovery account permitted him to lay the foundations for interpreting the colonial relationships between Spain and the Indies, inasmuch as it established the basic plan of the enterprise. The first part of his *Historia general* ends with the chapter "Praise of Spaniards," which provides an interpretive overview of the conquest and its results. The second part, titled *Conquista de México,* presents the conquest of Mexico as a model case of Spanish imperial expansion in the New World. Several chapters near the end of the second part are dedicated to an examination of the benefits that the conquest brought to the Indians. The narratives of the Columbian discovery and the conquest of Mexico allow us to examine how Gómara came to articulate an imperial mission for Spain in the Indies.

THE DISCOVERY AND THE HISTORICAL TRADITION

Initially, the accounts of Columbus's discoveries revolved around the recurrent theme of Christianity's struggle against the Muslims. The association of his first voyage with the Catholic Monarchs' victory in Granada is found in the Alexandrian bull of donation and in early editions of Columbus's letter, and clearly became a central theme for historians of the Indies. Reprints of this letter during the sixteenth century reveal that the discovery was considered part of a much larger account that went back to the eighth-century Muslim invasion of Spain. This narrative assigned a paramount place to King Ferdinand of Aragón as Spain's leader in the undertakings of the conquest of Granada, the expulsion of the Jews, and Christian expansion toward the East (Roa-de-la-Carrera 1998, 75–85).[2] Columbus was completely secondary before the figure of the great Catholic king, who was advancing the cause of Christianity.

As the Indies acquired greater political and economic importance, however, it became necessary to construct a new interpretation of the discovery that would address the larger process of colonial expansion. Peter Martyr's revisions to his *Decades* reveal how the account of the discovery began to be integrated within a larger narrative of colonization. At first, Martyr related the discovery without much temporal perspective, for the event was recent and he could only report on what had occurred up until the preparations of the second voyage.[3] At this point he merely underscored that the Catholic Monarchs expected to "ad Christi lege[m] tot nationes & simplices gentes facile trahi posse" [easily be able to draw so many nations and simple people to the law of Christ] (1966, 42), completely omitting some of the contentious themes that would draw greater attention from subsequent historians.[4] Because Martyr wrote about the news that came to the court, his way of telling the story changed as the character of the enterprise changed. By the third book of his *Decades*, however, he had stopped writing as if he were listing an aggregation of news items and began conveying the sense that these events formed part of a larger, independent historical process.[5]

Martyr's first decade exhibits evidence of successive additions and amendments, updating the text to conform to ensuing developments

unfolding in the New World. These rewritings brought new understandings of the events, thus superimposing various layers of narration. The original version of the decade, published in 1500, discussed
Columbus's voyages (books 1, 2, 3, and 6), the submission of Hispaniola's
native inhabitants and his quarrels with the Spaniards (books 4 through
7), the exploration of Tierra Firme after his third voyage (books 8 and
9), and native customs in Hispaniola (book 9). Ten years later, Martyr
realized that he needed to infuse his account with contemporary historical meaning. In the tenth book, Martyr added an epilogue addressed
to Iñigo López de Mendoza in 1510, in which his writing changed from
reporting a series of news items to constructing a full-fledged historical
narrative:

> *Magna laude digna est hac nostra te[m]pestate Hispania, quae late[n]tes
> hactenus tot Antipodu[m] myriadas nostris ge[n]tibus cognitas effecerit,
> ingenioq[ue] pole[n]tibus ampla[m] adeo scribe[n]di materia[m] praebuerit.
> Quibus ego iter aperui, cum ista nude vti vides collegerim, tum quia
> elega[n]tioribus nequeo vestibus quicqua[m] ornare, tum etia[m] quonia[m]
> calamu[m] vt historique scribere nu[n]qua[m] sumpsi, sed vt per epistolas
> raptim scriptas his a quoru[m] ma[n]datis referre pedem no[n] licebat,
> satisfacere[m] (1966, 76).*

> Spain is worthy of great praise in our time for making known to our
> people so many thousands of antipodes hidden until now, and
> providing ample writing material to those who have the talent, for
> whom I have opened the way, by collecting these things
> unembellished, as you see, not only because I am unable to adorn
> anything so elegantly dressed, but also because I never took up the
> pen to write historically, except to satisfy, with hurriedly written
> letters, the mandates of those one may not ignore.

The statement that Spain deserved to be praised for having revealed
"thousands of antipodes" to the world brings the text into historical
modality by answering the question: "What have the Spaniards accomplished in their travels?" In this revision, Martyr interjected himself as
a precursor who nevertheless did not intend to "write historically,"
but "to satisfy . . . the mandates" of the powerful. Thus he recognized
the limitations of his text to tell the story of the discoveries within an
encompassing narrative framework. Martyr began to discuss the exploration of the New World as a historiographical problem, fundamentally

because he realized the need to interpret these events within a larger process of expansion. Martyr seems to convey a sense of coherence at the end of this first decade when he described the Consejo de la Corte (the precursor of the Council of the Indies), followed with a brief mention of Columbus's fourth voyage to Veraguas (Panama) and other discoveries. Here he moved the story into two main directions: the institutionalization of government for the new lands and the continued opening of new regions to the Spaniards' knowledge, commerce, and dominion. When presenting a new framework that shifted the focus away from the Columbian voyages, Martyr implicitly was redefining the history of the discovery. This revised account prepared the way for emerging areas of knowledge that the Spanish explorations to the west had enabled.[6]

In addition to the sudden appearance of a historical context that markedly differed from that of the early Columbian explorations, the historian of the discovery faced other difficulties writing in the sixteenth century. Marcel Bataillon (1954) has attributed Martyr's exclusion of details about the discovery of Veraguas in the first decade to his desire to ingratiate himself with the crown.[7] Thus he explained the omission as Martyr's reaction to Diego Colón's lawsuit to reclaim his hereditary political and economic rights over the territories on the mainland discovered by his father. The brevity of Martyr's mention of the fourth voyage, however, is quite understandable when one recognizes that his purpose in this section was to provide a brief summary of ten years of history. His treatment suggests that although Columbus's first three voyages had a major influence on navigation, commerce, and politics in the new territories, the fourth was an insignificant contribution to the exploration of the continent. Moreover, Martyr explicitly endorsed Colón's legal position when he stated that "[v]aria diuersi nautae hoc dece[n]nio littora percurrerunt, sequuti tame[n] Coloni inuenta" [several different navigators have sailed the coasts in these ten years, but having followed the discoveries of Columbus] (1966, 75).

This is not to say that the lawsuits did not influence historiography, but these narrative accounts maintained their independence from what transpired in the legal proceedings. Bataillon used the Columbian litigation to explain not only Martyr's text, but also the histories of Oviedo and Gómara. He proposed that these authors, in support of the crown's position, attempted to prevent Tierra Firme and Veraguas from being associated with Columbus's discoveries. But Oviedo clearly referred to the "tercero viaje e descubrimiento que él hizo cuando halló la costa (e grandísima parte del mundo incógnita) llamada Tierra Firme general-mente" [third voyage and discovery that he made when he found the coast (and the largest part of the unknown world) generally called Tierra Firme] (1992, 1:58), and Gómara said Columbus landed on the main-land in the region of Paria on his third voyage and on the fourth sailed the coast from Cape Higueras to Nombre de Dios.

There is a difference between the purposes of judicial and historical inquiry: the former seeks to reach a decision and the latter an interpre-tation. When Oviedo and Gómara respectively mentioned the lawsuit, it was not in the context of the discovery of Tierra Firme or Veraguas, but in discussing the accusation that Columbus would have given up the voyage had it not been for the Pinzón brothers. Gómara briefly touched on this in his chapter on Columbus's death, but Oviedo made it part of his discovery account, adding:

> *Esto será mejor remitirlo a un largo proceso que hay entre el Almirante y el fiscal real, donde a pro e contra hay muchas cosas alegadas, en lo cual yo no me entremeto; porque, como sean cosas de justicia, y por ella se han de decidir (1992, 1:26).*

> This will be better remitted to a long proceeding that exists between the Admiral and the royal *fiscal*, where many things pro and con are alleged, in which I do not involve myself, for they are matters of justice and therefore must be adjudicated.

The case against Columbus only reveals that it was difficult to see an obvious correlation between his discoveries and subsequent explo-rations in the New World. The lawsuits questioned Columbus's contri-bution to Spanish expansion there. The first suit presented by Diego Colón reclaiming his rights over the mainland achieved the greatest resonance.[8] The *fiscal* or royal attorney tried to minimize the impor-tance of Columbus in the discoveries, but his arguments did not estab-lish narrative guidelines upon which historians of the Indies would construct their narratives. With sufficient artistic leeway to create Columbus's persona within the story, these historians did not need to deny his accomplishments. On the contrary, both Oviedo and Gómara made the recognition of his services to Spain a central theme in their discovery accounts.[9] The impact of the suits may be best appreciated in Las Casas's *Historia de las Indias*, the only text that discussed the case in detail. He criticized the *fiscal's* statements because they contradicted the notion that God had chosen Columbus for the undertaking (1988–1998, 3:523–527, 657–661).[10]

Las Casas suggested that the discovery was not the product of only one man's wisdom and will, but rather the constancy and achievements of Columbus as part of a providential plan. He used the Genoese sailor to arrive at an interpretation of God's will for the Indies, thus Columbus remained the main protagonist in his account of the discovery. Facing the question of how he could have gained knowledge of the Indies and exhibited such conviction and persistence in achieving his objective, Las Casas answered:

> *Pero, pues parece que Dios, antes de los siglos, concedió a este hombre las llaves deste espantosísimo mar y no quiso que otro abriese sus cerraduras oscuras, a éste se le debe todo cuanto destas puertas adentro ha sucedido y cuanto sucediere en todo género de bondad de aquí a quel mundo se haya de acabar (1988–1998, 3:697).*

> But, as it seems that God, centuries before, granted this man the keys to this most menacing sea and did not want another to open its obscure locks, to him is owed everything that has happened within these gates and that would occur in every kind of good from now until the end of the world.

Las Casas's did not simply present an account of a Columbian exploit, he drew upon a providential framework to reconcile the inconsistencies he saw within the discovery story. Thus the influence of the Columbian lawsuits upon historiography did not matter because both stemmed from a context of common inquiry that posed similar questions. These problems include, but are not limited to, the geographic identity of the territories explored by Columbus, as Edmundo O'Gorman suggested (1951, 1964, 1977).[11] He contended that "una vez concebido el primer viaje de Colón como una empresa descubridora del Nuevo Mundo . . . la dificultad fundamental estribará en explicar de qué modo pudo saber Colón de la existencia de las desconocidas tierras que se dice 'descubrió'" [once the first voyage of Columbus is conceived as an enterprise of discovering the New World . . . the fundamental difficulty will rest on explaining how Columbus could know of the existence of the unknown lands he says he "discovered"] (1951, 47). There is no doubt that situating these new territories in relation to the intellectual tradition became a dominant concern in the histories of the Indies. Persistent questions arose about the knowledge that the ancients had of these territories and how Columbus could have conceived of his project. These issues did not have an impact on the validity of his discovery, rather they involved constructing a fluid account that was not tied to the initial Columbian project. The historiography of the discovery was not focused on the account of the hermeneutical process of a geographical entity; the problem was presenting the discovery in an interpretive framework that permitted determining the role of Spain in the Indies.

The necessity of situating Columbus's discoveries had a hand in determining in what sense he had made the Indies accessible to the Spaniards. The discovery was presented as the beginning of a larger process of knowledge, exploration, domination, and evangelization of the Indies. That the discovery posed the problem of origins is appreciated in the fact that the references to Ferdinand of Aragón, the conquest of Granada, and the expulsion of the Jews found in the editions of Columbus's letter had nothing more than anecdotal value in sixteenth-century historiography. The historical referent of the triumph of Christianity over Islam had lost its explanatory power in relation to the discovery of the Indies—it was no longer about a few islands *supra Gangem* (beyond the Ganges). An illustrative example of this is found in the contrast between Las Casas's *Historia de las Indias* (written 1527–1559) and *Asia* (written 1539–1570, and incrementally published in 1552, 1553, 1563, and 1613) by João de Barros (1496–1570). Las Casas began his history with the "creation of heaven and earth," but Barros started with the Muslim conquest of Spain. Las Casas understood the history of the Indies as a story of redemption and criticized Barros for presenting the history of the Portuguese conquests and navigations toward the East as an account of war against infidels.[12]

Las Casas was not the only one facing the problem of giving coherence to the history of discovery. Oviedo had previously discussed two theories wherein Columbus "se movió al descubrimiento" [was driven to the discovery]. The first is the story of the "anonymous pilot," which he attributed to the masses and refuted on many occasions (1992, 1:15–16). Oviedo's version states that a caravel en route from Spain to England was blown off course in a storm and came across some islands in the Antilles but, when returning, part of the crew died on the voyage and the rest perished in Portugal, leaving the secret of the location of these lands in the hands of Columbus. Oviedo rejected this story as false under the principle that it was improper to assert something that was not certain:

> *Que esto pasase así o no, ninguno con verdad lo puede afirmar; pero aquesta novela así anda por el mundo, entre la vulgar gente, de la manera que es dicho. Para mí, yo lo tengo por falso, e, como dice el Augustino: Melius est dubitare de ocultis, quam litigare de incertis. Mejor es dubdar en lo que no sabemos que porfiar lo que no está determinado (1992, 1:16).*

> Whether this happened in this way or not, no one can truly say, but this story thus runs throughout the world, among the common people, in the manner that it is said. For me, I take it as false, and, as Augustine says, "Melius est dubitare de ocultis, quam litigare de incertis." It is better to question what we do not know than to argue about what is uncertain.

The second theory was formulated by Oviedo himself, who said that "Cristóbal Colom se movió, como sabio e docto e osado varón, a emprender una cosa como ésta . . . porque conosció, y es verdad, que estas tierras estaban olvidadas" [Christopher Columbus was driven, like a wise, learned, and daring man, to undertake something such as this . . . because he knew, and this is true, that these lands were forgotten] (1992, 1:17). Oviedo supposed that the Indies previously belonged to the dominion of Spain in the times of the mythical King Hesperus, basing his theory on the authority of "Seboso e Solino e Plinio e Isidoro" [Sebosus, Solinus, Pliny, and Isidore]. According to this version, Columbus drew upon the knowledge of these authors to develop his plan to sail west.[13] The problem that Oviedo confronted was relocating the origins of the discovery before Columbus in order to reconcile them with the construction of the Spanish empire.

In the *Vida del Almirante* (Life of the Admiral) (written ca. 1535–1539, originally published 1571), Fernando Colón dismisses the theory of ancient Spanish dominion over the Indies as conjecture. He associated Oviedo's hypothesis primarily with statements concerning the Hesperides attributed to Aristotle, and argued that the philosopher had utilized the verb *fertur* ("to be told") to present his story "como cosa dudosa y sin fundamento" [as something questionable and without foundation] (1985, 79). For Colón, myth ("what is told") could not serve as the foundation of an interpretation of the discovery: the historian must employ "diligencia y cuidado" [diligence and care] to "informarse y escribir la verdad" [inform himself and write the truth] (1985, 53). He dedicated chapters 5 through 9 of his *Vida del Almirante* to establishing the reasons that moved Columbus to embark on the enterprise of the discovery. After relating his stay in Portugal and the way in which he began to collect information, he proposed three motivating factors: "los fundamentos naturales, la autoridad de los escritores y los indicios de los navegantes" [natural foundations, the authorities of writers, and the evidence of sailors] (1985, 62). He carefully examined each of them in order to clarify Columbus's unresolved role in the discovery. This allowed him to show how his father could have conceived the idea of sailing west to Asia.[14] He resolved the historiographical problem by establishing the nature of Columbus's contribution:

> [L]o principal que había ofrecido antes que descubriese las Indias, lo había ya cumplido, que era mostrar que allí había islas y tierra firme, a la parte occidental; que el camino era fácil y navegable, la utilidad manifiesta, y las gentes muy domésticas y desarmadas. De modo que, habiendo probado él mismo todo lo referido, ya no faltaba más sino que Sus Altezas siguiesen la empresa, enviando gente que buscase y procurase entender los secretos de aquellos países. Pues estando ya abierta la puerta, cualquiera podría seguir la costa, como ya hacían algunos que impropiamente se llamaban descubridores, sin considerar que no descubrieron alguna nueva región, sino que siguen la descubierta, después del tiempo en que el Almirante les mostró dichas islas y la provincia de Paria, que fue la primera región de tierra firme que se halló (1985, 287).

The main thing that he had promised before discovering the Indies he had already fulfilled, which was to show that there were islands and mainland there to the west, that the way was easy and navigable, the utility manifest, and the people very tame and unarmed. In this way, after he had proved all this himself, there was now nothing left for Their Highnesses to do except to continue the enterprise, sending people to seek and try to understand the secrets of those countries. Now that the door was open, anyone could follow the coast, as some already did who improperly were called discoverers, without considering that they did not discover any new region, but that they continued the discovery, after the time in which the Admiral showed them the said islands and the province of Paria, which was the first region of Tierra Firme that was found.

He downplayed the importance of the identity of the discovered lands to affirm that his father had "opened the door" for continuing exploration of these regions. Central in his assertion is that Columbus had carried out the most important part of the process and then left the continuation of the enterprise in the hands of the monarchs. His contrast between Columbus and those improperly called "discoverers" emphasized the lack of continuity between Columbus's discoveries and the subsequent exploration and conquest of the New World. Fernando Colón's effort to clarify the life of his father and the origin of the discovery exemplifies the historiographical difficulties that this topic presented the sixteenth-century intellectual.

Of the two theories for the discovery that Oviedo had presented, the story about the anonymous pilot fared the best because of the doubts that the figure of Columbus and his discovery had generated. Even his son Fernando, far from refuting this theory, merely made the correction that it concerned a Portuguese man named Vicente Dias. On a voyage from Madeira to the island of Terceira in the Azores, Dias had seen an island toward the west. Later, he teamed up with a Genoese man to look for it without success, but until his death he never gave up the hope of finding it (Colón 1985, 75–76). With this clarification, Colón eliminated the aspects of this story that were prejudicial to his father and made it consistent with his attributing a central role in the discovery to Columbus.

Las Casas presented the pilot episode in a chapter whose long descriptive title concluded that it was "cosa dudosa" [something questionable] (1988–1998, 3:407–410). Nevertheless, in spite of his scruples as a historian, Las Casas felt profoundly attracted to this story and enumerated with great conviction the reasons why it seemed credible to him. First, he said that it was a rumor on the lips of everyone in Hispaniola, thus he supposed that someone must have heard it from Columbus himself. Then, he added that the natives of the island of Cuba remembered bearded white men having arrived before the Spaniards. Finally, he figured that the possibility that a ship could be blown off course to the Indies by a storm was sufficiently high considering the distance and the force of the currents. At the end of the chapter, Las Casas revealed that the story captivated him because Columbus "tan cierto iba de descubrir lo que descubrió y hallar lo que halló, como si dentro de una cámara, con su propia llave, lo tuviera" [was so certain he would discover what he discovered and find what he found, as if within a chamber, with his own key, he held it] (1988–1998, 3:410).

The main issue for Las Casas was to comprehend how Columbus, the man, could have accomplished such a transcendent act as the discovery. The analogy of him finding the Indies as if he held them in a chamber with his own key stresses the complex convergence of factors that came together in the crystallization of the project. Las Casas had in mind an account of redemption where the accidental and the chaotic achieved coherence under the wing of providence for which Columbus served as an instrument and, in a certain sense, a voice.

The history of the discovery presented the sixteenth-century historian with a problem of discontinuity between the project that Columbus initiated and the subsequent development of the Spanish empire in the Indies. The difficulty of establishing a nexus between these accounts lies in the fact that the enterprise was continually changing from the very beginning. The violent transformations that introduced the processes of Spanish and Portuguese expansion in the Atlantic posed the historiographical problem of providing an overarching structure of meaning for the events. To the eyes of the historian, the sudden emergence of a vast imperial horizon beyond the Mediterranean required origins that were consistent with this new reality. In addition to the problem of continuity, historians' readings of the Alexandrian bull of donation at the time addressed the issue of the conquest's legitimacy. Employing the bull to support the imperial rights of Spain made the discovery a critical point in their debates. Evaluating Columbus's role had direct repercussions on legal interpretations of the conquest. This can be found in the histories of Martyr, Oviedo, Las Casas, and Gómara for whom the Columbian discovery presented a historiographical challenge of considerable proportions.

Martyr began his history of the discovery with the day that Columbus "Ferna[n]do & Helisabethae Regibus Catholicis proposuit & suasit se ab occidente n[ost]ro finitimas Indiae insulas inue[n]tutu[s], si nauigiis & reb[us] ad nauigatione[m] attine[n]tib[us] instruerent" [proposed and persuaded the Catholic Monarchs Ferdinand and Isabel that to our west he would discover islands neighboring India, if they supplied ships and the things pertinent to navigation] (1966, 39). Focusing on Columbus's agency, one might expect Martyr would proceed to show how he achieved his goals. Instead, he exposed the corruption and power struggles that developed between Columbus and some of the Spaniards who accompanied him.[15] Subsequently, Las Casas explored this same thread in his *Historia de las Indias* to interpret the providential design for the Indies. Oviedo, on the other hand, resolved the problem by saying that the Indies had previously belonged to King Hesperus and therefore the rights of Spain did not emanate from Columbus's discovery.[16]

This is the historiographical climate in which Gómara set out to write his *Historia general.* Marcelino Menéndez y Pelayo said that "[p]or lo tocante a los primeros descubrimientos, Oviedo fue su principal fondo, con lo cual dicho se está que no añade nada nuevo, salvo tradiciones y rumores vulgares, de origen oscuro y de poco fundamento" [for what concerns the earliest discoveries, Oviedo was his principal source, so needless to say, he adds nothing new except traditions and common rumors of obscure origin and of little foundation] (1942, 95). In a similar manner, Robert Lewis has stated that "[t]he greatest number of similarities between the histories of Gómara and Oviedo appear in their accounts of the discovery of the New World by Columbus and the early Spanish actions in the Caribbean" (1983, 116). A comparison of these texts not only reveals that Gómara created an account completely different from Oviedo, but that he conducted a program of inquiry and research that contributed elements that were not found in other accounts.[17] Gómara did more than recycle old sources in a new account, he rethought the problem of the discovery and tried to present it in a narrative form that adhered to the objectives of his *Historia general.* The problematic character of the historiography of the discovery demanded intense debate and reflection on the part of sixteenth-century historians, and Gómara was no exception.

THE HUMBLE BEGINNINGS OF THE EMPIRE

Gómara drew upon many sources for his chapter dedicated to the discovery. The list includes the Capitulations of Santa Fe, Columbus's letter, the Alexandrian bull of donation, the story of the anonymous pilot, authoritative texts from antiquity, the Columbian litigation, the histories of Martyr and Oviedo, accounts of the Portuguese voyages in Africa, Columbus's biography, and Sepúlveda's *Democrates secundus.* With the exception of the bull of donation, Gómara left only faint traces of these texts, but without question he subtly put them into play. He deployed an intricate critical and textual apparatus to relate the discovery as a history of the origins of empire. This interpretive maneuver allowed him to make his discovery account consistent with subsequent developments in the Indies.

Gómara began his account with the story of the anonymous pilot in a chapter titled "el Descubrimie[n]to primero de las Indias" (The first discovery of the Indies). In Gómara's version, a Portuguese vessel coming from "Ethiopia" was blown off course to the Indies by an easterly wind. The pilot and three or four others barely made it back to port but then perished a short time later. Columbus had put the survivors up in his home, where they informed him about the new lands before they died. Thus Columbus's 1492 voyage constituted a "second" discovery after this pilot's fortuitous first landing. Gómara referred to the Indies as the lands "nueuame[n]te vistas, y halladas" [newly seen and found] at the end of the chapter to reinforce the notion of the dual discovery (1552, 1:10r). When suggesting that the Indies were "found" more than once, Gómara was challenging accounts that focused on Columbus's persona.

The story of the anonymous pilot naturally led to questioning Columbus's reputation as a discoverer, but Gómara tried instead to redefine his place in the historical account. In other words, instead of supplanting Columbus with the unknown pilot, Gómara wanted to establish a relationship between both accounts. Gómara redistributed their roles in terms of conceiving the project, finding lands, writing down what was seen, presenting the news, and leaving a record of the event. Interweaving each of these moments gave shape and meaning to the episode. The account of this "first discovery" constituted a "beginning" that would achieve its full historical significance at a later time:

> *E aqui como se descubriero[n] las Indias por desdicha de quien primero las vio, pues acabo la vida sin gozar dellas. Y sin dexar, a lo menos sin [h]auer, memoria d[e] como se llamaua[.] Ni de donde era. Ni que año las hallo. Bien que no fue culpa suya, sino maliçia de otros, o inuidia de la que llaman fortuna. Y no me marauillo de las historias antiguas, que cuenten hechos grandissimos por chicos, o escuros principios, pues no sabemos quien de poco aca hallo las Indias, que tan señalada: y nueua cosa es. . . . Solamente concuerdan todos en que falleçio aquel piloto en casa d[e] Christoual Colon. En cuyo poder quedaron las escrituras de la carauela. Y la relacion de todo aq[ue]l luengo viaje con la marca, y altura de las tierras, nueuame[n]te vistas, y halladas (1552, 1:10r).*

Behold how the Indies were discovered to the misfortune of the first one who saw them, for he ended his life without enjoying them. And without leaving, at least, any surviving record of his name, or where he was from, or what year he had found them. Although it was not his fault, but rather the malice of others, or the envy of what they call fortune. And I am not surprised by the ancient stories that tell of the greatest acts through small and obscure beginnings, for we do not know the one who a short time ago found the Indies, which is such a prominent and new thing. . . . Only everyone concurs that the pilot died in the house of Christopher Columbus, in whose power were left the logs of the caravel and the story of that long voyage with the mark and latitude of the newly seen and found lands.

It is quite clear from Gómara's commentary that he considers "discovery" and "reporting" to be codependent activities. In addition to the common act of finding, discovery involved recording and informing the public. As the pilot was unable to leave any record (his name, place of origin, the year it occurred), his discovery failed to have any impact, nevertheless there was something tangible linking his voyage to the Columbian discovery. Gómara could properly speak of a "first discovery," not so much because of the pilot's voyage, but because he had left the ship's logs with the lands' "mark and latitude" in the hands of Columbus. This is to say, Columbus's discovery owed specific information about the route to the Indies and their location to the anonymous pilot's "first discovery." Discovering, however, concerned the generation of public knowledge, which the "first discovery" did not achieve. Thus the "first discovery" allowed Gómara to reinterpret the "greatest acts" of the discovery through its "small and obscure beginnings."

The concept of a beginning resolves the paradox of a dual discovery, which then appears as an event that developed in stages. The justification for this operation comes from "ancient stories" where "obscure beginnings" can explain larger historical developments. In this way Gómara developed a model for his account of the origins of the empire. He treated the story in terms of a relationship between myth and history by juxtaposing a story of imprecise — and unverifiable — occurrences and another of known events. The issue was whether the account was possible, not so much that it had actually taken place. When he said, "And I am not surprised," he was resorting to the authority of those "ancient stories" to present the story of the pilot as plausible. His problem is fundamentally interpretive: the historian must establish the likelihood, significance, and logic of events.

In his chapter titled "Quien era Christoual Colon" (Who Christopher Columbus was), he established that the Genoese mariner put up the moribund pilot during his stay in Madeira and it was then that he likely had learned about the Indies (1552, 1:10r–v). Gómara, however, did not try to present this story as the only definitive version. Rather, he contrasted the likelihood of a discovery inspired by the unknown pilot with one where Columbus was the sole mastermind. Gómara set the account of the pilot that he favored against the belief that "Colon alcançara por sçie[n]çia donde las Indias estaua[n]" [Columbus found out through science where the Indies were] (1552, 1:10v). He judged it improbable that Columbus, having conceived of the idea on his own, would not have attempted the discovery earlier with the Genoese.[18] His objective was not to emphatically establish a causal relationship between the "first discovery" and that of Columbus, but rather to propose a debate over the meaning of the discovery. He was concerned with confronting simultaneously two alternative accounts of the discovery in order to determine the more viable historiographical construction. Gómara represented the discovery as a fragmented process because this allowed him to reconstruct it as a meaningful whole.

Columbus could be the "learned" man who conceived of the discovery based on his wisdom and study, or the shrewd, "well-informed" man who applied his faculties to assembling an undertaking that presented enormous obstacles to its completion. The first had the capacity of interpreting books, discovering the meaning of things, and applying his knowledge to reality. The second was able to carry out what he planned. Gómara responded to the question of "who Columbus was" in the following manner:

> *No era doto Christoual Colon. Mas era bien entendido. E como tuuo notiçia de aq[ue]llas nueuas tierras por relacion del piloto muerto, informose de [h]ombres leydos sobre lo que dezia[n] los antiguos açerca de otras tierras, y mu[n]dos. (1552, 1:10v).*

> Christopher Columbus was not gifted, but he was well informed. And as he had information about those new lands related to him by the deceased pilot, he was informed by men who read what the ancients said about other lands and worlds.

Determining that Columbus was "well informed" is much more than a simple resolution to a minor point in the biography of the Genoese mariner. Gómara devoted the entire chapter titled "Por q[ue] se llamaro[n] Indias" (Why they are called Indies) to discussing whether his project was in fact to get to India (1552, 1:12r–v). Responding to the question about the origin of the name of the Indies, Gómara established a distinction between India and Ethiopia, locating the latter between the Nile and the Red Sea.[19] In this way, he could separate Columbus from the conception of the project of getting to India by sailing west and endorse the account of the pilot. According to Gómara the pilot came on a return voyage from India, that is, not the "gran india, que tambien nombra[n] oriental" [great India, that they also call the East], but "De la India pues del Preste Gia[n], do[n]de ya contratauan portogueses" [from the India then of Prester John, where the Portuguese already were trading] (1552, 1:12v).[20] Because the pilot would have generically named the new lands "Indies," Columbus kept the same toponym. The privilege of naming has in this case the profound significance of defining the origins of the discovery: it concerns accidental acts whose purpose is beyond the will of one man.[21]

Gómara gave credit to both Columbus and the unknown pilot for the discovery. Although the pilot left Columbus his notes about the location of the new lands, the latter's diligence earned him fame for the event. Gómara stressed Spain's debt of gratitude to him for the Indies, for he had the capacity and understanding necessary to transform an "obscure" act into something "distinguished." In other words, the Columbian discovery was a remarkable deed because of its public and political impact. In fact, Gómara's review of the discoverer's life in his chapter "La muerte de Christoual Colon" (The death of Christopher Columbus) stressed his place in the public spaces and memory of Spain:

> [A]ue[n]turose a nauegar en mares, y tierras, q[ue] no sabia, por dicho de vn
> piloto. Y si fue de su cabeça, como algunos quiere[n], meresce mucha mas
> loa. Como quiera q[ue] a ello se mouio hizo cosa de gra[n]dissima gloria. Y
> tal q[ue] nu[n]ca se oluidara su no[m]bre. Ni españa le dexara de dar
> sie[m]pre las gracias, y alaba[n]ça q[ue] merescio. Y los reyes catolicos
> do[n] Ferna[n]do, y doña Ysabel, en cuya ve[n]tura, no[m]bre, y costa, hizo
> el descubrimiento, le diero[n] titulo, y officio de almira[n]te p[er]petuo de
> las Indias. Y la re[n]ta q[ue] co[n]uenia a tal estado, y tal seruicio, como
> hecho les [h]auia. Y a la [h]onra q[ue] gano (1552, 1:15v).

He dared to navigate seas and lands he did not know on the word of a pilot. And if it was from his own mind, as some wish, he deserves much more praise. Whichever way he was moved to do it, he did something of the greatest glory, and such that his name would never be forgotten. And Spain would not fail to always thank him and give him the praise that he deserves. And the Catholic Monarchs *don* Ferdinand and *doña* Isabel, in whose fortune, name, and expense he made the discovery, gave him the perpetual title and position of Admiral of the Indies, and the revenue that corresponded to such a status and such service as he had done them, and the honor that he had won.

There is no definitive account, nor does there need to be. Gómara allowed for the possibility that Columbus conceived of the discovery in "his own mind," but the story of the pilot permitted him to deal with the inconsistencies that he observed within the Columbian biography itself. Fame, honor, and royal favors are Columbus's rightful share in this story. In Gómara's opinion, he is worthy of acts of veneration appropriate for a hero: graces, praise, glory, and remembrance. But what is meritorious about Columbus is *carrying out* the discovery, not *conceiving* it.

The key point in Gómara's account of the discovery is Columbus's reception in the court and the favors he was granted by the monarchs.[22] In contrast, the chapter relating the discovery itself contains no more than a summary description of the voyage and little commentary or interpretation. Columbus's return brings about the point of anagnorisis, that is, the act of recognition that formulates the identity of both the discoverer and what he discovered. Thus it enables the transition between the *obscure beginnings* and the *distinguished act of the discovery* by presenting it as a conception of the project realized after the fact. Gómara described Columbus's return in his chapter titled "La honra y mercedes que los reies catolicos hizieron a Colon por [h]auer descubierto las Indias" (The honor and favors that the Catholic Monarchs did Columbus for having discovered the Indies). His account exalts the fame acquired by Columbus and the interpretations that the spectators made on his return. In Gómara's interpretation, fame carries with it the act of recognition:

[F]ue muy honrado, y famoso: porque salian a verle por los caminos a la fama de [h]auer descubierto otro mundo, y traer del grandes riquezas. Y *[h]ombres de nueua forma color, y traje. Unos dezian que [h]auia hallado la nauegacion que Cartagineses vedaron. Otros, la que Plato[n] en Cricias pone por perdida con la tormenta, y mucho cieno que crecio en la mar. Y otros que [h]auia cumplido lo que adeuino Seneca en la tragedia Medea, do dize, verna[n] tie[m]pos de aqui a mucho que se descubriran nueuos mundos. Y entonces no sera Tyle la postrera de las tierras (1552, 1:11v–12r).*

He was quite honored and famous, because they came out to see him on the roads for the fame of having discovered another world, and bringing back great riches, and men of a new form, color, and dress. Some said that he had found the navigation that Carthaginians prohibited; others, the one that Plato in *Critias* established as lost with the storm and much silt that accumulated in the sea; and others that he fulfilled Seneca's prophesy in the tragedy *Medea*, where he says, there will come times far in the future when new worlds will be discovered, and then Tyle will not be the furthest of lands.

Those who assign fame to Columbus are making an interpretive maneuver, for they are projecting their take on the meaning of the acts that merit this. Therefore, the acquisition of fame necessarily brings out a hermeneutic dynamic embedded within the development of the events. Gómara presented this aspect of recognition under the expression "they came out to see him on the roads for the fame of having discovered another world, and bringing back great riches, and men of a new form, color, and dress." The spectators mentioned the Carthaginians, Plato, and Seneca. They reenacted the account of the "learned" Columbus, which focused the meaning of the discovery on his persona. In contrast, Gómara's preference for the "well-informed" Columbus, which he associated with the story of the anonymous pilot, suggests that the moment of recognition still had not arrived. Columbus's invitation to the court of the monarchs is the central interpretative instance in Gómara's history of the discovery. In this moment, Gómara poses the question of the discovery's conception and assembles the different fragments into a coherent narrative.

The hermeneutic of recognition is resolved by the monarchs' reading of the account that Columbus presented them. Their reaction to Columbus's verbal report reveals the historical significance of the discovery and assigns a place to the discoverer in this story:

Estuuieron los reyes muy ate[n]tos a la relacion, q[ue] de palabra hizo Christoual Colon, y marauilla[n]dose de oyr que los indios no tenian vestidos, ni letras, ni moneda, ni hierro, ni trigo, ni vino, ni animal ninguno, maior que perro. Ni nauios grandes, sino canoas, que son como artesas, hechas de vna pieça. No pudieron sufrirse quando oieron que alla en aquellas islas, y tierras nueuas, se comia[n] vnos [h]ombres a otros. Y que todos eran idolatras y prometiero[n], si dios les daua vida, d[e] quitar aquella abominable inhumanidad. Y desarraygar la idolatria en todas las tierras de Indias, que a su mando viniessen. Voto de christianisimos reies, y que cumplieron su palabra. Hizieron mucha honra a Christoual Colon, manda[n]do le sentar delante dellos, que fue gran fauor, y amor Ca es antigua costumbre de nuestra España estar siempre en pie los bassallos, y criados, delante el rey por acatamiento de la autoridad real. Confirmaronle su priuilegio de la dozena parte d[e] los derechos reales. Dieronle titulo, y oficio, de almirante de las Indias. Y a Bartolome Colon de adelantado. Puso Christoual Colon alrededor del escudo de armas, que le concedieron, esta letra.

Por Castilla, y por Leon.
Nueuo mundo hallo Colon (1552, 1:12r).

The monarchs were very attentive to the verbal report Christopher Columbus made and were astonished to hear that the Indians had no clothes, letters, money, iron, wheat, wine, any animals larger than a dog, or large ships, except canoes, which are like troughs made from a log. They could not bear it when they heard that there in those islands and new lands, some men ate others, and all of them were idolaters, and they promised, if God granted them life, to stop that abominable inhumanity. And eradicating idolatry in all the lands of the Indies that would come under their command, the most Christian monarchs vowed and carried out their word. They did much honor to Christopher Columbus, ordering him to sit before them, which showed great favor and love. For it is an ancient custom in our Spain for vassals and servants always to stand before the king in deference to royal authority. They confirmed his privilege of one twelfth of the royal share. They gave him the title and position of Admiral of the Indies and Bartholomew Columbus that of *adelantado*. Christopher Columbus put these words on the coat of arms they granted him:

For Castile and for León,
A new world Columbus found.

In this section, Gómara staged the monarchs' reception of the let-ter that Columbus wrote upon returning from his first voyage. By making it an oral report, the interaction between Columbus and the monarchs clearly presents the moment of anagnorisis. This is a powerful point in the text because it is in sharp contrast with the account of the "learned" Columbus that Gómara placed in the mouths of those who came out to see him along the way. In addition, this reenactment of the encounter between Columbus and the monarchs sets in relief the dialogical aspect of the production of meaning in the story and makes it clear that it is in the monarchs' response that the discovery is conceived and defined.[23]

In Gómara's account the monarchs are the ones who grant rewards to Columbus and establish the moral obligation of intervening in the Indies. Faced with Columbus's description of the Indies, the monarchs "were astonished to hear that the Indians had no clothes, letters, money, iron, wheat, wine, any animals . . . , or large ships" and "could not bear it when they heard that there in those islands and new lands, some men ate others." Gómara highlighted the customs that made the Indians look barbaric from a European perspective. When focusing on the monarchs' reaction to this representation of barbarity that was completely anathema to their system of values, he gave them the role of conceiving the desire to bring about change by stopping these customs. Thus Gómara has the monarchs define a mission for the Spaniards to carry out in the New World.

This mission coincides with the one that Sepúlveda had formulated in his *Democrates secundus* where he based the Spaniards' rights of conquest on the principle of natural slavery (1997, 55–56). The basic view that Gómara and Sepúlveda share is that of stopping the crimes of the Indians (such as idolatry, human sacrifice, and cannibalism) in order to implant a new social reality:

> [U]t iam pridem accepta christiana religione fiunt. . . . [T]um litterarum et doctrinarum praeceptoribus tum morum ac verae religionis magistris publice datis. . . . [I]sti barbari Hispanorum imperium accipere iubentur lege naturae . . . quo virtuti, et humanitas, veraque religio omni auro et argento pretiosior habetur (1997, 97).

> Some time ago they began to accept the Christian religion. . . . Now they have been given public instructors of letters and sciences as well as teachers of customs and the true religion. . . . Such barbarians are ordered to accept the Spanish empire according to the law of nature . . . for virtue, civilization, and true religion are considered more precious than any gold and silver.

The scene of the encounter between Columbus and the Catholic Monarchs gives coherence and unity to the colonizing process. The history of the discovery is that of the origins of the empire: it explains the domination of the New World by Spain. The monarchs propose to eliminate inhumanity and eradicate idolatry from the lands of the Indies. Although Columbus's account of the discovery would basically be one of finding lands and gold, the monarchs articulate an approach to the inhabitants. Once Gómara had closed the account of the "honor and favors" received by Columbus, he proceeded to clarify "Why they are called Indies." Then, he finally added the account of "The donation that the pope made of the Indies to the Catholic Monarchs," which includes the text of the Alexandrian bull of donation. The political action of the monarchs and the pope completes the sequence of the discovery story by legitimating Spanish sovereignty.

The subject whose agency brings together the various fragments making up the discovery's history is divine providence. Gómara read in the discovery a fulfillment of the providential design for Spain and, in the conquest and evangelization projected in the interpretive and political activity of the monarchs, the satisfaction of the terms stipulated in the bull of donation. When commenting about the royal treasurer Luis de Santángel's financial contribution to Columbus's first voyage, Gómara made his providentialist reading of the discovery clear:

> *Dos cosas notaremos aqui. Una que con tan poco caudal se [h]ayan acrescentado las rentas de la corona real de Castilla en tanto como le vale[n] las Indias. Otra que en acabandose la conquista de los moros, que [h]auia durado mas de ochocientos años, se começo la de los indios, para que sie[m]pre peleassen los Españoles con infieles, y enemigos de la santa fe de Iesu Christo (1552, 1:11r).*

We will note two things here. One is that with so little wealth the royal crown of Castile's revenue has increased by as much as the Indies are worth. The other is that after completing the conquest of the Moors, which had lasted more than eight hundred years, the conquest of the Indians was begun so that Spaniards would always fight infidels and enemies of the holy faith of Jesus Christ.

The contrast between "little wealth" and what "the Indies are worth" reiterates the interpretive model of the "humble beginnings" applied to the story of the anonymous pilot. Gómara presents a historical pattern where the intervention of providence explains the various fortuitous events of the discovery. His providentialist view is clearly revealed in his second point where the telos of the "holy war" situates the discovery within the perspective of universal history.

When constructing the history of the discovery as an account of origins, Gómara subordinated the action, vision, and will of the anonymous pilot and Columbus to the providential meaning of the story. Thus he was able to integrate the discovery within the larger development of the Spanish empire in the New World. The hermeneutic obscurity of its "beginning" required a way of translating it into a narrative of origins. The theory of a dual discovery made it possible to create the retrospective portrayal of an obscure beginning that liberated the account from the inconsistencies and limitations of the Columbian story. Considering Columbus's hermeneutic inadequate, Gómara looked to the Catholic Monarchs to put forth the imperial mission.

EXCHANGE AS A SYSTEM OF COLONIZATION

Gómara's discovery account constructs an idea of benefit that could be achieved in the Spaniards' activities of exploration and conquest. Various kinds of action were articulated by the Catholic Monarchs whose role served to infuse the story with ethical and political meaning. They proposed to remove injustices and sins from the Indians at the same time that they honored and rewarded Columbus for his services. This representation of the discovery summarily put forth the notion of a common good that could be attained through the colonization of the New World. The Indians' cultural, religious, and material shortcomings could be supplied by the Spaniards, who in turn would enjoy their natural resources and manual labor. Along with this idea of mutual benefit, Gómara explained how exchange made it possible to simultaneously attain the goals of civilizing, evangelizing, and profiting through colonization. In fact, this exchange between Spaniards and Indians would consistently include all the various activities transforming colonial life in the New World.

Las Casas's *Historia de las Indias* offers a good point of contrast to help us comprehend the balance that Gómara tried to strike between these imperial activities. The Dominican historian associated the origin of the Spaniards' abuses in the Indies with the discovery, plunder, and ransom that characterized the kind of colonial relationships that the Portuguese had established in West Africa (1988–1998, 3:459–493). Ac-

cording to his account, the beginning of these expeditions was linked
to the war against the Moors:

> *En este tiempo, el dicho rey don Juan de Portogal determinó de pasar con*
> *exército allende del mar contra los moros — donde tomó la ciudad de*
> *Cepta — llevando consigo al infante D. Enrique, su hijo, el menor de tres*
> *que tenía; el cual, según las historias portoguesas, era muy virtuoso, buen*
> *cristiano y aun virgen. . . . Este infante comenzó a tener inclinación de*
> *inquirir y preguntar a los moros, con quien allí tractaba, de los secretos*
> *interiores de la tierra dentro de Africa. . . . [C]uanto el infante curioso era en*
> *preguntar, por adquirir noticia de los secretos de aquella tierra . . . tanto*
> *más su inclinación se encendía y mayor deseo le causaba de enviar a*
> *descubrir (1988–1998, 3:460).*

At this time, the said king *dom* João of Portugal decided to go with
his army across the sea against the Moors — where he took the city
of Ceuta — bringing with him the *infante dom* Henrique [Prince
Henry the Navigator], his son, the youngest of the three he had,
who, according to the Portuguese histories, was very virtuous, a
good Christian, and even a virgin. . . . This *infante* began to have the
inclination of inquiring and questioning the Moors, with whom he
had dealings there, about the inner secrets of inland Africa. . . . The
more curious the *infante* was in questioning to acquire information
about the secrets of that land . . . the more his inclination was
ignited and caused him greater desire to dispatch expeditions of
discovery.

The initial project of religious struggle radically changed course
with the curiosity awakened in the *infante* for ascertaining the secrets
of Africa. Prince Henry began to send maritime expeditions beyond
Cape Não, the first of a chain of natural barriers impeding the exploration of the Atlantic coast of Africa. After Cape Não came Cape Bojador.
The process of overcoming these barriers created its own dynamic. The
objective was always to ascertain what was beyond each cape, but the
sea currents presented obstacles for which the Portuguese were not
prepared. The sailors who failed to accomplish their assigned exploration objectives dedicated themselves to ravaging the land and ransom-
ing slaves on their return voyage. Las Casas believed that the Portuguese had been shortsighted in thinking that they could legitimately
plunder the land under the assumption that it belonged to Moors, for
these regions did not represent a threat to Christianity.[24]

The key moment occurred in 1434, when Gil Eanes successfully passed Cape Bojador and encountered a land "fertilísima y digna de poblar" [most fertile and worthy of settling], gathered some plants, and brought them back to the *infante* as proof of his discovery (1988–1998, 3:466). Las Casas explained that eight years later the Portuguese enterprise gained momentum when its economic potential became evident:

> *En el año de mill y cuatrocientos y cuarenta y dos, viendo el infante que se*
> *había pasado el Cabo del Bojador y que la tierra iba muy adelante, y que*
> *todos los navíos que enviaba traían muchos esclavos moros con que pagaba*
> *los gastos que hacía y que cada día crecía más el provecho y se prosperaba*
> *su amada negociación, determinó de enviar a suplicar al Papa Martino*
> *quinto . . . que hiciese gracia a la Corona Real de Portogal de los reinos y*
> *señoríos que había. (1988–1998, 3:468–469).*

In the year 1442, the *infante* seeing that Cape Bojador had been passed and that the land went on much further, and that all the ships that he sent brought many Moorish slaves, which paid for the expenditures he made, and that each day the profits grew more and his beloved business was prospering, he decided to send a request to Pope Martin V . . . to grant the royal crown of Portugal the favor of the kingdoms and domains that were there.

Las Casas described a process in which human complacency led to overlooking increasingly greater abuses in the voyages of discovery until the desire of riches completely took over the enterprise.[25] The excessive weight that material interests began to assume in the activities of exploration brought about a gradual process of moral degradation. He attributed the plunder and violence of the Portuguese expeditions to human imperfection:

> *Porque desta naturaleza o condición imperfecta somos los hombres,*
> *mayormente en esta postrera edad: que donde no sacamos provecho para*
> *nosotros, ninguna cosa nos agrada de todo lo que los otros hacen; pero*
> *cuando asoma el propio interese, o hay esperanza de él, tornamos presto a*
> *mirar las cosas con otros ojos (1988–1998, 3:470).*

Because of this nature or imperfect condition, we are human, especially in this last age, where we are not profiting ourselves, we are not pleased with anything others do; but when our own interest arises, or there is hope for it, we quickly turn around to look at things with other eyes.

Interpreting these acts according to canon law (Pennington 1970; Benson 1976; Adorno 1992d, 4-6), Las Casas established a contradiction in his narrative between Portuguese colonial practice and the legal tenets of Christian tradition.

Las Casas denounced these abusive practices because he noted that they served no other purpose than to satisfy the material interests of the Portuguese. He did not deny the Christian objectives of the Portuguese enterprise; rather he questioned the legality of its practices and the deviation from its original ends. The initial intention of struggling against Muslims rapidly gave way to the extraction of wealth without examining the justice of the means. Military and religious considerations yielded to economic impulses and the enterprise came to be dominated by the quest for riches. Las Casas examined the origins of Portuguese expansion into Africa in order to dismantle its legal justification.

Gómara, on the other hand, based his interpretation of events on the postulate of the inequality between Spaniards and Indians. This inequality works as a narrative principle of integration, establishing equilibrium between modes of juridical, political, military, economic, and religious conceptualization. This can be understood by comparison to the way João de Barros treated the episode in which Eanes presented the *infante* a barrel of earth and some plants that looked like the roses of Saint Mary. According to Barros,

> [S]e gloriáua as ver, como se fora alguu[n] fructo & móstra da térra de
> promissam . . . & pedia a nóssa senhora cujo nome aquellas héruas
> tinha[m], que encaminhásse as cousas daquelle descobrime[n]to pera louuor
> & glória de deos & acresçentame[n]to de sua sancta fe (1932, 22).

> He was delighted to see them, as if it were some product and sample
> from the Promised Land . . . and he asked Our Lady — whose name
> those plants received — to guide matters concerning that discovery
> for the praise and glory of God and the growth of his holy faith.

The roses served to validate what the discoverer reported and led the *infante* to an epiphany that revealed the imperial destiny of Portugal in Africa. Here the delivery of a sample allows a prince to make decisions about a newly discovered territory without physically having to be there. The dynamics of exchange (plunder and ransom) on the African coast made the *infante*'s epiphany a powerful substitute for a direct experience of the land. The desire to extend Christianity, manifested after the fact in the roses of Saint Mary, conceals the abuses that the Portuguese committed in Africa.

Gómara applied this same interpretive principle in his account of the discovery of the Indies when he said that Columbus "[t]omo diez indios, quare[n]ta papagaios, muchos gallipauos[,] conejos, . . . batatas, axies[,] maiz, . . . y otras cosas estrañas, y diferentes de las nuestras, para testimonio de lo q[ue] [h]auia descubierto" [took ten Indians, forty parrots, many turkeys, rabbits, . . . potatoes, chili peppers, maize, . . . and other things, strange and different from ours, as testimony of what he had discovered] (1552, 1:11v). Columbus's report to the monarchs was accompanied with objects that served as samples from the land: "Presento a los reyes el oro, y cosas que traya del otro mundo. Y ellos, y quantos estauan delante, se marauillaron mucho en ver todo aquello, exceto el oro, era nueuo, como la tierra, donde nacía" [He presented the monarchs gold and things that he brought from the other world, and they and everybody who were present marveled greatly at seeing that everything, except for the gold, was new, like the land from which it came] (1552, 1:12r). The monarchs reacted with both astonishment and outrage to the objects and the account presented by Columbus. In this case, the proof not only established the existence of the Indies, but also initiated a hermeneutic in which Isabel and Ferdinand observed what was different about the men, animals, and things brought back by Columbus. These specimens permitted them to decide on the necessity of intervening in the Indies and their reaction of wonderment and disdain gave them an incentive to act. In this way, they formulated an imperial project defined by what was different about the Indies: it was necessary to supply what the Indians lacked (clothing, letters, money, iron, wheat, wine, beasts of burden, ships) and to eliminate their practices and customs considered idolatrous and inhuman.

Here the process of exchange, mobilization, and displacement of worlds and objects is recorded as the narrative foundation of the colonial relationship. The monarchs' interpretive prerogative establishes their position of privilege and authority vis-à-vis the Indies and other territories; thus empire becomes a prerequisite for trade. These activities of exchange, taking place within culturally specific assumptions about value, create disparities between the Spaniards and the Indians, who are regarded as deficient in the areas of customs, governance, and religion. Gómara's narrative construction of the empire can be correlated with Vitoria's legitimate titles of conquest. Vitoria's *Relectio de*

Indis includes a title called "naturalis societatis et communicationis" [natural society and communication], according to which:

> *Hispanis licet apud indos barbaros negotiari, sine patriae tamen*
> *incommodo, importantes merces, quibus illi carent, etc., et efferendo inde*
> *aurum et argentum vel alia quibus illi abundant; nec illorum principes*
> *possunt impedimento esse quominus subditi exerceant commercia cum*
> *hispanis, etc. (1967, 76).*

> It is lawful for the Spaniards to trade with the barbarous Indians,
> but without harm to their country, bringing merchandise there that
> they lack and taking away from there gold, silver, or other things in
> which they abound. And their rulers may not impede their subjects
> from engaging in commerce with the Spaniards.

If the Indians violated this title, then the Spaniards had the right to wage war against them, "spoliare illos et in captivitatem redigere et dominos priores deponere et novos constituere" [despoiling them and reducing them to captivity and deposing their previous lords and constituting new ones] (1967, 85).

Gómara, in turn, shares Vitoria's notion of exchange in which riches are extracted in return for supplying what the Indians lack, but he goes further when utilizing it as the narrative foundation of the conquest. He regards conquest and exchange (either as gifts or in trade) as processes that establish a dynamic of interaction that reflects the Spaniards' superior understanding of objects. Gómara portrays scenes of exchange where the Indians' disadvantage before the Spaniards sets the colonial relationship in motion. Those who have better knowledge get to control the situation and dictate its terms. This can be observed in Gómara's account of the voyage of Ferdinand Magellan (Fernão de Magalhães, 1480–1521) where he described several encounters with the native inhabitants. He utilized this narrative to interpret the imperial practices of the Spaniards in the voyages of discovery.

In the first of these encounters, the Spaniards took a Patagonian by force back to their ships.[26] The sailors treated him as if he were an object under observation:

> *Beuio bien del vino. [H]vuo pauor de verse a vn espejo. Prouaron que*
> *fuerça tenia, y ocho [h]ombres no lo pudieron atar. Echaronle vnos grillos,*
> *como que se los dauan para lleuar. Y entonces bramaua. No quisso comer de*

puro corage. Y muriose. Tomaron para traer a España la medida, ya que no podia[n] la persona. (1552, 1:51v).

He drank his wine well. He was terrified when he saw himself in a mirror. They tested his strength, and eight men were unable to restrain him. They put shackles on him, as if they were giving them to him to carry, and then he roared. He refused to eat out of sheer rage and he died. They took his measurements to bring back to Spain, for they were unable to bring back the person.

After describing the Patagonian's responses to the sailors' experiments, Gómara abruptly informs us of his violent death. In his ironic statement that "[t]hey took his measurements to bring to Spain, for they were unable to bring back the person," Gómara seems to be calling attention to the inhumanity of the situation: the Patagonian's misery and the tragedy of his death.

A similar episode on the island of Cebu in the Philippines took a very different turn. After crossing the Pacific, Magellan tried to ascertain the judgment and abilities of the native inhabitants in this new region.[27] This involved a test of strength that would set the rules for future interaction between the parties. Magellan clad a man in armor to show the inhabitants that blows from a lance and sword could not penetrate it. Gómara tells us: "Los de la isla se marauillaron de lo vno, y de lo otro. Mas no tanto quanto los nuestros pensaron" [Those of the island marveled at the former and the latter, but not as much as our men thought] (1552, 1:52v). The Filipinos' lack of astonishment extinguished the sailors' hope that the natives were cognitively inferior and ironically anticipated the deaths of Magellan, his successor Juan Serrano, and various Spaniards.[28] Gómara insinuated that the Spaniards' knowledge of metals did not give them a significant advantage over the Filipinos because they were unable to instill fear with their weaponry.

The *Historia general* contrasts experiences in the Atlantic and the Pacific based on the type of exchange that transpired between Europeans and native inhabitants. A revealing case occurred after Juan Sebastián de Elcano had taken over the expedition and the explorers were invited to trade on the island of Borneo. The Spaniards decided to present their diplomatic mission to the king, bearing clothing, fabrics, needles, a glass, and a cup as presents. Gómara noted their reaction when they were brought to the royal palace on elephants and saw the streets lined with men armed with swords, lances, and shields:

Viendo los españoles tanta maiestad, tanta riqueza, y aparato, no alçauan
los ojos del suelo, y hallauanse muy corridos con su vil presente. Hablauan
entre si muy baxo de quan diferente gente era aq[ue]lla que la de Indias. Y
rogauan a dios q[ue] los sacasse con bien de alli. (1552, 1:54r)

The Spaniards seeing so much majesty, so much wealth and
property, did not raise their eyes from the floor, and felt very
ashamed of their despicable gift. They spoke among themselves very
softly about how different these people were from those of the Indies.
And they prayed to God that he would get them out of there
unharmed.

This passage is fundamental for appreciating the narrative logic that
Gómara applied in his interpretation of the history of the Indies. The
instance of exchange was central for establishing the dynamic developing between Europeans and natives; in other words, it was the hermeneutical principle that founded the imperial relationship. In this case,
the Spaniards committed the error of operating in the Pacific as if they
were in the Americas and found themselves in an embarrassing situation of not representing their diplomatic mission with the proper dignity. The passage shows that, for Gómara, the knowledge of objects in
imperial encounters could provide a explanation of the conquest and
colonization of the Indies.

It is also important to note that Gómara's constructions of these
scenes were not found in any of the accounts that circulated in Europe
about the Magellan-Elcano trip. Information about the circumnavigation of the globe had been essentially transmitted through Transylvanus
Maximilianus's *De Moluccis Insulis,* Antonio Pigafetta's *Le Voyage,* and
Peter Martyr's fifth decade.[29] One might suppose that Gómara either
drew upon survivors' testimonies or deliberately fabricated these episodes. In any case he bothered to incorporate these details within his
narration of the Magellan-Elcano voyage. The sense of irony with which
Gómara infused these encounters reveals his critical vision about the
discoverers' expectations of easy enrichment.

Gómara also explains indigenous submission as the result of exchange in the conquest of Mexico. Glen Carman has pointed out that
Cortés's discourses with the native inhabitants served to reaffirm the
hierarchies presupposed by the conquest (1992, 235; 1993, 175–176). The
conquistador's messages and statements to Motecuhzoma specifically
took place in the larger context of acts of exchange. Gómara began

contrasting the methods of Francisco Hernández de Córdoba and Juan de Grijalva (who both merely reconnoitered the land despite noting its richness) with those of Cortés (who decided to conquer and settle).[30] In his chapter titled "Oracion de Cortes a los soldados" (Cortés's speech to the soldiers), Gómara had Cortés tell his men: "Por tanto otra forma, otro discurso, otra maña [h]emos de tener que Cordoua, y Grijalua. . . . Y aqui yo vos propongo grandes premios, mas embueltos en grandes trabajos" [Therefore we must take another way, another course, another tact than Córdoba and Grijalva. . . . And here I propose to you great rewards, but enveloped in great hardships] (1552, 2:6v). When comparing Córdoba and Grijalva with Cortés, he contrasted barter with conquest, that is, a form of trade with settlement and the subjugation of the native population. Moreover, he alluded to another way of exchange that Cortés began to practice with native Mesoamericans.

What Gómara had in mind appears in the chapter titled "El buen acogimiento que Cortes hallo en san Juan de Ulhua" (The good reception that Cortés got in San Juan de Ulúa) (1552: 2:15v–16r). The Spaniards traded gold in exchange for objects such as glass beads, pins, mirrors, and scissors, which had little value to them. Gómara commented that the Indians "quedaron con ello tan pagados, y ricos, que no se veyan de plazer, y regozijo. Y aun creyan que [h]auian engañado a los forasteros, pe[n]sando que era el vidrio piedras finas" [felt so satisfied and wealthy with this that they were overwhelmed with pleasure and joy. And they even believed they had tricked the foreigners, thinking that glass was a precious stone] (1552, 2:16r). He contrasted the image of their naiveté with the shrewdness of Cortés, who seems to have had complete control over the situation:

Visto por Cortes la mucha cantidad de oro que aquella gente traya y trocaua tan bouamente por dixes, y niñerias, ma[n]do pregonar en el real que ninguno tomasse oro so graues penas, sino q[ue] todos hiziessen que no lo conocian, o que no lo querian. Porque no pareciesse que era codicia. ni su intencion, y venida, a solo aquello encaminada. Y assi dissimulaua para ver que cosa era aquella gran muestra de oro. Y si lo hazian aquellos indios por probar si lo [h]auian por ello (1552, 2:16r).

Cortés, seeing the great quantity of gold that the people brought and exchanged so foolishly for trinkets and trifles, ordered it proclaimed in his camp that, under serious penalties, no one may take gold, that everyone instead should act as if they did not acknowledge or want it, so that it would not seem that they were greedy or that their intention and coming were only directed at that. And he pretended in this manner in order to see whether the Indians were making that great display of gold merely to test them.

Gómara's Cortés not only knew the value of objects, but also concealed his desire for gold and was preoccupied with ascertaining whether the natives acted with any degree of sophistication in their exchanges with the Spaniards. He later added that Teudilli, the lord of Cotosta, offered his respect to Cortés by burning incense and bloodied sticks. This comment is significant because it suggests that the Indians received the Spaniards as gods. The delivery of gifts and sacrifices allowed Gómara to present the theory that the Indians thought Cortés was Quetzalcoatl. The clash of two systems of knowledge led to the Mesoamericans' unequal relationship with the Spaniards.[31]

Gómara used scenes of exchange to document stages of progress in the conquest of Mexico. First, in San Juan de Ulúa, Cortés met with Teudilli (1552, 2:15v–16r), who received him with gifts and offerings. Cortés used the occasion to have his interpreters, Jerónimo de Aguilar and Marina, ask him for a meeting with Motecuhzoma to give him a message from the king of Spain. The chapter "El presente y respuesta q[ue] Motecçuma embio a Cortes" (The present and response that Motecuhzoma sent Cortés) (1552, 2:16v–17v) relates that his ambassadors brought the conquistador an extraordinary gift with their lord's reply accepting the king of Spain's friendship and offering Cortés provisions for his men but excusing himself from the meeting. Having initially failed to gain access to the emperor of Mexico, Cortés moved to establish an alliance with the lord of the nearby community of Cempoala, who sought deliverance from Motecuhzoma's rule. In the chapter titled "Lo que dixo a Cortes el señor de Cempoal" (What the lord of Cempoala said to Cortés) (1552, 2:20v–21v), the two conspired to form a coalition against the Mexicans under the conquistador's protection. They sealed their pact with an exchange of gifts, and the lord gave Cortés eight noble ladies to take as wives "en prenda de amor, y amistad perpetua y verdadera" [as a token of love and true, perpetual friendship] (1552, 2:21v).

In Quiahuixtlan, Cortés forced the lord of the town into open rebellion against Motecuhzoma by imprisoning his tribute collectors and then secretly freeing two of the prisoners. He used them as messengers and sent them to the Mexican emperor to offer his friendship and request once more to meet with him. Thus he was able to reestablish communication with Motecuhzoma who, although still refusing to meet with him, sent him more presents and thanked him for saving his men. The emperor also asked Cortés to have the Cempoalans free the two other prisoners still being held and agreed to pardon their lord's offense of detaining his collectors. Cortés sent messengers to assure the town that Motecuhzoma would not dare to hurt them while they remained under his protection and to declare them free from the Mexicans. Strengthening his ties with both lords in this two-way exchange allowed him to act as a broker between the conflicting parties. These moments of exchange also defined the bonds that Spaniards and Indians were creating with each other. It was not just a simple act of taking gold and other objects in return for something worthless, but rather the promise of a permanent relationship that Gómara interpreted as a gesture of submission.

While Cortés was advancing toward Tenochtitlan to force a meeting with Motecuhzoma, the Mexican emperor was gradually ceding power to his adversary. He sent messages and presents until he finally delivered to the conqueror the sovereignty over his territory. In the chapter "La embaxada que Motecçuma embio a Cortes" (The embassy that Motecuhzoma sent Cortés) (1552, 2:31v), the Mexican emperor dispatches more presents to the approaching conquistador and offers himself as a tributary on the condition that he not come to Tenochtitlan. Cortés rejects this proposal and, making his way into the Aztec capital, he finally meets with Motecuhzoma. In "La oracion de Motecçuma a los Españoles" (Motecuhzoma's speech to the Spaniards) (1552, 2:40v–41v), an exchange of gifts takes place between the leaders, and subsequently the emperor offers his obedience to Cortés. In "La oracion que Motecçuma hizo a sus caualleros dandose al rei de Castilla" (The speech that Motecuhzoma made to his men giving himself to the king of Castile) (1552, 2:53v–54r), he orders his lords to become vassals of the Castilian king. A few days later Cortés requests from Motecuhzoma a contribution to finance the wars that the king of Spain was waging in Europe. In "El oro y joyas que Motecçuma dio a Cortes" (The gold and jewels that Motecuhzoma gave Cortés) (1552, 2:54r–v), the Mexican emperor was to collect a large treasure from various tributary towns and to present what would be his last gift to the Spanish conqueror. Gómara constructed a progressive sequence of exchanges of words and objects in which the dynamic of the relationship created between Spaniards and Indians gave way to the gradual appropriation of territory.

JUSTICE AND THE DYNAMICS
OF INTERCULTURAL RELATIONS

The systems of knowledge about objects that Gómara observed in imperial encounters shaped colonial relationships by creating a space of subordination for the Indians. The violence and abuses committed by the conquistadors appear in the *Historia general,* in part, as a consequence of the vulnerability of native communities. For Gómara, the Indians were susceptible to violence because their modes of knowledge limited their capacity to relate to their invaders. The success of Spanish explorers, conquistadors, and settlers depended on their ability to manage a wider perspective of the world. The native individuals who developed positions of resistance or collaboration in the *Historia general* specifically faced the problem of evaluating their Spanish aggressors. In his *Democrates secundus,* Sepúlveda (1997, 66) criticized the Mexicans for their "ignaviam, inertiam et ruditatem" [cowardice, inactivity, and crudity] in confronting Cortés's invasion.[32] Gómara's *Historia general* shared this defamation of the native population, but went on to situate it within the context of ethics and exchange.

The protocols of action established in royal instructions for the conquests are a central aspect of the ethical apparatus that Gómara attributed to the crown.[33] The Requirement was consistently employed in Tierra Firme by Pedrarias Dávila, in México by Fernando Cortés, and in Peru by Francisco Pizarro. It is interesting to note that Gómara does not explicitly mention the Requirement, perhaps because it was a controversial legal instrument criticized by both conquistadors and missionaries.[34] Oviedo (1992, 3:227–232) questioned it because he thought it was impossible for the Indians to understand. He related with skepticism an encounter that he had with Palacios Rubios, where he asked him "porque él había ordenado aquel Requerimiento, si quedaba satisfecha la conciencia de los cristianos con aquel Requerimiento; e díjome que sí, si se hiciese como el Requerimiento lo dice" [why he had drawn up that Requirement and if the conscience of Christians was satisfied with that Requirement; and he told me yes, if what the Requirement says was done] (1992, 3: 230). Las Casas, in turn, criticized the legal foundation whereby their obedience was demanded and explained that it was merely a subterfuge to avoid the repercussions of the Laws of Burgos for harming the native population (1988–1998, 5:1980–2003, 10:44–45).

Gómara understated the relevance of the Requirement by presenting it as a sermon rather than a formal mechanism of conquest. The conquistadors were clearly following the protocol of conquest in his account, but Gómara presented the act of "requiring" as an attempt to communicate the evangelical purpose of the conquest to the Indians. The emphasis that Gómara gave the doctrinal content of the Requirement over its juridical dimension ignores the fact that these encounters were primarily coercive acts employing a legal tool of subjugation. He thus erases the institutional aspect of colonial violence to present it as the result of a dynamic created by intercultural contact. Most historians date the creation of the Requirement between 1512 and 1514 (Gibson 1966; Parry 1971; Hanke 1974; Zavala 1988; Seed 1995), but Gómara traced it back to the instructions provided for the expeditions of Alonso de Ojeda and Diego de Nicuesa in 1508. In fact, he never spoke of the Requirement as such, but rather alluded to the instructions given to the conquistadors to carry out their conquests. Gómara's descriptions of their contents, however, correspond to the actions involved in the Requirement:

> *A Diego de Nicuesa, y Alonso de Hojeda, que fueron los primeros conquistadores de tierra firme de indias, dio el rey vna instrucion de diez, o doce capitulos. El primero que les predicassen los euangelios. Otro que les rogassen con la paz. El otauo que queriendo paz, y fe, fuessen libres, bien tratados, y muy priuilegiados. El nono que si perseuerassen en su idolatria, y comida de [h]ombres, y en la enemistad los catiuassen, y matassen libremente. Que hasta entonces no se consentia (1552, 1:30r).*

> To Diego de Nicuesa and Alonso de Ojeda, who were the first conquistadors of Tierra Firme in the Indies, the king gave an instruction of ten or twelve chapters. The first was that the gospels would be preached to them. Another was that they would ask them for peace. The eighth was that they, wanting peace and faith, would be free, well-treated, and very privileged. The ninth was that, if they persisted in their idolatry, eating humans, and enmity, they would be captured and killed freely, which up until that time was not allowed.

The three basic points—preaching, requesting peace, and punishing resistance—would suggest that the instructions of Ojeda and Nicuesa incorporated the Requirement or at least contained its essential elements. Gómara in fact identified them with the instructions of Pedrarias Dávila: "Mandole guardar la instrucion de Hojeda, y Nicuesa . . . que requiriesse mucho, y solenemente, a los indios con la paz, y amistad, antes de hazerles guerra" [He ordered him to follow Ojeda's and Nicuesa's instructions . . . to ask the Indians many times and solemnly for peace and friendship, before waging war against them] (1552, 1:36v). Thus Gómara would be situating the composition of the Requirement around 1508, three or four years before the earliest dating accepted today.[35] According to Gómara's version, the use of the Requirement would have been in place in all the conquests conducted in the continental territories of the Indies. More importantly, it would predate the Laws of Burgos (1512) and even the criticisms of *fray* Antonio de Montesinos (1511) concerning the *encomenderos'* abuses. Gómara treated these instructions as part of Spanish imperial policy, disassociating them from the legal debates concerning the conquests and especially the juridical criticisms of the Requirement. Moreover, Gómara's emphasis on the content of the instructions underscores that the conquistador had to make an effort to enter into communication with the indigenous communities by peaceful means and establish relations of friendship.

José Rabasa (2000, 10–11, 84–96) considers the Requirement part of a "machinery of terror" created to preserve the colonial order. Its persuasive power rested in the threat of military force; therefore, it exercised symbolic violence upon the Indians who were left with no option but to submit to the conquistadors. Rabasa (2000, 85) also suggests that colonial legislation tended to maintain the basic model of the Requirement. The Ordinances of 1526 refined the parameters of the acceptable uses of force through the ideology of peaceful conquest. We must take into account, however, that this readjustment of the Requirement denied legitimacy to actions that the conquistadors and settlers were still carrying out in the Indies. It served poorly as a mechanism for concealing colonial violence, for in the long run it strengthened the platform for denouncing and criticizing the conquest. Inasmuch as it prohibited the previous procedures of conquest, the ideology of peaceful conquest created a problem, not a solution, for developing a hegemonic discourse. Gómara's portrayal of the Requirement as a sermon was an attempt to limit the legal implications of his conquest narratives, and his lack of arguments justifying the Spaniards' abuses left their infamy exposed.

Gómara focused his attention on the role of the Indians who reacted critically to the actions of the conquistadors. Peter Hulme (1994, 196–197) considers that the topos of the "savage critic" expresses the anxiety that accompanies the colonial project with respect to the forms of violence that it exercised on the native inhabitants. Gómara, in turn, employed the topos in order to relativize rational arguments against the conquest. He recorded discourses of resistance in order to suggest that they offered inadequate responses to the complex situations created in the interaction between Spaniards and Indians. When putting these criticisms in the mouths of Indians, Gómara basically questions their ability to comprehend the moral world of the conquistadors. In the *Historia general,* the topos of the "savage critic" always consists of a member of the native elite who was either collaborating with the conquistadors or responding to some form of coercion. The Indians' criticism is consistent with their position in the indigenous social hierarchy, but they do not represent a moral obstacle for the Spaniards. This seemingly dialogical element in his account represents a process of negotiation in which the Indians chose to either ally with or resist their invaders.

Gómara's understanding of the complexities found in verbal interplay between cultures is revealed in the indigenous reaction to *bachiller* Martín Fernández de Enciso's sermon. When Enciso was en route to meet Ojeda in Urabá in 1509, he stopped in Cenú to trade with the native inhabitants. After they showed up on the coast armed to offer resistance, Enciso tried to calm them down by communicating through an interpreter that he came in peace. But the natives rejected his peaceful offer and the *bachiller* proceeded to preach a sermon informing them of the reason for his coming. He explained

> como el santo padre d[e] Roma, vicario de Jesu Christo en toda redo[n]dez
> de la tierra, q[ue] tenia mando assoluto sobre las almas, y religio[n], [h]auia
> dado aquellas tierras al muy poderoso rey de castilla su señor. Y q[ue] yua
> el a tomar la posession dellas (1552, 1:39r).

> how the holy father of Rome, the vicar of Christ around the entire
> earth, who had absolute command over souls and religion, had
> given these lands to their lord, the very mighty king of Castile. And
> that he was going to take possession of them.

This sermon was consistent with the conquistadors' use of the Requirement and has been frequently cited as an example of the absurdity of the procedures employed by the Spaniards (Hanke 1974, 37).

The indigenous reaction, on the other hand, presents a rational criticism of the sermon and the foundations of Spanish dominion in the Indies. The Indians responded:

*Que deuia ser muy fra[n]co de lo ageno el padre santo, o reboltoso, pues
daua lo q[ue] no era suyo. Y el rey q[ue] era algu[n] pobre, pues pidia. Y el
algu[n] atreuido, q[ue] amenazaua a quie[n] no conocia (1552, 1:39r).*

That the holy father must have been very generous, or mischievous,
with what belonged to others because he granted what was not his.
And the king was some poor man because he was begging, and
[Enciso] rather impudent to threaten someone he did not know.

Enciso's reaction was to repeat the Requirement various times, threat-
ening to wage war against them and to take them as slaves; then, he
finally fought them. Gómara took their response directly from Enciso's
own account in his *Suma de geografía* (1519, [52]v). Las Casas recognized
the critical potential of this episode and paraphrased it in his *Historia de
las Indias* (in terms similar to those of Gómara) to criticize the use of the
Requirement by the conquistadors (1988–1998, 5:1999–2000). He claimed
that it was absurd to expect that the native inhabitants would be willing to submit themselves to a foreign king they did not know and from
whom they did not know what to expect.

The interest in Gómara's version lies in having recorded an indigenous criticism that a European reader could recognize as a valid refutation of the legal foundations employed in the Requirement. In fact,
Oviedo (1992, 119, 142–143) omitted the entire episode in his *Historia
general y natural*. Martyr related in his *Decades* that the Indians had surrounded them for three days, but once they communicated with one of
the native servants brought by the Spaniards, they kindly received them
(1966, 80). He explained that the Indians had previously been assaulted
by Ojeda's and Nicuesa's bands and thought that Enciso also came to
rob them. When they discovered that Enciso came with a different plan,
they declared that it would be unjust to attack an innocent man if he
had not caused them harm. Then, they received him peacefully and
provided him with food. Las Casas (1988–1998, 4:1550–1552) used Martyr's
version to refute the accusations of bellicosity in which the laws enslav-
ing the Caribs had been based and argued that their rebellion was a
legitimate response to the injustices that they had suffered at the hands
of Ojeda and Nicuesa. Gómara's version, however, offered hardly any
concession to the criticism of the conquest. He ignored the peaceful
response of the Caribs and stated that they rejected Enciso's overtures.
His citation of the indigenous criticism of the Requirement did no more
than explain their rejection.

The criticism offered by the Indians questions the principles that Gómara presented as legitimate foundations of Spanish dominion in the Indies. On the basic level, they were violating Vitoria's title of "natural society and communication" by refusing to trade with the Spaniards. More specifically, the rationality of their criticism clashes with Gómara's interpretation of Christian juridical tradition and sacred history. The reaction of the Indians of Cenú is quite similar to the one Gómara attributed to Atahualpa in his response to the messages that Francisco Pizarro sent him and the sermon preached by *fray* Vicente de Valverde (1552, 1:63r–64v). In both cases, the Indians thought they possessed the means to expel these unknown invaders, but they ended up suffering the effects of the conquistadors' violence. Throughout the *Historia general* the indigenous inhabitants' unwillingness to accept the authority of the Spaniards reinforced the determination of the conquistadors to subjugate them by force.

One could argue that the expressions of prudence among the Indians serve to highlight the conquistadors' moral shortcomings, but criticisms of their injustices were commonplace in the works of other historians such as Martyr and Oviedo, which Gómara had read. Although the Indians assume the moral authority to resist the conquistadors, they make the mistake of underestimating the military power and capacity of their enemies. Seeing that these responses were insufficient to weaken the determination of the conquistadors, Gómara assumed that the native leaders lacked the perspective necessary for interpreting their invaders.

Gómara questioned the Indians' moral position as a focal point of resistance in the *Historia general,* not only because he thought that the Indians were mistaken, but also fundamentally because they were incapable of generating an effective defense against the advance of the conquistadors. A paradigmatic case in this respect is found in the account of the conquest of Darién. Panquiaco, son of the *cacique* Comagre, gave gold and slaves to a group of conquistadors led by Balboa in Antigua del Darién. When the Spaniards divided up the treasure they began to quarrel over their shares and Panquiaco severely criticized them:

Pa[n]quiaco entonces dio una puñada en el peso, derramo por el suelo el oro de las bala[n]ças, y dixo. Si yo supiera (christianos) q[ue] sobre mi oro [h]auiades de reñir, no vos lo diera. Ca soy amigo d[e] toda paz, y co[n]cordia. Marauillome de vuestra ceguera, y locura que deshazeis las joyas bien labradas por hacer dellas palillos. Y q[ue] sie[n]do ta[n] amigos

*riñays por cosa vil, y poca. Mas os valiera estar en vuestra tierra, q[ue] tan
lexos de aqui esta, si [h]ay alla ta[n] sabia, y polida ge[n]te como affirmais,
que no venir a reñir en la agena. Do[n]de viuimos co[n]tentos los grosseros,
y barbaros [h]ombres, q[ue] llamays. Mas empero si tanta gana de oro
teneys, q[ue] desassossegueis, y aun mateis, los q[ue] lo tiene[n], yo vos
mostrare vna tierra do[n]de os harteis dello. Marauillaro[n]se los españoles
de la buena platica, y razones de aquel moço indio. Y mas de la libertad
co[n] q[ue] hablo (1552, 1:32v).*

Panquiaco then punched the scale; the gold on the balance spilled
on to the floor, and he said, "If I knew you (Christians) would have
quarreled over my gold, I would not have given it to you, for I am a
friend of total peace and harmony. I am amazed at your
shortsightedness and madness because you melt down well-crafted
jewels in order to make little bars out of them. And being friends,
you quarrel over something so insignificant and small. It would be
better for you to stay in your own lands, which are so far away from
here, if there are such wise and refined people there as you say,
instead of coming here to fight in a foreign land where we, the
barbarous and rude men that you call us, live happily. However, if
you have so much desire for gold that you would become restless
and even kill those who have it, I will show you a land where you
will get sick of it." The Spaniards were stunned with the young
Indian's eloquent speech and reasons, and even more with the
liberty with which he spoke.

Panquiaco's criticism has a double reading. On the one hand, he
presented a powerful moral argument for questioning the motivations
and forms of the Spaniards' behavior in the conquest. His judgments,
in this sense, are perfectly adjusted to the ethical perspective of a European criticizing the conquistadors. On the other hand, Panquiaco offered them the opportunity of finding more gold, inciting in them the
same greed that he had just criticized. Instead of rejecting them,
Panquiaco became a collaborator of the Spaniards and reasserted their
agenda. Moreover, like the responses of other native leaders in the
Historia general, he confirms that the Indians lack interest in gold and do
not need it to maintain their lifestyle. The Europeans are the ones who
need it and can make use of the gold for commerce and capital accumulation. The moral criticisms of the conquistador do not create effective
resistance to colonization among the Indians in Gómara's account, principally because of their differences in culture and way of life.

The greatest advantage that Gómara attributes to the Spaniards is their control over the development of events. Their will to carry out the conquest combines with their ability to articulate a strategy, take advantage of small opportunities, manipulate situations, and take the Indians by surprise. These qualities assume a special significance for they are associated with the conquistadors' familiarity with the written word. Throughout the *Historia general* it is evident that Gómara sees in the lettered culture of the Spaniards the critical factor in determining their victory over the Indians. When Gómara related the deceptions and tricks that Cortés played on Motecuhzoma and the Indians of Cempoala in the *Conquista de México,* he attributed his success to his ability to machinate intrigue: "Bie[n] podia Cortes tener estos tratos entre gente q[ue] no entendia por do yua el hilo de la trama" [Cortés could easily have these dealings among people who did not understand what web he was weaving] (1552, 2:23v). The possibility of understanding that there was a plot beneath the surface suggests a knowledge of the world anchored in European political and diplomatic tradition, but above all the type of attitude that a European reader would associate with an education in history and literature.

Gómara's interpretation of the conquest argues that the Indians have a fundamental disadvantage because they lack the rudiments of reading and writing. In his account of the death of Cuauhtemoc, Gómara explained that an Indian named Mexicalcinco had revealed to Cortés that the indigenous leader was conspiring to kill him. The conquistador conducted a secret proceeding and decided to punish the guilty parties. Gómara described the Indians' astonishment at Cortés's swift response:

Y creian que la aguja, y carta de marear, se lo [h]auian dicho, y no [h]ombre ninguno. Y tenian por mui cierto que no se le podian esconder, los pensamientos (1552, 2:103v).

And they believed that the compass and the map had told him that, and not any man. And they were very certain that they could not hide their thoughts from him.

Gómara believed that the Indians attributed special powers to European technologies of representation, thus he portrayed them as a condition for colonization. The tricks of perception that the conquistadors played with the native inhabitants led him to affirm the superiority of European alphabetic culture:

Hiziero[n] tambien mucho al caso las letras, y cartas, que vnos españoles a
otros se escriuian. Ca pensauan los indios que tenian espirito de profeçia
pues sin verse, ni hablarse, se ente[n]dian, o que hablaua el papel. Y
estuuiero[n] en esto abouados y corridos (1552, 1:19r).

They also paid a lot of attention to the notes and letters that the
Spaniards sent to one another, for the Indians believed that they had
the gift of prophecy—given that they communicated among
themselves without seeing or speaking to each other—or that paper
spoke. And they remained stupefied and embarrassed about this.

Communication and exchange become the foundations of the conquest. The characteristics that Gómara employed to assert native cultural inferiority also determine the fundamental limitations of their resistance and explain the forms of interaction that they develop with the
Spaniards. Gómara thus associated the disparities between the two
groups with the more general ends of imperialism as justification for
the evils of Spanish colonialism.

SEARCHING FOR A COMMON GOOD:
IMPERIALISM AS A FORM OF RECIPROCITY

The *Historia general* engages in effective debate about the consequences
of the conquest and makes no attempt to conceal its destruction. The
issue then becomes interpreting Gómara's vision of the empire as a
space of negotiation and exchange that should lead to the common benefit of the colonizers and the colonized. I would argue that this allows
him to reconcile the military, political, economic, juridical, and religious
objectives of the empire. Moreover, thinking about the conquest in terms
of exchange offers him a narrative solution that permits him to talk
about the positive as well as the failures, errors, and abuses.[36] In "Praise
of Spaniards" Gómara points out some of the problems that the conquest had caused:

[F]uera mejor no les [h]auer tomado nada. Sino contentarse con lo que
sacauan de las minas, y rios, y sepulturas. No tiene cuenta el oro, y plata, ca
passan de sesenta millones, ny las perlas, y esmeraldas que [h]an sacado de
so la tierra, y agua. En comparacion de lo qual es muy poco el oro, y plata,
que los Indios tenia[n]. El mal que [h]ay en ello es [h]auer hecho trabajar
demasiadamente a los indios en las minas en la pesqueria de perlas, y en las

cargas. Oso dezir sobresto que todos quantos [h]an hecho morir indios assi, que [h]an sido muchos, y casi todos, [h]an acabado mal (1552, 1:121v).

It would be better to have not taken anything, and to be content with what was extracted from the mines, rivers, and burial places. The gold and silver is beyond counting, for it surpasses sixty million, and so are the pearls and emeralds that they have extracted from under the earth and water. In comparison to this, the gold and silver that the Indians had is very little. The evil in it is having made the Indians work too much in carrying loads, pearl fishing, and the mines. I dare say regarding this matter that all who have caused Indians to perish in this manner—who have been many and nearly all of them—have come to a bad end.

Gómara recognized that the plunder and death of the Indians had tainted the conquests, but the foundation of the colonial relationship was based on the future that it made possible. Convinced that Spain's sovereignty over the Indies was legitimate, he had to address these blemishes and explain how the empire could be beneficial for the New World. Gómara was obviously confronted with the dilemma of either abandoning colonialism or showing how it worked. He chose to accept the injuries as a necessary evil, assuming that the defects of the system would be fixed along the way. This argument might have allowed him to ease his conscience while continuing to support the oppression of Indians, but by exposing many outrages committed by the Spaniards he was also making his own claims difficult to accept. This explains how the *Historia general* could subsequently be used to attack the conquest. As Carman (1992, 1993) has persuasively argued, Gómara made a genuine effort to comprehend and interpret Spain's dominion over the Indies.

Gómara's discursive economy results from his awareness of the imperial culture developed in the Atlantic by Spain and Portugal. This culture of exchange and mediation of different worlds took a violent and destructive form, but it continued to be regarded as a locus of material and spiritual profit.[37] Gómara's narrative synthesis aspires to establish a historical foundation to characterize imperial practices. He explained the relationship between Spain and its colonies and the compatibility of discovery, exploration, conquest, and evangelization. Gómara sought equilibrium between the diverse interests and practices associated with colonization. Thus he used exchange as the principle of integration for reconciling the conquest with other imperial activities. In "Praise of Spaniards" Gómara presented the conquest as a relationship of reciprocity between Spain and the Indies:

> *Buena loa, y gloria, es d[e] nuestros reyes, y [h]ombres de España, que*
> *[h]ayan hecho a los indios tomar, y tener, vn dios vna fe, y vn bautismo. Y*
> *quitadoles la idolatria, los sacrificios de [h]ombres, el comer carne humana,*
> *la sodomia, y otros grandes, y malos pecados, que nuestro buen Dios mucho*
> *aborresce, y castiga. [H]an les también quitado la muchedumbre de mugeres.*
> *. . . [H]an les mostrado letras, que sin ellas son los [h]ombres como*
> *animales. Y el vso del hierro, que tan necessario es a [h]ombre. Assimismo*
> *les [h]an mostrado muchas buenas costu[m]bres, artes, y policia, para mejor*
> *passar la vida. Lo qual todo, y aun cada cosa por si, vale, sin duda*
> *ninguna, mucho mas que la pluma, ny las perlas, ny la plata, ny el oro que*
> *les [h]an tomado (1552, 1:121v).*

Good praise and glory belong to our monarchs and men of Spain, who have made the Indians accept and have one God, one faith, and one baptism. And abandoning their idolatry, human sacrifices, eating of human flesh, sodomy, and other great and evil sins that our benevolent God greatly abhors and punishes, they also have stopped their herding of women. . . . They have shown them letters, without which men are like animals, and the use of iron, which is so necessary to man. Likewise they have shown them many good customs, arts, and civility to better live their lives. All of which, and even each thing by itself, without any doubt, is worth much more than the plumage, the pearls, the silver, and the gold that they have taken from them.

Gómara saw in the conquest a process that could be interpreted as a transfer of objects, persons, texts, and knowledge between worlds. This exchange permitted him to represent the colonial relationship as a model of cultural interaction that created material as well as moral bonds. The variety of institutions (religious, legal, economic) that take part in the exchange defined the interests and obligations between the two communities in the formation of a social system (see Mauss 1990). Gómara presented a clearly utopian conception of colonial relations in which the introduction of Christian religion, letters, and technology had benefited the Indians, while the conquest simultaneously allowed the extraction of their resources. He showed this principle of exchange at work in the conquest of Mexico, which he considered an exemplary model for Spanish imperialism. He included a chapter explaining "Que libraron bie[n] los Indios en ser conquistados" (That the Indians were better off being conquered) (1552, 2:136v–137r), and another containing a long list of "Cosas notables q[ue] les falta[n]" (Notable things that they lack) (1552, 2:137r–v) where he highlighted the various improvements he thought that the conquest had brought to native life. As for instances in which the indigenous population had almost completely been decimated, Gómara stressed the steps taken by the crown to protect their well-being. Even in cases such as where the destruction of the Indians was unjustifiable, he continued to embrace this principle of improvement, focusing on the products, businesses, urban development, and institutions that Spaniards had introduced to the island.

Gómara's acceptance of the loss of life may be partly explained because he represented the Spanish imperial experience in positive terms, privileging the observable changes in his own material world. The presence of the riches from the Indies in Spain brought on a new awareness about the value of things. In the chapter "De las perlas" (On pearls), Gómara called attention to the way in which the pearls of the Indies had inundated Spain and he questioned social assumptions about their worth:

> *E ya todos traen perlas, y aljofar, [h]ombres, y mugeres, ricos y pobres.*
> *Pero nunca en prouincia del mundo, entro tanta perleria como en España. Y*
> *lo que mas es, en poco tiempo. En fin colman las perlas la riqueza de oro y*
> *plata, y esmeraldas que [h]auemos traido de las Indias. Mas considero yo*
> *que razo[n] hallaron los antiguos, y modernos, para estimar en tanto las*
> *perlas, pues no tiene[n] virtud medicinal. Y se enuejecen mucho. . . . Y no*
> *alcanço sino que por ser blancas. . . . Quiça es porque se traen del otro*
> *mundo . . . o porque cuesta[n] [h]ombres (1552, 1:109r).*

And now everyone wears gems and pearls—men and women, rich and poor. But never in any province of the world did so many pearls enter as in Spain and, moreover, in so little time. In short, the pearls, the wealth from gold and silver, and the emeralds that we have brought from the Indies abound. But I wonder why the ancients and moderns value pearls so much, for they have no medicinal virtue, and they deteriorate considerably. . . . And I cannot figure it out, unless it is because they are white. . . . Perhaps it is because they are brought from the other world . . . or because they cost men.

Gómara was struck that pearls had become a common possession among Spaniards and were esteemed even though there was little to say about

their properties. He supposed that their worth might lie in three possibilities: their whiteness, that they came from another world, or the
human cost of their extraction. His fascination with New World difference involved the recognition of the human tragedy brought on by
Spanish imperialism. He ascribed to these pearls the power to mediate
between worlds, either because of their transfer from one world to
another or by converting Indian lives into value.

Other sixteenth-century historians considered that the transatlantic
crossing infused a special charismatic quality to things that could be
equated with power or truth. In book ten of his fifth decade, Peter
Martyr described a revealing scene in this respect. He related a meeting that took place in his house that included the prothonotary apostolic legate Marino Caracciolo, the ambassador of Venice Gaspar
Contarini, the vice duke of Milan Tomasso Maino, and Cortés's secretary Juan de Ribera. In this meeting Ribera showed a variety of objects
brought back from Mexico to his guests who observed the materials
and the exquisiteness of their manufacture. In particular they admired
the stone work and "nullu[s] e nostris naturales magis ostendere vultus
humanos fassi sumus omnes" [they all confessed that none of our (crafts-
men) represents the human face in a more lifelike way] (1966, 202).
Then, Ribera had a young native boy come out, whom he had brought
back as a servant, who performed a parody of different indigenous
customs: wrestling, sacrifices, ceremonies, drunkenness, and so on (1966,
203–204). Martyr added that Ribera confirmed that the boy had given a
faithful representation, and based on this performance the Milanese
humanist went on to provide a description of Mexican culture.

This kind of cultural performativity also had an important place in
the *Historia general*. Gómara associated it with what he called the fame
or reputation of the Indies. One of the great spectacles he described
was related to Cortés's first return to Europe in 1528, which he presented in his chapter titled "Como vino Cortes a España" (How Cortés
came to Spain):

> *Embarco mil y quinientos marcos de plata, veinte mil pesos de buen oro, y
> otros diez mil de oro sin ley. Y muchas joyas riquissimas. Traxo consigo a
> Gonçalo de Sandoual, Andres de Tapia, y otros conquistadores de los mas
> principales, y [h]onrados. Traxo vn hijo de Moteççuma. Y otro de Maxixca,
> ya christiano, y don Lorencio por nombre. Y muchos caualleros, y señores
> de Mexico, Tlaxcallan, y otras ciudades. Traxo ocho bolteadores del palo,*

doze jugadores de pelota, y ciertos Indios, & Indias, muy bla[n]cos. Y otros enanos, y otros contrechos. En fin venia como gran señor. Y sin todo esto traia, para ver tigres, alcatrazes, vn aiotochtli, otro tlaquaci. . . . Y para dar, gran suma de mantas de pluma, y pelo. Ventalles, rodelas, plumajes, espejos de piedra, y cosas assi (1552, 2:113v).

He shipped fifteen hundred marks of silver, twenty thousand pesos of pure gold, and another ten thousand in substandard gold, and many of the richest jewels. He brought back with him Gonzalo de Sandoval, Andrés de Tapia, and others among the most principal and honored conquistadors. He brought a son of Motecuhzoma, and another of Maxixca, now Christian, *don* Lorenzo by name, and many gentlemen and lords from Mexico, Tlaxcala, and other cities. He brought eight acrobats, twelve ballplayers, and some Indian men and women, very light-skinned and others were dwarfs or crippled. In short, he came as a great lord. And apart from all this he brought jaguars, pelicans, an armadillo, and an opossum for show, . . . and a large sum of feathered and hair blankets, fans, bucklers, plumage, stone mirrors, and the like to give away.

Gómara emphasized the display of power and wealth projected by Cortés as the "great lord" in this gala. He brought not only extraordinary riches and a court of Spanish conquistadors and Mexican lords, but also a series of men and animals for show and objects to give away as presents. Cortés's entourage appears as a traveling exhibition and microcosm of the Mexican world for European public consumption. Undoubtedly it was a gesture of power, but also one of transferring pieces of reality from one side of the Atlantic to the other. This spectacle was not a passive entity in Europe; it recreated an experience of empire by opening a window into the New World.

Empire as exchange suggests the transformation of the world made possible by the material and cultural differences existing between Europe and the Indies. It is also a way of defining a civilizing mission—a common good that could be created for the communities entering into contact under Spanish colonial expansion. Gómara had to decide whether the forms of social organization that developed after the conquest had any merit. The difficulty of defending them was in evaluating the consequences of the conquistadors in the New World. Gómara condemned episodes such as the slaughter of Indians that the colonizers perpetrated in Hispaniola and Pedrarias Dávila's tyrannical warfare in Tierra Firme, and he exposed the moral turpitude of the conquistadors of

Peru. But when it came to examining the negative and positive results, he chose the image of the imperial enterprise that he drew from its "humble beginnings," established with Columbus and the Catholic Monarchs and brought to fruition by Cortés in the conquest of Mexico. In spite of relating these infamies, he still preferred to live in a world made possible by these reprehensible acts. He could have flatly condemned the empire, but he preferred to present reasons whereby his contemporaries could praise the Spaniards.

NOTES

1. The economic forces I am thinking of here are those that drove the globalization of the European world economy: the need to widen the territorial base and increase the supply of food, lumber, textiles, and currency to sustain demographic growth and the expansion of the European market (Wallerstein 1974).

2. See, for example, the Basel edition of Columbus's letter, which contains an illustration of King Ferdinand with the arms of Castile and Granada. The association of the discovery with the struggle against Islam reappeared more explicitly later in the edition of a play by Carlos Verardo (1494) about the conquest of Granada, which includes Columbus's letter. Likewise, Foresti's summary of the discovery in his *Supplementum* (1503) and the *Bellum christianorum principum* compilation (Remensis and Columbus 1533) clearly associated this letter with the theme of the opposition between Muslim and Christian worlds.

3. Martyr indicated that what he says in this book was told to him shortly after Columbus's departure in September 1493. He had earlier given little importance, however, to the discovery in a May 14, 1493, letter to his old protector Juan Borromeo (1990, 25). The fact that the letter addressed to Borromeo was dated in May of the same year suggests that Martyr attributed greater importance to the event during the preparations for Columbus's second voyage, probably because of the commotion that this would have caused in the Spanish court — a topic that Martyr discussed in some detail. The way Martyr relates the first voyage reveals a later writing, for he seems to be informed about Columbus's subsequent voyages, as Demetrio Ramos (1981, 16–18) has demonstrated.

4. Martyr did not mention the conflicts between Spain and Portugal over India and other recently discovered lands. Moreover, he completely omitted the long struggle that Columbus went through before gaining approval for his project. It is important to note that Bernáldez, in his *Historia de los Reyes Católicos*, mentioned the failure of the proposition made by Columbus to the king of Portugal, but he affirmed that the wise men of the court of the Catholic Monarchs listened to Columbus and approved his plan (1870, 1:359). In both accounts the discovery appears as a congruent historical development. The fact that

both narratives are contemporary suggest that the discovery did not present great interpretive challenges in this early phase.

5. Marcelino Menéndez y Pelayo saw in Martyr "one of the oldest and distinguished types of news journalism" (1942, 82). Among others, Manuel Ballesteros Gaibrois has reiterated this notion under the epithet "El primer periodista de la Historia Moderna" [the first journalist of modern history] (1987, 32–35). The term "journalist" alludes to the contemporary and informative character of his accounts. Martyr discussed contemporary topics in his *Opus epistolarium*, and his *Decades* may have been related to this epistolary, but the latter over time definitely shifted away from a focus on news items to take the form of an interpretive history of past events.

6. I intend to distance myself from the readings that Edmundo O'Gorman (1964) and Demetrio Ramos (1981) have made of Martyr's text. O'Gorman situated the *Decades* within "un largo proceso en el cual muchas inteligencias sagaces se debaten para concebir la existencia de un ente que no tenía cabida dentro del cuadro histórico y científico de la cosmovisión entonces vigente" [a long process in which many clever minds collaborated to conceive of the existence of an entity that had no place within the historical and scientific framework of the cosmovision of that time] (1964, 18). This process culminated in the announcement of a new world in Amerigo Vespucci's 1503 letter to Piero Lorenzo de' Medici and Martyr would have been its precursor (1964, 35–36). Ramos, in turn, has stated that what Martyr began would close with the triumph of the *Victoria*'s circumnavigation and Maximilianus's letter that "left antiquity behind" (1981, 53). Although I do not reject the validity of determining Martyr's place in the geographical identification of new territories, he was more influential in telling stories of exploration and colonization than in solving the cosmographical problem of the New World.

7. This line of interpretation has been continued by Paul Roche (1994), who analyzes the conflicts of interest that surrounded Columbian historiography in the sixteenth century.

8. The Columbian lawsuits lasted from 1506 to 1536 when Cardinal Loaysa (president of the Council of Indies) and Gaspar de Montoya (president of the Council of Castile) issued a final decision in Valladolid on June 28, 1536. There were at least eight verdicts, but subsequent complaints and appeals prolonged the conflict for several years. The most important one was issued on May 5, 1511, at Seville in which Diego Colón was granted the viceroyalty and his rights to one-tenth of the profits, as the crown had conceded to Columbus and his heirs at Santa Fe de Granada in 1492. This is the lawsuit cited and commented on by sixteenth-century historians. For more on these litigations, see the introduction of Muro Orejón (1967).

9. At the end of the synopsis of his discovery account, Oviedo stated: "Suya es esta gloria, y a solo Colom, despues de Dios, la deben los reyes de España

pasados e católicos, e los presentes y por venir; y no solamente toda la nasción de los señoríos todos de Sus Majestades, más aun los reinos extraños, por la grande utilidad que en todo el mundo ha redundado destas Indias" [His is this glory, and Columbus's alone, after God, which the past Catholic monarchs of Spain owe, and those present and yet to come, and not only the entire nation of all Their Highnesses' kingdoms, but even foreign kingdoms, because of the profit that has inundated the entire world from these Indies] (1992, 1:15). For Gómara's treatment of Columbus, see the chapter devoted to the mariner's death (1552, 1:15r–v).

10. Las Casas (1988–1998, 3:550) also attacked Oviedo for validating the *fiscal*'s opinion concerning the Pinzón brothers having urged Columbus to continue in the discovery.

11. O'Gorman understood "discovering" as an intentional act that consisted of interpreting territories within geographical knowledge. His position is that Columbus had the intention of arriving in Asia and therefore it is inappropriate to speak of discovery in his case. Vespucci, however, had discovered America because he affirmed that the new lands were a reality distinct from Asia. O'Gorman imposed his own historiographical agenda on the sixteenth-century texts when he affirmed that at issue was "el proceso hermenéutico a que pertenecen, es decir, como respuestas a una problemática fundamental que brota del apriorismo básico en que descansa dicho proceso" [the hermeneutical process to which (the texts) belong, that is to say, as responses to a fundamental problematic that arise from the basic a priori foundation on which the said process rests] (1951, 92). He supposed that the historians of the discovery intended to interpret the discovery in terms that necessarily were unrelated to experience. The weakness of this thesis lies in the belief that the sixteenth-century historian narrowly understood "discovery" as an act of giving a geographical identity to new territories. This belief led him to ignore other important aspects in Gómara's and Fernando Colón's accounts of the discovery, present the texts of Oviedo and Las Casas as cases that deviated from what he predefined as "a geographic-historical event" (1951, 130), and dismiss as metahistorical anything outside his interpretive framework (1951, 149). O'Gorman tried to impose a modern definition of the discovery upon sixteenth-century accounts taking the notion of scientific discovery as a model. The use of the word "discovery" by the historians of the sixteenth century, however, referred to the practice of navigation initiated by the Portuguese on the west coast of Africa, a known continent within the geographical tradition, being newly explored (Las Casas 1988–1998, 3:459–464).

12. Las Casas alleged that there was a difference between the Moors and inhabitants of the west coast of Africa, and the Turks and Moors of Barbary and the East against whom it was legal to wage war at any time (1988–1998, 3:468–477).

13. This hypothesis was strongly criticized by Fernando Colón in the tenth chapter of his *Vida del Almirante* and, later, by Las Casas in his *Historia de las Indias* (1988–1998, 3:410–428). Both drew upon a great number of authorities to dismantle Oviedo's argument. With respect to Gómara, he neither followed nor mentioned it because he rejected the idea that Columbus was a wise man.

14. O'Gorman attributed to Fernando Colón the proposition that Columbus "iba al descubrimiento intencional de, diríamos ahora, América" [was going about the intentional discovery of, we would now say, America] (1951, 111). This reading is not supported by the text of Colón who clearly attributed to his father the belief that "podía navegarse por el Occidente hasta el fin Oriental de la India; y que no era muy gran mar el que estaba en medio" [he could sail west until the eastern end of India; and that it was not a very large sea that was in between] (1985, 64). He stated that his father called the territories that he found "Indies" "porque eran la parte de la India allende el Ganges" [because they were the part of India beyond the Ganges] (1985, 63). He also indicated, albeit subtly, that his father was mistaken: "Esta autoridad y otras semejantes de este autor fueron las que movieron más al Almirante a creer que fuese verdadera su imaginación" [This authority and others similar to this author were the ones who most moved the Admiral to believe that his imagination was true] (1985, 66). Although he concealed and downplayed his father's errors, one can hardly say that he resorted to the "dialectical subtleties" that O'Gorman attributed to him (1951, 117).

15. Martyr's first eight chapters address the problems that arose in Hispaniola. In the fourth, he mentioned that Columbus decided to return to the court because *fray* Bernardo Buyl, Pedro Margarit, and others "ad Hispaniam corrupto animo discessisse comperit" [had gone back to Spain with corrupt animus] (1966, 54). Martyr developed this story fundamentally in relation to the account of Roldán's rebellion and Columbus's subsequent incarceration (1966, 64–67). Accusations of the Spaniards' tyranny against Columbus along with charges against his subordinates for crimes and abuses illustrate the kind of degradation that Martyr observed in the colonization of Hispaniola (1966, 56–65). His account of *cacique* rebellions tends to justify the war they waged against the Spaniards whether because of abuses and violations, a desire for liberty, or not being able to endure the burden of tribute. Although his view is not critical, his disenchantment is evident when he said that the natives "[c]ompertum est apud eos velut solem & aquam terram esse co[m]munem, neq[ue] meum aut tuum, malorum omnium semina, cadere inter ipsos. . . . Aetas est illis aurea" [are certain that the land, like the sun and water, belongs to everyone and that "mine" and "yours," the seeds of all evils, do not befall them. . . . For them it is the Golden Age] (1966, 53). Although Martyr's disenchantment seems to be more associated with the wars in Italy than those in the Indies, his attitude would have been more problematic if it had focused

on the Catholic Monarchs. Fernán Pérez de Oliva's *Historia de la invención de las Indias* of 1528—a synthesis of the first decade—specifically quotes Columbus's accusation that Roldán and his faction were "corrompidos de vicios" [corrupted by vices] when referring to what had occurred in the Indies (1991, 86).

16. Certainly, this is not an easy solution for Oviedo. The theory of the Hesperides demanded an examination of the authorities of antiquity for which he was not sufficiently prepared. This poor decision drew severe criticism from his detractors.

17. One could suppose that Gómara added rumors and reminiscences of participants, information brought up in litigation, and even items he may have consulted in the library of Fernando Colón, which he mentioned at the end of his chapter on Columbus's death.

18. The logic of this argument holds that the series of accidents preceding the discovery implicitly suggests that providence had provided the discovery to Spain. Columbus was in Madeira, but the Portuguese pilot who gave him the information died with the secret. Columbus tried to negotiate the discovery with the kings of England and Portugal but was rejected. Finally, in spite of the obstacles, Columbus reached an agreement with the Spanish monarchs.

19. Gómara was likely thinking about João II's 1487 embassy to Ethiopia. He commissioned Pêro da Covilhã and Afonso de Paiva to determine if there was a passage to Asia and to establish relations with Prester John. Paiva and Covilhã traveled by way of the Mediterranean, but only Covilhã got to Abyssinia in 1493. (After having gone to Calcutta in India and Sofala in East Africa, he learned of Paiva's death when he arrived in Cairo where he received the order to go to Abyssinia.) According to eleventh-century tradition, Prester John lived south of Lake Baikal; but unable to find him the Portuguese ambassadors identified the Abyssinian kings with his dynasty (Penrose 1952, 48–50).

20. It is uncertain whether Gómara at this point is referring to Portuguese trade in West Africa or is mistaken about the chronology of the Portuguese exploration of Abyssinia.

21. O'Gorman said that Gómara utilized the story of the anonymous pilot to present a Columbus who tried to reveal "regiones ignoradas y nuevas" [new and unknown regions] (1951, 64–67). The truth is that Gómara never bothered with explicitly affirming such a thing nor with precisely establishing what Columbus sought. When relating the Columbian discovery, Gómara said that the Spaniards asked about Cipango and that they believed that Cibao was Cipango. This shows that Gómara's explanation for the name of the Indies only denies that Columbus conceived of the project of getting to India by himself.

22. Gómara is not alone in this. Las Casas, in his *Historia de las Indias*, described the impact that Columbus had had since his arrival on March 4, 1493, in Lisbon, where "vino tanta gente a verlos y a ver los indios, que fue cosa de gran admiración" [so many people came to see them and to see the Indians

that is was quite an amazing thing] (1988–1998, 3:689). He presented a similar scene at his arrival in Palos where he was received "con grande procesión y regocijo de toda la villa" [with a large procession and cheers from the entire town] (1988–1998, 3:695). And on his trip from Seville: "Tanto comenzó la fama a volar por Castilla . . . muchos de los pueblos del camino por donde venía remotos, se vaciaban y se hinchían los caminos para irlo a ver y adelantarse a los pueblos a recibir" [The news began to fly throughout Castile: . . . many remote towns along his route were left emptied and people swelled the roads in order to see him and went on to the towns ahead to receive him] (1988–1998, 4:829). When describing the reception that the monarchs prepared for him in Barcelona, he said that "salió toda la gente y toda la ciudad, que no cabían por las calles, admirados todos de ver aquella veneranda persona ser la que se decía haber descubierto otro mundo" [all the people and the entire city came out, not able to move through the streets, amazed to see that revered person who was said to have discovered another world] and later he compared him to "un senador del pueblo romano" [a Roman senator] (1988–1998, 4:830). Another very similar account is found in the history that Fernando Colón wrote about his father (1985, 149–153). Each of these authors used these scenes for quite different hermeneutical purposes in their histories.

23. Glen Carman (1992) discusses the relationship between Gómara's *Historia* and Sepúlveda's *Democrates secundus*. His analysis of the discourses of the conquistador, principally those pronounced by Fernando Cortés, presupposes that "López de Gómara's history presents a mixture of voices that address the issues of the debate over the conquest" (1992, 226). Carman indicates that, in Gómara's *Historia*, Cortés's success as a conquistador is owed to the fact that he knew how to present the conquest in different ways to different people. In a similar manner, Columbus was incapable of establishing the true significance of the discovery and it fell to the monarchs to do so.

24. On Las Casas's criticism of the Portuguese, see Adorno (1992d, 8–9).

25. Rolena Adorno reads in Las Casas's *Historia de las Indias* a providentialistic view that "presented humankind with the challenge of making history the site of human conscience and frailty" (1992c, 19).

26. Magellan left on September 20, 1519, from San Lúcar; he sailed along the east coast of South America and anchored between March and August 1520 in the Bay of San Julián in Patagonia to cross the Strait of Magellan between October 21 and November 28 that year. His encounter with the Patagonians occurred at San Julián.

27. Magellan arrived at Cebu on April 7, 1521, after having passed by the Ladrones Islands in March.

28. Magellan died in an attack at Mactan on April 27. Juan Serrano succeeded him but was captured on May 1 by natives at the instigation of

Enrique, a slave of Magellan who served as interpreter. Enrique had been reprimanded and threatened in an insulting way by Serrano a few days earlier.

29. Transilvanus Maximilianus touched on these encounters superficially. Pigafetta's account is more substantial and provides a detailed version of the exchanges in Patagonia, Cebu, and Brunei; however, his account does not coincide exactly with Gómara's and it lacks the interpretive slant of the *Historia general*. Maximilianus's *De Moluccis Insulis* was first published in 1523, in Cologne by Cervicornus, in Paris by Viart, and in Rome by Calvo. Except for Calvo's 1524 reprint, the text only reappeared accompanying other works: with Pigafetta's letter in the Italian translation of *Le voyage* (*Il viaggio,* Venice: Luca-Antonio Giunta, 1536), with the *Omnium gentium mores, leges, & ritus* by Johann Boemus (Antwerp: Jan Steels, 1542), and within the *Primo volume* in Ramusio's collection (Venice: The Heirs of Luca-Antonio Giunta, 1550). Pigafetta's letter was only published in a French translation made from an Italian manuscript (*Le Voyage,* Paris: Simon de Colines, ca. 1525), along with Maximilianus's account in *Il viaggio,* and in Ramusio's collection. Peter Martyr's fifth decade was not published until 1530 by Miguel de Eguía in Alcalá de Henares. The letters of Maximilianus and Pigafetta would subsequently be used by Oviedo, who paraphrased the latter (1992, 2:229–237). On these editions of Maximilianus's letter see JCBL (1980, 523/7–9, 524/13, 542/3), on Pigafetta (525/12), on *Il viaggio* (536/14), and on Ramusio (550/31).

30. Gómara said that "[s]i Juan de Grijalua supiera conocer aquella buena ventura, y poblara alli, como los de su co[m]pañia le rogauan, fuera otro Cortes. Mas no era para el tanto bien. Ni lleuaua comission de poblar." [if Juan de Grijalva had been able to recognize such good fortune, and had settled there as those in his company begged him, he would have been another Cortés. However, he was not meant for such wealth, nor did he have instructions to settle] (1552, 1:26r).

31. On this dimension of exchange, Davíd Carrasco (2000, 210) has shown that Mesoamericans' interpretation of Cortés through the myth of Quetzalcoatl resulted from the creation of a shared cultural space in the conquest of New Spain.

32. Sepúlveda's statement refers to Cortés's entry into Tenochtitlan and Motecuhzoma's capture: "Cortesius autem ad hunc modum urbe potitus, tantopere cotempsit hominum ignaviam, inertiam et ruditatem, ut terrore iniecto non solum coegerit regem et subiectos ei principes iuguum et imperium Hispanorum regis accipere. Sed regem ipsum propter suspicionem conscientiae patratae in quadam eius provincia quorundam Hispanorum necis, in vincula coniecerit, oppidanis stupore et ignavia quiescentibus, et nihil minus quam sumptis armis ad regem liberandum conspirantibus" [Cortés, in turn, after having thus occupied the city, greatly scorned the cowardice, inactivity, and crudity of these people, as he not only terrorized the king (Motecuhzoma) and

his principal subjects into accepting the yoke and empire of the Spanish monarch, but put the king himself in chains, on suspicion of complicity in the death of some Spaniards in a certain province of his, to the amazement and idleness of his citizens, indifferent to the situation and concerned with anything but taking up arms to free the king] (1997, 66).

33. On the Requirement, see Chapter 2.

34. Patricia Seed (1995, 92–93) associates the Requirement with the procedures of the Islamic *jihad* on the basis of a comparative study of Christian and Muslim legal traditions. She shows how Las Casas used the Requirement's ascendancy in Islamic law to question the procedure.

35. Silvio Zavala (1988, 488), however, has stated that it possibly had been read for the first time in Ojeda's expedition in 1509. This would challenge assertions that the Requirement was composed as a response to the criticisms of Montesinos (Seed 1995).

36. Jonathan Loesberg has suggested that in the *Conquista de México* divine and secular narrative strands coexist without reconciliation (1983, 253). One of the narratives would focus on the conversion, and the other on a voyage of discovery. I agree with Carman (1993, 105–106) who has argued that Loesberg's hypothesis does not explain the political and narrative consistency of Gómara's text. For Gómara, political subjugation was the prelude of the conversion.

37. Gómara's conception of empire comes close to what Stephen Greenblatt, in his reading of the Columbian texts, has called Christian imperialism. According to Greenblatt, "this discursive economy brings opposites into the closest conjunction with one another and yet leaves the heart of their relation a mystery" (1991, 70). He assumes that material and spiritual ends were ethically incompatible. Gómara, however, tried to persuade his readers that these imperial ends were in fact complementary. Greenblatt has proposed that there is something inherently debased in the conquest accounts of colonial texts (1991, 128). The problem with his analysis is that when discussing the texts of the discovery and the conquest in terms of their comprehension or ignorance of the other, he loses sight of the function of these texts within the process of colonial expansion (see Mignolo 1995, 313).

CHAPTER 4

Gómara and the
Destruction of the Indies

Carneades . . . entre otras cosas dixo a los romanos que tan necesaria era la injusticia para la fuerza de su República que si ellos habían de guardar justicia en restituir lo que en el mundo tenían usurpado, que les sería necesario volver a morar en chozas como moraron en sus principios.

Carneades . . . among other things said to the Romans that injustice was so necessary for the strength of their republic that if they had to preserve justice by restituting what they had usurped in the world, they would have to go back to living in shacks as they had in the beginning.

—Pedro Mexía, *Coloquios*

Cest l'or, cest or auquel chacun te[n]d, chacun vise, pour lequel nuyt & iour ce miserable monde vit en continuelle peine & tourment de corps & d'ame. Cest or lequel accompagné de l'arge[n]t n'a moindre auctorité ne puissance sur terre que le soleil & la lune ont au ciel.

It is gold, the gold that everyone seeks, to which everyone is drawn, for which night and day this miserable world lives in constant pain and torment of body and soul. It is the gold that accompanied with silver has no less authority or power over the earth than the sun and the moon have over the sky.

—*L'histoire de la Terre Nevve du Perù*

RULING THE INDIANS: THE KING AND HIS DESPOTS

In the first preceding epigraph, Pedro Mexía cited Carneades's statement about the Roman Empire because he was attempting to prove that in certain cases it was necessary for the state to tolerate injustice in order to avoid greater evils (1947, 155). Other examples that Mexía discusses in his dialogue "Del porfiado" (The stubborn one) include soldiers lying, stealing, and destroying property in a just war to prevail over their enemies; a man killing his unfaithful wife to avenge adultery; and authorities allowing prostitution to avoid greater harms to society. His sources on the defense of injustice among ancient philosophers were Augustine's *De civitate Dei,* Cicero's *De re publica,* and possibly Lactantius's *Divinae institutiones.*[1] All three narrate a debate between Gaius Laelius and Lucius Furius Philus, where the former argued that "[e]st quidem vera lex recta ratio naturae congruens" [true law is indeed right reason in agreement with nature] and is "diffusa in omnes" [extended to all], and the latter said that "the government cannot be carried on without injustice" (Cicero 1928, 184–217). Laelius defended conquest, arguing that by defending their allies the people of Rome had gained dominion over the whole world, and that nature had granted dominion to everything that is best. In contrast, Philus's quotation of Carneades stressed the incompatibility between imperial conquest and justice. Both Augustine and Lactantius criticized Philus's arguments on justice but also objected to the plunder of the Roman conquests (Augustine 1957–1995, 1:217–227, 293–299; Lactantius 1994, 150–154). Mexía's endorsement of Carneades's statement strikes a compromise between the moral rejection of conquest among the first fathers of the church and questioning the wisdom of justice. How did Carneades's stance concerning the Roman Empire's dependence on injustice reflect on the story of Spanish colonization in the New World? As royal chronicler and the House of Trade's cosmographer, the erudite Mexía was well acquainted with the disputes regarding the legality of the conquest.[2]

The second epigraph, from *L'histoire de la Terre Nevve du Perù* (The history of the New World of Peru) (1545, 4v), highlights the desire for gold and silver as the engine driving Spanish expansion in the Indies. Not only was this assumption about human action present within the mindset of sixteenth-century readers, but also the stories of exploration and conquest themselves attributed these motives to the Spaniards. This may help us to understand why somebody like Mexía would have been willing to condone the shortcomings of the empire. If the extraction of gold and silver was viewed as the mobilizing force of colonization, then the ideologies justifying Spanish imperialism for the sake of conversion or the betterment of Indian life had to account for the meaning of the pursuit of wealth within their narratives. Gómara tried to resolve the ethical contradictions posed by the inconsistency between the ends and means of colonizing the Indies. The question he confronted was whether it was appropriate for Spaniards to employ the native inhabitants of the New World as an instrument for acquiring wealth. His response to this problem took on special meaning in the context of criticisms concerning the treatment of the native population and the legal foundations of Spanish imperialism.

The debates about the capacity of the Indians, the legitimacy of the conquest, and the survival of the *encomienda* set a problematic precedent for formulating a coherent narrative of colonization. Most of these debates transpired in oral form, but written sources allow us to identify certain instances that played a central role in determining the responsibilities of the monarchy in colonial governance.[3] A decisive moment came in 1511 after the famous sermon of *fray* Antonio de Montesinos, who accused the *encomenderos* of mortal sin because of the way they treated the native population.[4] His allegation was a threat to the legitimacy of Spanish authority in the New World and to the salvation of the king and his subjects engaged in the colonizing enterprise. His criticisms led the authorities and colonists in Hispaniola to complain to the king, who prohibited the friars from speaking about Indian matters in or outside the pulpit and threatened to expel the Dominicans from the island if they disobeyed his order. Montesinos nevertheless went to Spain to inform the court about conditions in the *encomiendas*, leading the king to convene a commission in Burgos to determine what would be best in terms of the treatment and conversion of the native inhabitants. This commission included the Dominican friar Matías de Paz, a canonist at the University of Salamanca, and Juan López de Palacios Rubios, a legal expert on the Royal Council. Both of them wrote separate treatises on the juridical foundations of Spanish rule in the New World, which articulated the basic legal principles that would guide war and governance in the Indies for at least the next fifty years.[5] At the same time, however, they laid the framework for subsequent criticisms of Spanish colonialism.

Although the treatises of Palacios Rubios and Paz were not published during the sixteenth century, they came to influence public discourse through the promulgation of colonial legislation and Las Casas's denunciations of the injustices committed by the conquistadors and the *encomenderos*. In 1516 Las Casas presented a report to Cardinal Francisco Ximénez de Cisneros, who was then regent of Castile, in which he requested that both treatises be published, suggesting that they juridically demonstrated that "los indios son hermanos y libres y como tales deben ser tratados" [the Indians are brothers and free and should be treated as such] (Zavala 1954, xvi). Although Palacios Rubios and Paz tried to justify Spanish dominion over the Indies, their treatises also defined the nature of this authority and the responsibilities that the colonizers had toward the native inhabitants. Their ideas concerning the liberty and treatment of the Indians as individuals, based on Aristotelian political theory and the legal discourse on slavery, established the theoretical foundations of legitimate colonial rule.

Their treatises, in fact, were the first to formally apply Aristotelian theory to determine whether the monarchs' authority over the Indians was despotic or royal in nature.[6] According to Aristotle, despotic rule corresponds to the type of authority exercised over a tool or a slave as an instrument to carry out an action for the benefit of the owner or master. On the other hand, royal or constitutional rule involves the exercise of authority among equals, who are free to act for the purpose of obtaining what they consider beneficial. The difference between the slave and the equal rests in the equal having the capacity to think about his own well-being, but the slave merely obeys. Both Palacios Rubios and Paz rejected the legitimacy of despotic authority over the Indies, with the latter concluding:

> *Por la autoridad del Sumo Pontífice, y no de otra manera, le será permitido a nuestro católico e invictísimo monarca gobernar a los sobredichos indios con imperio real, mas no despótico, y retenerlos así perpetuamente debajo de su dominación (1954, 223).*

> By the authority of the Supreme Pontiff, and in no other manner, our Catholic and most triumphant monarch will be permitted to govern the aforementioned Indians with royal but not despotic rule and to retain them perpetually under his domination.

Paz went on to establish principles to guide the governance of the native population "with royal rule," thus proposing a notion of justice in colonial administration.

> *[P]ara que el alma del Rey cristianísimo no sufra detrimento en tan extensas tierras, sino que viva eternamente con Cristo, procure ampliar, dilatar y amplificar su fe en aquellas regiones, y propóngase no dominar o enriquecerse, sino la salvación de las almas de sus moradores (1954, 258).*

> So that the soul of the most Christian king would not suffer detriment in such extensive lands but rather live eternally with

Christ, he should endeavor to extend, expand, and amplify his faith
in those regions, and not set about to dominate or enrich himself,
except in the salvation of the souls of their inhabitants.

Although promoting the spread of Christianity has traditionally been
recognized as an incentive for the missionary friars to defend the Indians (Hanke 1974, Seed 1993a), Paz established an even more stringent
guiding principle for Spanish colonialism: the king could not seek to
extend his dominions or enrich himself. The quest for wealth and power
therefore rendered the subjugation of indigenous communities illegitimate and made it necessary to prove that the activities carried out in
the New World had the purpose of achieving the salvation of the native population. Paz also proposed a particular policy to achieve this
objective. Along with bishops, priests, and missionaries, the king should
send

> *personas seglares, destacadas en el verdadero gobierno y celo de la fe, que*
> *sepan procurar lo que convenga, no a sus propios intereses, sino a la*
> *república, y que no sean codiciosos, ni ladrones ni avaros, sin permitirse*
> *que allá moren hombres blasfemos y grandes criminales (1954, 258).*

> secular persons, prominent in true governance and zeal for the faith,
> who would know how to provide what was appropriate, not for
> their own interests, but for the republic, and who would not be
> greedy, thieves, or misers, or permit blasphemous men and great
> criminals to live there.

Paz and Palacios Rubios formalized the legal foundations of Spanish
imperialism. When they established the rights of the king to subjugate
the natives, they also established the administration's responsibilities
toward the native inhabitants, making it imperative to guarantee their
common good. This potentially offered supporting arguments for questioning the ethical integrity of the methods and procedures of Spanish
expansion, thus creating an obstacle for the construction of a discourse
of domination. Because despotic governance of the native population
was not recognized as a legitimate option, it was necessary to show
that individual interests had not guided the process of conquest and
colonization in the Indies. In fact, the concept of common good played
a central role in Spanish colonial discourse in judging the merits of the
enterprise. This ethic of colonization created the conditions whereby the
legitimacy of Spanish imperialism began to be questioned elsewhere in

Europe during the sixteenth century and laid the foundations of the "Black Legend."[7] Royal governance imposed judicial obligations for which the monarchs would be held accountable. The criticism against personal interest acquired such importance that in 1571 the Spanish crown commissioned Antonio de Herrera y Tordesillas to write a history of the Indies,

> *para que sopiesen las naciones estranxeras que todos estos Catholicos Reyes e sus Consexeros, an complido con la Bula del Pontyfice, e que non an atendido a desfrutar aquellas nuevas tierras como lo discen; e que para que la ynfamia desta Nacion de crueldad e de avarycia se restabrase, mostrando que non es xusto que las malasobras de pocos escurezcan las buenas de muchos (CDIA 1864–1884, 37:107).*

so that foreign nations would know that all these Catholic Monarchs and their advisors have complied with the pontiff's bull, and that they have not sought to enjoy those new lands as it is said; and so that this nation's infamy of cruelty and avarice would be put to rest, showing that it is not fair that the misdeeds of a few obscure the good deeds of the many.

The allegation of having made use of the land and committed acts of avarice and cruelty basically constituted an accusation of despotism. This type of criticism greatly concerned the crown, for it represented a serious attack on its claims of authority and legitimacy in the empire. In Herrera's time the crown chose to address this issue by blaming individual subjects instead of facing up to its responsibilities to the native communities. The decision to blame the "misdeeds of a few" for the problems created during the colonization, however, suggests the importance that these accusations had from an ethical and political perspective. One can hardly avoid asking why the crown selected such a weak option to respond to international criticism. Surely the conditions that left the colonial enterprise in such a vulnerable position were present in the tradition of Spanish colonial discourse.

THE INFAMY OF SPAIN AND THE CONQUISTADORS

The infamy of imperial Spain was a prominent historiographical concern in Las Casas's *Brevísima relación* and Gómara's *Historia general,* both published in 1552. The accusations of avarice and cruelty against the conquistadors, outlined with particular clarity in these texts, constituted the basis of subsequent criticisms denouncing Spanish conduct in the Indies. The *Brevísima relación* was particularly damaging to Spain's reputation, for instead of questioning the legitimacy of its New World empire, it informed the emperor of "las matanzas y estragos de gentes inocentes y despoblaciones de pueblos, provincias y reinos, que en ellas se han perpetrado, y que todas las otras no de menor espanto" [the massacre and destruction of innocent people and the depopulation of communities, provinces, and kingdoms, which have been perpetrated there, and everything else no less astonishing] (1988–1998, 10:33). Las Casas explained in his prologue addressed to Prince Philip that he had decided to publish his work out of an obligation of conscience "por no ser reo, callando, de las perdiciones de ánimas e cuerpos infinitas, que los tales perpetraran" [to not be an accomplice, remaining silent about the loss of countless souls and bodies, which the like perpetrate] (1998–1998, 10:32). Presenting his work as an act of conscience advising the king so that appropriate measures would be taken, Las Casas clearly revealed the contradictions between the actions of the conquistadors and the ideological system that justified colonization.

Las Casas characterized the conquistadors as cruel and greedy tyrants who had subverted justice to their own personal interests. His allegation of despotism suggested that the conquistadors had acted outside the margins set for the common good and contradictory to the norms of administering justice within royal government. He stated that the conquests were "inicuas, tiránicas, y por toda ley natural, divina y humana, condenadas, detestadas e malditas" [iniquitous, tyrannical, and, by all natural, divine, and human law, condemned, detested, and wicked] (1988–1998, 10:32). The problem for him was the procedures that had been employed to incorporate the native inhabitants as vassals of the crown, for they consisted of "despedazallas, matallas, angustiallas, afligillas, atormentallas y destruillas por la estrañas y nuevas e varias e nunca otras tales vistas ni leídas ni oídas maneras de crueldad" [dismembering, murdering, molesting, beating, torturing, and destroying them by strange, new, varied, and other manners of cruelty never before seen, read, or heard] (1988–1998, 10:34). Las Casas attributed the destruction of the native population of the Indies, on the one hand, to the wars that the Spaniards unjustly waged against the native inhabitants to subject them to their authority and, on the other hand, to the slavery inflicted upon them after being conquered. He explained that the conquistadors were motivated *por tener por su fin último el oro y henchirse de riquezas en muy breves días, e subir a estados muy altos e sin proporción a sus personas (conviene a saber) por la insaciable codicia e ambición (1988–1998, 10:35).*

by having gold as their ultimate objective and engorging themselves with wealth in a very short time, and climbing to very high statuses without proportion to their persons (one should know) through insatiable greed and ambition.

Throughout his *Brevísima relación* Las Casas revealed a gradual process of degradation whereby the conquistadors and settlers had not only increased the levels of violence, but came to shamefully disobey the laws that had been employed to legitimate Spanish colonialism.

Las Casas's writings demonstrate how the process of colonization had been carried out in violation of the same legal principles that tried to justify it. He identified a common discursive base between hegemonic perspectives and his opposition to the conquest, which allowed him to demonstrate that the colonial enterprise relied upon forms of social action that could not be executed without suffering some kind of moral decay. Inasmuch as legal discourse made it advisable to curtail the actions of the conquistadors, it forced a critical evaluation of the human and social cost of the undertaking in the Indies. Las Casas's criticisms presented his sixteenth-century readers with the dilemma of either rejecting the further authorization of conquests or accepting the resulting transgressions. Idealizations of the conquest that privileged the use of peaceful methods of conversion had a place in Las Casas's discourse because they allowed him to show that there were alternatives to war, but the conquistadors invariably chose the quickest and easiest method of securing economic profits.

Las Casas's formal accusation of tyranny established a critical perspective about the conquest its supporters could not easily shake. The connection he made between the illegitimate use of violence and the greed of the Spaniards was a powerful argument that the colonial enterprise had been conducted in a despotic manner. Although part of his argument questioned the legal foundations of the conquest, his most salient criticism alleged that the conquistadors had openly disobeyed royal laws. The *Brevísima relación* revealed that most of the conquests had violated the principles of just war and that the gravity of the crimes had increased over time (1988–1998, 10:85–88). The Spanish crown had been unable to adequately monitor colonial activity, which explains why

Las Casas also argued that the only solution was to put an end to the conquests. Claiming that all of the conquests had been unjust, he was supported by a historiographical tradition that had already recognized the cruelty and greed of the colonizers.

The infamy that befell Spaniards with the publication of the *Brevísima relación* was corroborated by Peter Martyr's *Decades*. Martyr blamed the destruction of indigenous peoples in the Caribbean on reckless Spaniards who ignored the monarchs' orders. The scandalous reports of abuses committed against the Lucayos stemmed in part from the Spaniards' violations of the laws concerning slavery. Martyr explained that the Lucayos believed that after atoning for their sins in colder climates their souls would travel south to meet their diseased ancestors in a land of delights. The Spaniards tricked them by saying that they came from the regions where the Lucayos thought they would go after death and that they would lead them to their ancestors. Once on the ships, they were brought to Hispaniola as slaves where they died from either overwork or suicide. Their docility made it impossible to justify their enslavement from a legal standpoint because slavery was a punishment reserved for captives of a just war. Concerning the Spaniards, Martyr concluded that "sub praetextum auge[n]d[a]e religionis moueri se fatea[n]tur habita ratione, ad ambitiosam auaritia[m] & vim se co[n]uertant" [under the pretext of proclaiming that the desire to extend their religion motivates them, they succumb to ambitious greed and violence] (1966, 222).

Martyr claimed that these events caused an enormous scandal in the court, thus showing that the Spaniards' behavior was unacceptable in hegemonic sectors of the colonial administration. At that time he was a member of the Council of the Indies and had direct knowledge of matters pertinent to the government of the colonies. In addition, his *Decades* had circulated through Europe in Latin editions that widely informed the public of the Spaniards' abuses. Therefore this pattern of atrocities was beyond question both inside and outside Spain and the colonizers' practices could hardly be considered marginal. These allegations were also confirmed in the brutal power struggles among the conquistadors themselves. The civil wars of Peru had shown how the crown's legal reforms could lead to open rebellion, with the *encomenderos* breaking off their loyalty to the emperor and waging war against royal officials. In all these cases, whether the abuse of the native inhabitants or internecine conflict, the conquistadors' desire for wealth appeared to be the principal cause of the problems.

The Spaniards' greed and cruelty were also unavoidable themes in Gómara's conquest narrative. More than just negative behavioral traits, they characterized the Spaniards' acts as tyrannical in the legal sense. In his account of the conquest of Mexico, he had difficulty dealing with episodes where the conduct of Cortés or his men violated the legal principles of the conquest. Two of the most notable cases of this are the massacre at the Great Temple in Tenochtitlan carried out by Pedro de Alvarado and the torture of Cuauhtemoc ordered by Cortés. Both of these acts were so well documented that Gómara had to treat them as questionable, even unacceptable, conduct for a conquistador. The fact that he did not try to deny or justify them reveals the seriousness that he attributed to the application of legal norms in his representation of the conquest. From Gómara's standpoint, both actions constituted a source of infamy for the conquistadors and compromised the integrity of the conquering enterprise. The charges of cruelty that weighed on the conquistadors' actions, however, could not simply be dismissed; they required the examination and evaluation of the historian.

In his chapter titled "Como dieron tormento a Quahutimoc para saber del tesoro" (How they tortured Cuauhtemoc to learn about the treasure) (1552, 2:86v), Gómara claimed that the conquistadors "acordaron dar tormento a Quahutimoc, y a otro cauallero, y su priuado" [decided to torture Cuauhtemoc and another gentleman and his assistant] after the capture of Tenochtitlan because they could not find the gold that they had left in the city or any trace of Motecuhzoma's treasure (1552, 2:86v). Cuauhtemoc's torture was far from being an innocuous act, for Gómara himself explained that "[a]cusaron esta muerte a Cortes en su residencia como cosa fea. E, indina de ran [*sic*] gran rey. Y que lo hizo de auaro, y cruel" [they charged Cortés with this death in his *residencia* (that is, the official review of his royal service) as something hideous and inappropriate for such a great king and that it was done out of avarice and cruelty] (1552, 2:86v). The text does not conceal the legal implications of the acts or the weak excuses of Cortés:

> *Mas el se defendia con que se hizo a pedimiento de Julian de Alderete,*
> *tesorero del rey. Y porque pareciesse la verdad. Ca dezian todos que se tenia*
> *el toda la riqueza de Motecçuma. Y no queria atormentalle por que no se*
> *supiesse (1552, 2:86v).*

But he argued in his defense that it was done at the request of Julián de Alderete, the king's treasurer, and so the truth would be revealed.

For everyone said that [Cortés] had all of Motecuhzoma's wealth, and he did not want to torture him because this would be become known.

The use of torture, at this time, was only considered acceptable to bring about justice, thus Gómara had no choice but to condemn the act. In his chapter titled "La muerte d[e] Quahutimoc" (The death of Cuauhtemoc) (1552, 2:103v–104r), he explicitly added that Cortés's decision to kill the Mexican leader in Honduras had brought infamy upon the Spaniards:

> [P]orque dixesse del tesoro de Moteçuma, le diero[n] tormento. El qual fue vntandole muchas vezes los pies con azeite, y poniendoselos luego al fuego. Pero mas infamia sacaron que no oro. Y Cortes deuiera guardarlo viuo como oro en paño, que era el trunfo [sic], y gloria, de sus vitorias. Mas no quiso tener que guardar en tierra, y tiempo tan trabajoso (1552, 2:103v).

> To get him to talk about Motecuhzoma's treasure, they tortured him, which involved anointing his feet many times with oil and then putting them in the fire, but they got more infamy than any gold. And Cortés should have kept him alive like gold in a sheath, as he was the triumph and glory of his victories, but he did not want to have to guard him in such a difficult land and time.

The infamy of Spaniards was no trivial matter because it implied that the actions they had committed were worthy of condemnation from a moral and legal standpoint. Although Gómara celebrated the conquest of Mexico, he had to acknowledge fault in Cortés's conduct because omitting this episode might have put in question the veracity of his entire narrative. Recognizing Cortés's error as an isolated incident, he could maintain his overall positive representation of the conquest.

In his account of the massacre at the Great Temple, Gómara discussed the uprising of the Mexicans against the conquistadors in terms that were openly unfavorable to the Spaniards. In his chapter titled "Las causas de la rebelion" (The causes of the rebellion) (1552, 2:60r–v), he presented a list of different arguments offered by the conquistadors to explain the Mexican revolt while Cortés was absent from Tenochtitlan. Among the many explanations he provided, Gómara also mentioned the one accusing Pánfilo de Narváez of inciting Motecuhzoma to rebellion, which Cortés had used in his second *carta de relación*. Although

Cortés had conveniently omitted any reference to the massacre in his letter, Gómara chose the most damaging version of the episode from a legal perspective. The account he privileged not only presented the massacre as an unjustified act, it also clearly put the weight of responsibility on the greed of the conquistadors, particularly Pedro de Alvarado:

> *Pero la principal fue porque pocos dias despues de ido Cortes a Naruaez vino cierta fiesta solene, que los Mexicanos celebraua[n]. Y quisieron la celebrar como solian. Y para ello pidieron lice[n]cia a Pedro de Aluarado, que quedo alcayde, y teniente por Cortes, porque no pensasse, a lo que ellos dezian, que se juntauan para matar los Españoles. Aluarado se la dio co[n] tal que en el sacrificio no interuiniesse muerte de [h]ombres. Ny lleuassen armas. Juntaronse mas de seyscientos caualleros, y principales personas, y aun algunos señores en el te[m]plo maior. Otros dizen mas de mil. Hizieron grandissimo ruydo aquella noche co[n] atabales, caracoles, cornetas, huessos hendidos, con que siluan muy rezio. . . . Estando pues bayla[n]do aquellos caualleros Mexicanos en el patio d[e]l templo d[e] [H]uitzilopuchtli, fue alla Pedro de Aluarado. Si fue de su cabeça, o por acuerdo d[e] todos, no lo sabria dezir. Mas que de vnos dizen que fue auisado que aquellos indios, como principales de la ciudad, se [h]auian juntado alli a concertar el motin, y rebelion, que despues hizieron. Otros, que al principio fueron a verlos baylar, bayle tan loado, y famoso. Y viendolos tan ricos, que se acodiciaron al oro que trayan a cuestas. Y assi tomo las puertas con cada diez, o doze, españoles. Y entro el dentro con mas de cinquenta. Y sin duelo, ni piedad christiana, los acuchillo. Y mato. Y quito lo que tenian encima (1552, 2:60v).*

But the main [reason] was because a few days after Cortés left to meet Narváez there was a certain solemn festival that the Mexicans celebrated. And they wished to celebrate it as they usually did. And therefore they asked Pedro de Alvarado for permission, who was warden and lieutenant for Cortés, so that he would not think, as they said, that they were assembling to kill the Spaniards. Alvarado consented as long as they did not bear arms or slay men in the sacrifice. More than six hundred gentlemen and important persons, and even some lords, assembled at the Great Temple, others say more than a thousand. They made the greatest noise that night with drums, conches, trumpets, and bone flutes that whistle very loud. . . . While the Mexican gentlemen were dancing in the courtyard of Huitzilopochtli's temple, Pedro de Alvarado went there, whether it was his own idea or agreed to by all, I cannot say. But some say that he was warned that those Indians, as leaders of the city, had assembled there to coordinate the uprising and rebellion, which subsequently they conducted. Others said that at first they went to see them perform a dance so exalted and famous, but seeing them so wealthy, they coveted the gold that they wore. They blocked the entrances with ten or twelve Spaniards at each. [Alvarado] went inside with more than fifty, and without sorrow or Christian piety, he stabbed and killed them, and took what they had on them.

Gómara made it clear that the Indians had taken all the appropriate measures to conduct their festival with the authorization of Alvarado himself. He explained that they were caught unarmed, which removed any suspicion of them instigating the rebellion. In Gómara's eyes the slaughter carried out "without sorrow or Christian piety" had no other purpose than to take their gold. The gravity of this case rests in the likelihood that Gómara's readers could interpret the Indian uprising as a legitimate rebellion provoked by an act of tyranny. In fact, this was the same point that Las Casas had made in his *Brevísima relación* to state that the Mexicans had cause for a just war against the Spaniards (1988–1998, 10:51). As in the case of Cuauhtemoc's torture, Gómara preferred to openly present the incident as unjust, rather than trying to justify or omit its problematic aspects in his narrative.

Endeavoring to present the conquest as the foundation of Spanish imperialism, Gómara needed to work with the histories of infamy that were already recorded in public discourse. Infamy for greed and cruelty was not just a matter of reputation in conquest narratives, it also challenged the legitimacy of colonial rule. The problem could not be resolved simply by ignoring the historical record of events, for this would compromise the integrity of the account. Attempting to deny the abuses committed by the conquistadors would cast suspicion on the historian for colluding in the acts of despotism. Concealing or approving of the abuses were not acceptable options for Gómara. The history of Spanish colonialism in the Indies made it imperative to acknowledge that the conquistadors and settlers were motivated by personal interest and the desire for wealth. The greatest difficulty that Gómara faced was finding a way to convince his readers that the conquistadors' tireless quest for wealth was compatible with a notion of common good. Gómara had the difficult task of offering a positive evaluation of the conquest at a time when the conquistadors had lost their position as the moral and economic force that drove the colonizing enterprise.

Gómara found a philosophical solution to his problem in Sepúlveda's *Democrates secundus*. Sepúlveda's argument concerning natural slavery was particularly powerful because it brought the debate to the realm of natural law. He argued that anything done according to natural law was also just according to divine law (1997, 46). This enabled him to bypass canon law and state that various types of dominion were based on natural law. If nature ordained that the perfect must rule over the imperfect, then slavery founded on reason had its basis in natural law according to the hierarchies of nature (1997, 64). This hierarchical principle allowed him to justify the evils of colonialism with Aristotle's notion of "conditional action," whereby it was legitimate to tolerate evil to avoid the occurrence of greater harm.[8] Sepúlveda provided the example of a bad king who is tolerated to protect the institution of the monarchy because nature dictates selecting the lesser evil (1997, 58–59). Inasmuch as he argued that servitude was necessary for the protection of human society, he claimed that it was just to choose Indian slavery as the lesser evil (1997, 108).

In addition to Aristotle's *Politics*, Sepúlveda's ideological defense of Spanish imperialism mirrors very closely Laelius's analysis of dominion to justify conquest and slavery under the Roman Empire, as Cicero had put forth in *De re publica* (1928, 212–215). In fact, the ethics and epistemology of Roman stoicism allowed him to work out the equivalence of divine and natural law that would make conquest acceptable from a Christian perspective. Assuming that, as Laelius put it, men, through "ratio recta" [right reason], arrive at an interpretation of nature that is "diffusa in omnes, constans, sempiterna" [extended to all, unchanging, everlasting], then it follows that empire has the mission of extending its "superior" laws around the world.[9] Thus Sepúlveda's treatise articulated a powerful argument for extending Spanish rule to other nations, based on the mission that the Spaniards were carrying out in the Indies.

The task of universalizing the rule of natural law among the peoples of the world made it necessary, however, to define certain ethical boundaries within which the Spaniards could legitimately impose their dominion on the Indians. Sepúlveda's treatise explicitly discussed the problem of tyrannical governance of the colonies. He underscored the need to resolve the issue of abuses in order to preserve Spain's legitimate authority in the Indies. Regarding those perpetrated in the Caribbean, Sepúlveda thought that a just prince should try to prevent such out-

rages from occurring again in order to avoid infamy and divine condemnation. His view of the Spanish empire within the international
context made the Christian prince the guardian of an order in which
reason directed human action to achieve the common good (1997, 133).
It seems that his broader intent was to respond to the criticism of Spanish imperialism within Europe. In fact he wrote his treatise in the form
of a dialogue between Democrates, a Spaniard, and Leopoldus, a Ger-
man influenced by Lutheran ideas.[10] Democrates concludes that justice
forbids ruling with greed or cruelty or making servitude intolerable.
The principle of avoiding outrages provided a way of determining when
human losses could no longer be considered the choice of a lesser evil.
Sepúlveda sought to provide Spanish colonialism with a philosophy of
guiding principles of action and some criteria for protecting its reputation as a Christian enterprise.[11]

Gómara's conquest narrative shared Sepúlveda's imperialist precepts, but he confronted the additional problem of having to recount
examples of infamy. Although Sepúlveda rationalized colonial inequality to justify Indian slavery, Gómara needed to construct an account
that made sense of the problems caused by conquistadors in the native
communities. His account agrees with Las Casas's *Brevísima relación* in
terms of the basic acts committed, but the authors differed over issues
such as whether the conquest was legal, what conquistador behavior
was considered acceptable, what the Indians were like, and what steps
should be taken for the just governance of the New World. Whenever
possible, Gómara emphasized the record of the crown and its officials
in the duties of empire-building, particularly with regard to promoting
justice and evangelization. Justice and religion, however, lost ground
to the pursuit of wealth and sexual desire that characterized Spaniards'
behavior in key episodes of Gómara's conquest account.

IMPERIALISM AND DESIRE

The account of building an imperial society ruled by the principles of
justice supposed the subordination of the Spanish colonists to the will
of the king. This story, however, could not be written without making
the king and his royal officials responsible for the abuse and destruction of the indigenous communities. A major problem in the colonization of the Indies was the resistance of the Spanish settlers to obeying
the orders of the king. Exercising royal authority in the New World

not only involved obtaining the obedience of the native inhabitants, it also meant controlling the conduct of the Spanish residents, who were in the position of negotiating the kind of obedience that they would lend to royal decrees and crown officials. As Martyr suggested in his account of the destruction of the Lucayos, once the Spaniards found themselves far from the authorities, they forgot about the king's instructions and orders (1966, 222).[12] Gómara attempted to create an understanding in terms of the most appropriate ways of implementing royal policies in the colonies, but in his view the king lacked absolute authority. The legal conceptions of the period maintained that the king's authority was divinely ordained for the benefit of the community; therefore, his legislative power was constrained by the values of the community expressed in various laws and customs (Zavala 1954, xxxii–xliv). In the case of conflict, public utility determined the most acceptable solution. Gómara's account of the conquest reframed the debate in terms of a discussion about the most appropriate course of action to achieve the public good according to Iberian juridical tradition.

Gómara presented the difficulties that the Spaniards confronted in the enterprise of the Indies in his account of Columbus's voyages and the colonization of Hispaniola. His discussion of the empire's beginnings was set apart from the rest of the first part of the *Historia general*, which had maintained a sequential geographical order. In this way, Gómara projected its significance within the organization of the narrative and assigned to Hispaniola the particular importance of being the "principio y madre" [beginning and mother] of the discovery of the Indies (1552, 1:20r). Monique Mustapha (1994) has pointed out that the *Historia general*'s account of the Columbian voyages and the colonization of Hispaniola is central and serves as a fundamental paradigm that seems to frame Gómara's narrative of other conquests. She explains that this section creates a scenario upon which the conquest continually recommences. In a more concrete sense, Gómara's narrative takes the occupation of Hispaniola as the foundation for the expansion of the empire to the rest of the islands and the continent.

After discussing the Columbian discovery, Gómara stated that "[a] fama de las riquezas d[e] Indias, y por ser buena la armada, y por sentir tanta gana en los reyes, [h]vuo muchos caualleros, y criados d[e] la casa real, que se dispusieron a pasar alla" [because of the reputation of the Indies' riches and the expedition being good, and sensing so much desire in the monarchs, there were many gentlemen and servants of the royal house who were disposed to go there] (1552, 1:13v). Thus he portrayed the massive mobilization of Spanish settlers in Columbus's second voyage as a response to the expectations of wealth that they hoped to find in the discovered lands. The expression "reputation of the Indies' riches" captured the public image of the Indies that Gómara considered to be the fundamental incentive setting the colonial enterprise in motion as well as the economic motivation for the conquistadors. Service to the king was realized in terms of their interest to benefit individually from the resources of the Indies. This pattern of action reached its peak with the sexual conduct of the Spanish settlers who violated the native women. When Columbus returned to the island, he found that Navidad, the fort he had founded on his first voyage, had been destroyed. Gómara claimed that the discoverer "supo que los [h]auian muerto a todos los indios, porque les forçauan sus mugeres, y les hazian otras muchas demasias, o porque no se yuan, ny se [h]auian de ir" [learned that the Indians had killed them all because they raped their women and committed many other outrages, or because they would not go away and they were not going to] (1552, 1:13v). At this point a pattern emerges of abuse followed by native resistance, not only against the "outrages" of individual settlers, but against the colonial project in general.

The resistance offered by the native inhabitants was less of a concern to Columbus than punishing the offenses committed by the colonists. Gómara said that he had applied excessive rigor in disciplining some of the Spaniards who had acted with disrespect toward his brother Bartholomew and "hecho mal a indios" [done evil to the Indians] (1552, 1:13v). Columbus had hanged some Spaniards for mistreating the Indians, but Gómara, although acknowledging that the discoverer was applying justice, privileged the opposition voiced by *fray* Bernardo Buyl "para estoruar muertes, y afrentas de Españoles" [to prevent the deaths and affronts of Spaniards] (1552, 1:13v). At the end of the chapter, Gómara stated that the monarchs had reprimanded Columbus for the punishments he had carried out and ordered him "que [h]vuiesse de alli adelante mansamente con los españoles, que los yuan a seruir tan lexos tierras" [henceforth to be lenient with the Spaniards who went out to serve them in such faraway lands] (1552, 1:14r). His observations clearly went against the application of justice among the colonists because of the circumstances in which the occupation of the Indies unfolded. Columbus's desire to administer justice in Hispaniola was met with the colonists' challenges to his authority. He was bound to fail because he depended on their services to militarily control the island. On this point, Gómara clearly favored being "lenient" with the Spaniards over respecting the rights of the native population.

It would be plausible to read Gómara's narrative of rape and abuse as an expression of colonial desire, along with other Europeans writers who "sought to intrigue, impress, and arouse their (typically, male) readers, employing fantasy, invention, exaggeration, bragging, and projection" (Wood 1998, 11). Such a reading would require some caution on our part, however, for the *Historia general*'s emphasis on the gruesome consequences of these rape stories makes this action far from appealing.[13] The Spanish colonists' situation on Hispaniola further deteriorated because of their contraction of syphilis and the resistance of the native population. The chapter titled "La ha[m]bre: dole[n]cias, guerra, y vitoria que tuuieron los Españoles por defender sus p[er]sonas y pueblos" (The famine, ailments, war, and the victory that the Spaniards achieved in order to defend their persons and communities) (1552, 1:14r–v) established the foundations upon which the success of Spanish imperialism in the Indies emerged. Gómara explained that the Spaniards attacked the indigenous communities to supply themselves with food and "arrebataua[n] mugeres, q[ue] les pegaro[n] las bubas" [carried off women, who gave them *bubas*] (1552, 1:14r). In his chapter "Que las bubas vinieron de las Indias" (That *bubas* came from the Indies) (1552, 1:17r–v), he identified the disease by the French, Neapolitan, and Spanish terms used at that time to denote syphilis. Gómara claimed that the colonists contracted the disease from the women of Hispaniola and then spread it to Europe through their contact with prostitutes who in turn infected Spanish soldiers who went to Italy.

His account of native resistance, on the other hand, is divided into two moments: (1) when the Indians stopped planting thinking that Spaniards would abandon the island for lack of food, and (2) the Indians' attack on the fort where the settlers had taken refuge "por ve[n]gar la injuria d[e] sus mugeres & hijas" [to avenge the injury to their wives and daughters] (1552, 1:14r). The survival of the colony in Hispaniola was threatened by the very abuse inflicted by the colonizers—the syphilis they contracted from their violation of the native women and the Indians' rebellion in response to the colonizers' plundering them and raping their women. The Spanish settlers' appetite for sex and wealth plays a dominant role in Gómara's account, but instead of being the object of criticism, he saw it as a necessary condition to achieve the objectives of imperial policy. Gómara's concession to the colonizers' abuses is apparent when he emphasized the defeat of the native lord Guarionex in 1498 as the moment in which the success of the colonial enterprise became plausible. The conditions for bringing about colonization are clearly defined in Gómara's assessment of the victory: "Con este vençimiento, . . . fueron los españoles tenidos en gran estima. Y començaron a mandar los indios, y a gozar la tierra" [With this defeat, . . . the Spaniards were held in great esteem. And they began to rule the Indians and enjoy the land] (1552, 1:14v). Their fear of the Spaniards' military power was, in Gómara's point of view, what guaranteed their obedience but, more importantly, it also seemed necessary to him that the colonizers were able to "enjoy the land."

It is difficult to establish how far Gómara would go in overlooking the injustices of colonization. We have already seen how his objections to the punishments meted out by Columbus revealed his tolerance toward abuses committed against the Indians. Evidently Gómara privileged subduing the native inhabitants through war, even when they had just cause to rebel against the Spaniards. He was not promoting the creation of a social system based on injustice, but rather he hoped that some form of readjustment would take place. When discussing the destruction of the native population of Hispaniola, he openly stated:

> [L]os españoles abrieron muchos indios a cuchilladas en las guerras. Y aun en las minas. . . . Hiziero[n] los esclauos en la reparticio[n]. Por la qual como trabajauan mas de lo que solian, y para otros, se murieron, y se mataron todos (1552, 1:18v).

> The Spaniards slashed open many Indians in the wars, and even in the mines. . . . They made them slaves in the *repartición*, whereby, because they worked more than they were accustomed to, and for other people, they all died or were killed.

According to Gómara, the responsibility for the destruction of the Indies fell clearly upon the Spanish colonizers. He claimed that the catastrophic decline of the native population was so great that it had been reduced from one and a half million to only five hundred inhabitants. He painted a devastating picture:

> Unos murieron de ha[m]bre, otros de trabajo, y muchos de viruelas. Unos se matauan con çumo de yuca, y otros, co[n] malas yeruas. Otros se ahorcauan

de los arboles. Las mugeres hazian, tambien ellas, como los maridos, que se colgauan a par dellos. Y lançauan las criaturas con arte, y beuida, por no parir a luz hijos, que siruiessen a estranjeros (1552, 1:18v).

Some died of hunger, others from overwork, and many from smallpox. Some killed themselves with yucca juice and others with poisonous plants. Others hanged themselves from trees. The women also hanged themselves together with their husbands. And they aborted their unborn with skill and potion so as not to give birth to children who would serve the foreigners.

Starvation, overwork, disease, and mass suicides eloquently reveal the scope of destruction that Gómara observed in the social system. His conclusion pointed to one of the structural problems in the enterprise of the Indies: "Açote debio ser que Dios les dio por sus pecados. Empero grandissima culpa tuuiero[n] dello los primeros por tratallos muy mal, acodiçiandose mas al oro que al proximo" [It had to be the scourge that God gave them for their sins. But the (Spaniards) had the greatest blame for treating them so badly, coveting gold more than their neighbor] (1552, 1:18v). In spite of his allusion to divine punishment, Gómara ultimately attributed the depopulation of Hispaniola to Spanish greed. The colonists' appetite for wealth created the conditions that released the destructive potential of the colonial enterprise. In spite of being conscious of the injustices, Gómara presented a summary of the benefits brought by colonialism "para q[ue] todos conozca[n] qua[n]ta differe[n]cia, y ve[n]taja haze la tierra con mudar pobladores" [so that everyone would know how different and profitable switching inhabitants makes the land] (1552, 1:20r). Although he blamed Spaniards for the abuses they committed, it seems that he simply did not regret the destruction of the native population.

The colonization of Hispaniola provided the basic model for what would transpire in the rest of the Caribbean. Gómara lamented that "[e]s Jamaica, como Haiti, en todo. Y assi se acabaron los indios" [Jamaica is like Haiti in every respect and thus the Indians died] (1552, 1:25r–v); in Puerto Rico, the Spaniards "atendiero[n] mas a su prouecho que al de los isleños" [cared more about their profit than the islanders] (1552, 1:23r); and in Cuba, "[m]urieron muchos d[e] trabajo, y hambre, muchos de viruelas. Y muchos se passaro[n] a nueua España, despues que Cortes la gano. Y assi no quedo casta dellos" [many died from overwork and hunger, many from smallpox. And many went to New

Spain after Cortés had seized it. And thus there was no trace left of them] (1552, 1:26v–27r). Gómara did not try to conceal the evils of colonialism, thus contributing his share to Spanish infamy in the Indies.

These patterns of abuse and destruction extended beyond the principal islands of the Caribbean to wherever the Spaniards set foot in the New World. In some cases Gómara affirmed that the colonizers acted "contra la ley, y voluntad del rey" [against the law and will of the king] (1552, 1:20v); in others, "despoblaron, y destruyero[n] pueblos, y [h]ombres" [they depopulated and destroyed communities and individuals] (1552, 1:28v) and "faltan muchos Indios con las primeras guerras, y poca justicia que [h]vuo al principio" [many Indians are gone because of the early wars and the little justice there was in the beginning] (1552, 1:108r). Gómara's account of the exploration and conquest of the Indies contained the basic arguments for a powerful critique of Spanish imperialism. He defused potential criticism of his account of the destruction of the Lucayos with an argument that he reiterated in "Praise of Spaniards": "Dize[n] que todos los christianos q[ue] catiuaron indios y los mataron trabajando, [h]an muerto malamente. O no lograron sus vidas, o lo que con ellos ganaron" [They say that all Christians who enslaved the Indians and worked them to death have died horribly, or did not succeed in life or in what they gained with them] (1552, 1:21v).

Gómara's discussion of many early explorations characterized the colonial enterprise as an effort to find a passage to the Spice Islands. This project ended, however, when Charles V sold his rights of conquest to the king of Portugal. In his chapter titled "Repartition of the Indies and the New World between Castilians and Portuguese" (1552, 1:56r–57r), Gómara stressed that the Moluccas or Spice Islands fell within the boundary of the Spanish sphere of influence according to the papal donation. Here the king's decision to leave them in the hands of the Portuguese diminished the possibility of making the competition for spices the purpose of the imperial enterprise. The plan of creating a global empire was retained as a narrative axis in the *Historia general*, but the objective of conquering and settling the Indies came to be dominant.

Gómara insisted that "[q]uien no poblare no hara buena conquista. Y no conquistando la tierra no se conuertiera la gente. Assi que la maxima del conquistar [h]a de ser poblar" [whoever will not settle will not conduct a good conquest, and not conquering the land, the people would not be converted, therefore the maxim of the conquistador must be to settle] (1552, 1:23v). Attaining the native inhabitants' obedience before converting them thus emphasized the incorporation of new territories by Spanish settlers exercising military force. The central developments of this process in the *Historia general* are the conquests of Darién, Peru, and Mexico. With the exception of Mexico, Gómara questioned the colonizers' capacity to conduct themselves according to principles of justice.

In the conquest of Darién, Gómara stressed Balboa's role in subjugating the native lords and finding a passage to the Pacific Ocean. The Castilian court had eagerly sought a route to the region of the spices, but Spanish expeditions had failed to find one until the Magellan-Elcano voyage. Gómara did not object to Balboa's violent behavior when he tortured and sicced his dogs on the Indians under the pretext of punishing their sodomy but with the real intent of getting their gold. His first victim was Pacra, whose death, Gómara claimed, was celebrated by the Indians themselves as a just punishment for an evil ruler. But Balboa's application of justice was not the purpose of his course of action as revealed in the torture of Tumanama, with whom he had "tantas, y mas querellas" [as many or more complaints] than with Pacra (1552, 1:36r). Gómara explained that Balboa "[r]eprendiole asperamente, amenazolo mucho. . . . Empero todo era fingido por contentar a los querellantes, y sacarle su tesoro" [harshly reprimanded him, making many threats. . . . But it was all staged to satisfy the plaintiffs and take away his treasure] (1552, 1:36r). Although Balboa had bypassed his own justice for the love of Tumanama's treasure, Gómara approved of the services he had lent the crown. Balboa seemed to be gifted with a religious motivation for carrying out the conquest and was celebrated in the court for having subdued the region and opened the way to the Pacific.

The conquest of Darién, however, was far from being a positive episode in Spanish colonialism. Balboa had tortured the native inhabitants and fed them to the dogs in the lands ruled by Chiape, Pacra, and Tumanama, although he had also created alliances with native lords and left the region subjected to the authority of the king. Pedrarias Dávila, however, brought the violence and destruction to a new level. Although he had been entrusted with "la conuersion, y buen tratamiento de los indios" [the conversion and good treatment of the Indians] (1552, 1:36v), Gómara claimed that,

por deseo de oro, aperreo muchos indios de don carlos Panquiaco, seruidor
del rei amigo de españoles, a quien se deuian las albricias del sur. Despojole
tambien a el, y atormento ciertos caciques, & hizo otras crueldades, y
demasias, que causaro[n] rebelion de indios, y muerte de muchos españoles
(1552, 1:37r).

out of a desire for gold, he turned the dogs on many of the Indians of
don Carlos Panquiaco, servant of the king who was friendly to the
Spaniards, to whom they owed the good news about the south. He
also robbed him and tortured some *caciques,* and committed other
cruelties and outrages, which caused the revolt of the Indians and
the death of many Spaniards.

Pedrarias had caused injuries to the Indians who were already subjects
of the crown, thus acting like a tyrant. Gómara attributed Pedrarias's
violence to his desire for gold, placing greed as the driving force of
colonization. He presented a process where injustice was openly
practiced and its recurrence became an integral part of the colonial
enterprise.

This interpretation reappears in Gómara's account of the conquest
(1525–1533) and civil wars (1539–1548) in Peru, a key region in the development of the Spanish empire. The episodes of this conquest reiterated the pattern established in Hispaniola of syphilis, ill-gotten wealth,
injustices committed against the Indians, and power struggles between
the conquistadors. Syphilis took on an emblematic quality, representing the moral degradation of the Spaniards. Gómara stated that they
"renegauan de la tierra, y de quien a ella los traxo, viendose tan feos"
[detested the land and the one who brought them there, seeing themselves so ugly] (1552, 1:62r), but they had no way of returning to Panama
on their own. He even described that their warts were "ta[n] grandes
como nuezes, y muy sangrientas" [as big as nuts and quite bloody] and
broke out on their "cejas, narizes, orejas, & otras partes de la cara, y
cuerpo" [eyebrows, noses, ears, and other parts of the face and body]
(1552, 1:62r). Yet, in spite of the toll that death, disease, and starvation
had taken among the Spaniards, their leader Francisco Pizarro decided
to deny them the option of returning to Panama in order to continue
the enterprise. What motivated Almagro and Pizarro to conquer that
territory was, according to Gómara, "la muestra de piedras, y oro, que
los naturales tenian" [the evidence of the precious stones and gold that
the natives had] (1552, 1:60v).

In the course of events, native resistance first emerged after the plunder and rapes carried out by the conquistadors on the island of Puna. The incident was a problematic beginning for the conquest of Peru. Gómara admitted that initially the ruler of Puna had peacefully received them and only later "ordeno de matar los españoles por lo que hazian en las mugeres, y ropa" [ordered the killing of Spaniards for what they did to their women and clothing] (1552, 1:62v). Pizarro managed to capture him before he could injure the conquistadors, but the damage to the enterprise of the conquest had already been done. When Pizarro freed the prisoners held by the ruler to gain Atahualpa's friendship, instead of praising the Spaniards, they reported "como los christianos se aprouechauan de las mugeres. Y se tomaua[n] qua[n]ta plata, y oro topauan" [how the Christians took advantage of the women and how much silver and gold they found was taken] (1552, 1:62v). According to Palacios Rubios's doctrine, the Indians only had to submit themselves to Christians "cuando conocieron y descubrieron sus intenciones" [when they knew and discovered their intentions] (1954, 34). This principle justified the resistance of the ruler of Puna and Atahualpa against the conquistadors in Gómara's account. In fact, Las Casas often used the very same type of argument in his *Brevísima relación*.[14] The conduct of Pizarro and his men described by Gómara invalidated any claim of legitimacy in the use of violence on the part of the Spaniards.

Patricia Seed (1995, 98) has stated that the failure of Spaniards to comply with the legal precepts of the Requirement in the conquest of Peru horrified political and religious officials in Spain. Particularly serious was the massacre carried out in Cajamarca after Atahualpa had dropped a bible that *fray* Vicente de Valverde had placed in his hands. Francisco de Vitoria commented that the incident "made his blood run cold" (Seed 1995, 98). The massacre was completely unjustified because the sole objective had been to capture the indigenous leader. One important detail is the fact that none of the Indians fought back against the Spaniards. Gómara said that the Indians were stabbed without offering resistance because they did not receive Atahualpa's order to attack. It was a bloodbath of such proportions that Gómara presented it as an absurd expression of violence: "Murieron tantos porque no pelearon. Y porque andauan los nuestros a estocadas, que assi se lo aconsejaua fray Vicente, por no quebrar las espadas, hiriendo de tajo, y reues" [So many died because they did not fight back, and because our men went about stabbing them head on, as *fray* Vicente advised them not to break their swords by slashing from side to side] (1552, 1:64v). The frivolity with which the conquistadors conducted the massacre of Cajamarca becomes even more shocking when we learn about the orgiastic discovery made possible by Atahualpa's capture. Gómara commented that, in addition to the enormous treasure, the conquistadors "[h]allaron en el vaño, y real de Atabaliba cinco mil mugeres, que aunque tristes y desamparadas, holgaron con los christianos" [found in Atahualpa's privy five thousand women who, although sad and helpless, had sex with the Christians] (1552, 1:64v).

Although it is difficult to establish whether Gómara was the least bit concerned with the human cost of the conquest, his representation of the conquistadors of Peru lacks any heroic element. They were motivated by the desire for wealth and did not aspire to any higher purpose. Gómara found nothing to commend in their actions from an ethical and moral standpoint, for they did not achieve any social benefit. They only pursued their own individual interests, driven by their appetite for pleasure. The fall of the Inca dynasty occurred in little time with the deaths of Huascar and Atahualpa, both attributed to Spanish greed. According to Gómara, Huascar and Atahualpa were already involved in a civil war for the succession of the Inca empire when the conquistadors arrived. At the same time that the Spaniards captured Atahualpa, his officers had captured his brother Huascar, who was considered the legitimate heir of Huayna Capac, the previous Inca. Atahualpa tried to acquire his freedom by paying a ransom in gold to the Spaniards and while he was in prison he ordered Huascar's assassination to remain in control of the empire. Huascar, on the other hand, tried to save himself by asking Hernando de Soto and Pedro del Barco to accompany him to Cajamarca and he offered them even more treasures than Atahualpa for restoring his kingdom and freedom. Gómara concluded that Soto and Barco had the opportunity to save him, but "quisieron mas el oro del Cuzco, que la vida de Guaxcar" [they wanted Cuzco's gold more than Huascar's life] (1552, 1:65v).

Gómara portrayed Atahualpa's death as the result of accusations made by Felipe, the conquistadors' interpreter, but he attributed the decision to kill him to Spaniards who considered him a threat to the control they had acquired over his kingdom. Gómara claimed that Pizarro "d[e]termino matarlo por quitarse de cuidado. Y pensando q[ue] muerto ternia[n] menos que hazer en ganar la tierra" [decided to kill him to be on the safe side and thinking that with him dead they would have less to do to seize the land] (1552, 1:66v). This decision was reprehensible to Gómara, but he concluded that "[n]o [h]ay que reprehe[n]der a los que le mataron, pues el tiempo, y sus pecados los castigaron despues. Ca todos acabaro[n] mal, como en el proceso de su [h]ystoria vereis" [it is not necessary to reprimand those who killed him because time and their sins punished them later. For all of them ended horribly, as you will see in the course of their story] (1552, 1:66v). In this way Gómara painted a picture of masculine appetites out of control in which the sexual and economic conduct of the conquistadors was only rewarded in temporal success.

Gómara regarded the desire for riches driving the colonial enterprise as a general condition of life in the world. When he discussed the return of the conquistadors of Peru to Spain, Gómara explained that "[e]n fin traxeron casi todo aquel oro de Atabaliba. E [h]inchieron la contratacion de Seuilla de dinero, y todo el mu[n]do de fama, y desseo" [in short, they brought back all that gold from Atahualpa and flooded the commerce of Seville with money and the entire world with fame and desire] (1552, 1:66v). It was a world where the appetite placed no limits on the accumulation of wealth, and the appearance of new treasures stimulated the desire to obtain even more. As no point of satisfaction was ever reached, human action also lacked limits for attaining the objects of desire.

The male conquering subject found himself controlled by desire so much that his violence was not only directed at the native inhabitants but also at other conquistadors. Gómara went on to describe the bloody civil wars between the Spaniards who struggled to retain their power. After relating the story of nearly ten years of continuous violence in Peru, he concluded by attributing the disorder "a la malicia y auaricia de los [h]ombres" [to the malice and avarice of men] (1552, 1:104v). From Gómara's perspective, the picture of widespread corruption that dominated Peru ultimately made it difficult to tell the story:

> Començaron los vandos entre Piçarro, y Almagro por ambicion. Y sobre quien gouernaria el Cuzco. Empero creciero[n] por auaricia. Y llegaron a mucha crueldad por ira, & inuidia. Y plega a Dios que no duren como en Italia Guelfos, y Gebelinos. . . . Muchos [h]an dexado al rei porque no les tenia de dar. Y pocos son los que fueron siempre reales [sic], ca el oro ciega el sentido. Y es tanto lo del Peru que pone admiracion. Pues assi como [h]an

seguido diferentes partes [h]an tenido doblados coraçones. Y aun lenguas.
Por lo qual nunca dezian verdad sino quando hallauan malicia.
Corrompian los [h]ombres con dinero para jurar falsedades. Acusauan vnos
a otros maliciosame[n]te por mandar, por [h]auer, por vengança, por
embidia, y aun por su passatiempo. Matauan por justicia sin justicia. Y
todo era por ser ricos. Assi que muchas cosas se encubrieron, que conuenia
publicar (1552, 1:104v).

> The feuds between Pizarro and Almagro began because of ambition
> and over who would govern Cuzco, but they increased because of
> greed and became very cruel out of rage and envy. And I pray to God
> that they do not last like the Guelphs and Ghibellines in Italy. . . .
> Many have left the king because he was not going to give them
> anything. And few are those who remained loyal, for gold blinds the
> senses, and so much so in Peru that it causes wonder. For just as
> they have joined different factions, they have had double-crossing
> hearts and even tongues, whereby they never told the truth except to
> be malicious. With money they corrupted men to adjudicate lies.
> They accused one another maliciously for power, for wealth, for
> vengeance, for envy, and even for fun. They killed through justice
> without justice. And it was all to become rich men. Thus many
> things were covered up, which was appropriate to make known.

The corruption of the public record of events made it problematic for
Gómara to provide a positive account of Spanish imperialism in Peru.
Although he attempted to defend the conquest, all he could present
was violence and degradation. The conquistadors whose senses have
been blinded by gold came off as pathetic representatives of Spain's
colonial mission in the New World.

Gómara cannot help but tell the story of a morally crippled empire
sorely in need of a discourse of domination. Some passages in the *Historia*
general characterized religion as the motivating force in the conquistadors' actions, but their intention of evangelizing tended to be absent or
else taken for granted. With regard to the duty of bringing Christianity
to the New World, Gómara stressed that the crown took charge of
sending missionaries for the religious instruction of the native inhabitants. The achievements of the conquistadors were measured in the steps
they took to ensure the territorial control of the Indies and the Indians'
obedience. Considering conquest a precondition for evangelization,
Gómara opposed Las Casas's doctrines of peaceful missionization and
criticized him strongly for his failure in Cumaná (1552, 1:43v–44r). He

ridiculed him for having offered to increase royal revenues without having the necessary experience or knowledge to carry out his promises.

Gómara thought that Indians could not be won over without the aid of military conquest. He narrated the death of *fray* Luis Cáncer de Balbastro in Florida as an exemplary case that proved the inappropriateness and impracticality of forms of colonization that excluded the use of force. Gómara explained that, after the death of Hernando de Soto in Florida, many asked to conquer it; but Philip refused their offers, "aconsejados del su co[n]sejo de Indias. Y de otras personas que con buen zelo, a su parecer contradezian las conquistas de las Indias" [advised by his Council of the Indies and other persons, with good zeal, whose opinions opposed the conquests of the Indies] (1552, 1:23v). Instead, he sent Cáncer to "conuertir la gente, y traerla a seruicio, y obediencia del Emperador, con solas palabras" [convert the people and bring them to the service and obedience of the emperor, with mere words] (1552, 1:23v). The mission, however, ended with the death of the missionary who, according to Gómara, was then eaten by the Indians. From Gómara's perspective, the case proved that peaceful methods were completely ineffective:

> *Muchos que fauorecieron la intincion de aquellos frayles conoce[n] agora que por aquella via mal se pueden atraer los indios a nuestra amistad. Ni a nuestra santa fe. Aunque si pudiesse ser mejor seria (1552, 1:23v).*

> Many who favored the intention of those friars now know that in this way they can hardly attract the Indians to our friendship and our holy faith, although it would be better if it could.

Gómara's political pragmatism with respect to the colonization of the Indies may have contributed to creating a sense of secularity that many critics have noted in his narrative.[15] The patterns of abuse and destruction associated with the conquistadors' greed are sufficiently clear in his account, but this critical dimension of the *Historia general* has attracted little attention. Although he celebrated the subordination of the indigenous communities, Gómara was still able to praise the measures taken by the crown to protect the natives from the conquistadors' abuses. His commentary on the promulgation of the New Laws seems to take on an ingratiating quality in his elegies of the emperor: "Sabie[n]do el emperador las desordenes del Peru, y malos tratamie[n]tos que se hazian a los indios, quiso remediarlo todo, como rei justiciero, y zeloso del seruicio de dios, y prouecho de los [h]ombres" [The emperor, know-ing about the disorder in Peru and the mistreatment of the Indians, wished to remedy it all as a just king, zealous in the service of God and the benefit of men] (1552, 1:82r). This position is consistent with the monarchical theories of power where the king is a guardian of justice who must negotiate with the interests of the communities under his authority. Gómara regarded the legal reforms of 1542 as Charles's ef-fort to implant justice in the Indies. He expected that these laws would strike a difficult balance between the well-being of the Indians and the aspirations of the colonizers to dominate them.

LORDSHIP AND MASCULINITY

The case of the conquest of Mexico (1519–1521) offers a unique excep-tion to the general picture of abuses and greed that dominates the rest of the *Historia general*. Gómara reserved this account for a separate vol-ume so he could narrate it in greater detail. He thought that "[l]a conquista de Mexico, y conuersion de los de la nueua España, justamente se puede, y deue, poner entre las [h]istorias del mundo, assi porque fue bien hecha como porque fue muy gra[n]de" [the conquest of Mexico and the conversion of New Spain can justly and should be placed among the histories of the world, because it was accomplished well and be-cause it was quite grand] (1552, 2:1v). His contemporaries had good reason to question his motivations for portraying it as an exceptional achievement, because he had been Cortés's chaplain in Spain (Oviedo 1992, 4:265; Las Casas 1988–1998, 5:1870–1871, 2251, 2256, 2382, 2466–2472). He was paid by Martín Cortés to write it (Lewis 1983, 330), but his adulation of the conqueror does not sufficiently explain his positive assessment of the conquest. Las Casas, who considered all the con-quests illegal, referred to the situation in Mexico, out of all the regions of the Indies, as "un poco menos malo . . . porque allí, y no en otra parte, hay alguna justicia (aunque muy poca)" [a little less dreadful . . . because there and nowhere else, there was some justice (although very little)] (1988–1998, 10:87). Gómara may well have had some reason to use the conquest of Mexico as a model of colonization based on the information he had available from previous accounts or his interviews with colonists.

Gómara emphasized the tempered use of violence employed by Cortés, whom he depicted following appropriate legal procedures and planning his actions rationally to obtain the collaboration or submission of the native inhabitants. Cortés's own account in his *Cartas de relación* provided a narrative precedent where the use of violence had been calculated according to the political or military situation of each moment. With few exceptions throughout the account, the use of violence was characterized as undesirable and limited to a minimum necessary for achieving the ends of the conquest. It was a conquest exemplifying prudence and military prowess. The conquistadors' advance only brought destruction to the native communities who resisted being subjugated by the conquistadors. Although Gómara narrated the slaughter of a great number of Indians, this violence was codified through religion, reason, and law. In fact Cortés often appeared preaching to the native inhabitants and claiming evangelization as one of the most important purposes of his coming.

The conquistadors' appetite for gold and sex is still part of the account, but the detriment of plunder and rape in the indigenous communities is conspicuously absent. When arriving at Cozumel, Cortés won the trust of the native lord by treating his wife "[h]onestamente" [respectfully], after having found her alone with her children (1552, 2:7v). The good treatment that Cortés gave the inhabitants of Cozumel set the foundations for his subsequent success, because it allowed him to gain the friendship of the *calachuni,* who concluded that "aquella gente estrangera era buena, y amorosa" [those foreign people were good and loving]. Thanks to this, Cortés would obtain the collaboration of the Indians to find Jerónimo de Aguilar, who would then play a decisive role in informing Cortés about the native inhabitants and in communicating with them with the assistance of *doña* Marina. When the Indians of Tlaxcala submitted to the authority of the conquistadors, Gómara said that they did so because they thought that "su libertad seria menos quebrada, sus personas, sus mugeres mas miradas, y no destruydas sus casas ny labra[n]ças. Y si alguno los quisiesse ofender, defendidos" [their liberty would be less weakened, their persons and their women more secure, and their houses and fields not destroyed, and they would be defended if anyone wished to attack them] (1552, 2:33v). Gómara's representation of Cortés's sexual self-restraint in the conquest serves a legitimizing purpose, but it does not have the effect of erasing colonial desire by disavowing gendered violence.[16] He did not try to conceal the appetites that drove the Spaniards in the conquest of Mexico; rather he showed that Cortés was able to deter the opportunities for abuse in favor of his objective of drawing the Indians to the service of the Spaniards. In this sense, Gómara insisted on calling the reader's attention to how Cortés's way of operating differed from other conquistadors, as in the case of the Potonchan:

> *No menor alabança merecio en esto Cortes que en la vitoria. Porque en todo se [h]vuo cuerda, y esforçadamente. Dexo aq[ue]llos indios a su deuocio[n]. Y al pueblo libre, y sin daño. No tomo esclauos, ny saqueo. Ny tampoco rescato, aunque estuuo alli mas de veynte dias (1552, 2:14v).*

> Cortés did not merit less praise in this than in the victory, for in everything he acted prudently and bravely. He left those Indians to their devotion and the community free and unharmed. He did not take slaves, plunder, or ransom, even though he was there for more than twenty days.

Cortés also had an appetite for riches, but he was able to channel it so that it did not obstruct his relations with the Indians. When the lord of Tabasco subjected himself to the Spaniards, Gómara said that "entregaronse en su poder, y de los españoles, ofreciendoles la tierra, la hazienda, y las personas" [they delivered themselves into his and the Spaniards' power, offering them land, wealth, and persons] and he added that "Cortes los recibio, y trato muy bien. Y les dio cosas de rescate con que se holgaron mucho" [Cortés received and treated them very well, and gave them things in return that greatly pleased them] (1552, 2:14r). The conquistador used the situation to create a bond with the Indians where a sense of reciprocity was affirmed. He surely intended to take advantage of them, but he eliminated the kind of detriment and abuse that aroused native resistance in other conquests. I have already mentioned how Cortés, concerned with concealing their greed, ordered his men not to accept any gold or let on that they wanted it, or even knew what it was, so as not to alert the Indians to their true intentions (1552, 2:16r). In a similar manner, he hid his greed when asking Motecuhzoma's messengers to tell their leader that "tenemos yo y mis compañeros, mal de coraçon, enfermedad que sana con [oro]" [my companions and I have a disease of the heart, a sickness that is cured with gold] (1552, 2:16v). The conquistadors' desire for gold was essential to sustain the conquest because it fueled their determination to vanquish native resistance and confront any adversities. Gómara was able to portray this appetite as an acceptable aspect in the production of colonial relationships because of his notion of conquest as exchange.

Gómara saw the conquistador as an intensely masculine figure preoccupied with reaffirming his patriarchal authority. Karen Vieira Powers (2002, 7–8) explains that this "discourse of sexual conquest" erases female subaltern agency through its "language of male ownership, of male conquest, of female betrayal, and of women's promiscuity" as well as through its portrayals of female rape and victimhood.[17] Gómara's portrayal of Cortés's mastery over female honor in the conquest of Mexico articulates the full range of possibilities described by Powers within this kind of discursive economy. Nowhere is this more apparent than in the case of Cortés's conflict with Diego de Velázquez, the governor of Cuba, over women and property in the chapters titled "Algunas cosas que acontecieron en Cuba a Ferna[n]do Cortes" (Some things that happened in Cuba to Fernando Cortés) (1552, 2:3r–v), "La diligencia y gasto que hizo Cortes en armar la flota" (The diligence and expense that Cortés made in preparing his fleet) (1552, 2:5r–v), and "Como fue Cortes hecho gouernador" (How Cortés was made governor) (1552, 2:95v–96r). After the conquest, the two men engaged in prolonged litigation in the Spanish court over who would govern the territory. Each of them based their claims on having borne the cost of preparing the fleet. According to Gómara, it was Cortés who primarily financed the undertaking, spending two thousand *castellanos* in gold and putting himself into debt. Velázquez, on the other hand, had sought out Cortés because "[t]enia poco estomago para gastar, siendo codicioso. Y queria embiar armada a costa agena" [being greedy, he had little stomach for spending money and wanted to send the fleet at someone else's expense] (1552, 2:5r). Gómara declared that Juan de Grijalva had taken possession of the land in San Juan de Ulúa in the name of Velázquez, but the author also recognized the rights of his patron, Cortés, to govern Mexico.

Gómara depicted Cortés's life before the conquest as a gradual social accession toward becoming a figure of authority. Instead of accepting land and a home to settle down in Santo Domingo, Cortés preferred to go in search of gold. His services to Velázquez in the war against Anacaona won him an *encomienda* and the position of notary in Azúa, where he dedicated himself to "granjerias" [enterprises] (1552, 2:2v–3r). After taking part in Velázquez's conquest of Cuba, Cortés settled down in Santiago de Baracoa and amassed some wealth in livestock and mining. He had achieved a position of importance on the island with Velázquez entrusting him with businesses and the construction of the mint and a hospital. Eventually, however, Cortés lost the governor's favor in a case involving two of the few Spanish women in Cuba at that time. After the Juárez sisters arrived on the island, Cortés began to court the one named Catalina. She demanded that he marry her, but he was not willing to fulfill his promise of matrimony.[18] Velázquez, who was courting her sister, also pressured Cortés, but he still refused. According to Gómara, this predisposed the governor to believe his relatives' accusations of conspiracy against the conquistador. Velázquez had him arrested, but he escaped and sought refuge in a church to avoid execution or deportation from Cuba. Finally, the governor asked him to be friends again and Cortés "se caso con la Catalina Xuarez porque lo [h]auia prometido, y por viuir en paz. Y no quiso hablar a Diego Velazquez en muchos dias" [married Catalina Juárez because he had promised to and in order to live in peace. And he refused to speak to Diego Velázquez for many days] (1552, 2:3v).

Gómara's account of the reconciliation between Cortés and Velázquez emphasized the bond of mutual fear and trust that was created between them. According to Cortés, he presented himself before Velázquez and

> *dixo q[ue] no venia sino a saber las quexas que del tenia. Y a satisfazerle, y a ser su amigo, y seruidor. Tocaronse las manos por amigos. Y despues de muchas platicas se acostaron juntos en vna cama. Donde los hallo a la mañana Diego de Orellana (1552, 2:3v).*

> said that he did not come except to know the complaints he had about him, and to satisfy him, and to be his friend and servant. They shook hands as friends and after much conversation they slept together in a bed where Diego de Orellana found them in the morning.

Gómara's version irritated Las Casas because he portrayed his patron as a man of status in Cuba (1988–1998, 5:1870–1872); but it is interesting that Gómara characterized this meeting between the two as an act of male bonding. Their competition as masculine figures gets resolved with an expression of what Eve Sedgwick (1985) has termed homosocial desire.[19] Sleeping together established their trust in spite of the threat that they represented to each other. The relations that each had with a Juárez sister appear as an expression of their dominant sexual role;

therefore, Cortés challenged Velázquez's masculine authority. Their encounter then established that their relationship was one between equals within the homosocial code of the conquistadors.

Gómara understood the conquistador's masculinity as the social foundation of his power. Here, women functioned as objects of exchange that served to define the bonds between men. We can read this "traffic in women" as taking part in the production of a colonial sex and gender system in the manner that Gayle Rubin (1975) has analyzed within kinship systems. It is irrelevant to ascertain whether this is a conscious move in Gómara's narrative, for it symbolically articulates the status of the conquistador.[20] Pedro Carrasco (1997, 90) explains that the donation of women served among indigenous peoples to create and maintain political relations, but Gómara interpreted these gestures as an act of submission to the conquistadors. Polygyny gave a strong political meaning to broad notions of kinship in Mesoamerican communities, but for Spaniards, however, the notion of marriage as an alliance between large kin groups had been replaced by single male lineages in the late Middle Ages (Gaunt 2001). Instead of grasping the notion of reciprocity implied in the Indians' behavior, Spaniards treated these gifts as a confirmation of their privileged access to honor in conquest activities. Insofar as honor defined the social hierarchy for the Spaniards within a patrilineal system, it comes as no surprise that they would understand these donations as a marker of their precedence rights over Indian communities (Burkett 1978, 105–106; Gutiérrez 1984, 1994). The internal hierarchy of the conquistadors as a group would also become manifest in the narrative through differences in the kinds of access they had to women, either Spanish or indigenous, among themselves.

Gómara recounts that when the lord of Tabasco agreed to submit to the Spaniards he delivered twenty female slaves to Cortés whom the conquistador decided to distribute among his men as *camaradas*, that is to say, mistresses.[21] Among these women was *doña* Marina, also known as La Malinche, whom he would later ask to serve as his secretary and interpreter (1552, 2:16r–v).[22] Gómara made it clear that her help was essential for Cortés to communicate with native lords in the conquest of Mexico, even to the extent that Indians identified him by her name. When Cortés returned from Honduras, he sent messages to every Indian town along the way letting them know that he would pass by in his journey back to Mexico. Gómara playfully linked her name to his authority among the Indians when he said that "[t]odas ellas se holgaron mucho que por su tierra passasse Malinxe, que assi le llamauan. Ca le tenian en grandissima estimacion por [h]auer ganado a Mexico Tenuchtitlan" [all of them were glad that Malinche would pass by their land, for they held him in high regard for having conquered Mexico-Tenochtitlan] (1552, 2:109v). Later Bernal Díaz also stated that her collaboration was the foundation of the conquest and added that more than just an aide and translator, she became the mother of his son (1982, 60–70).

Gómara narrated the main stages of Cortés's biography through incidents linked to his involvement with women. First, when he was about to leave for the New World with Nicolás de Ovando, the new governor of Hispaniola, Cortés was forced to delay his departure because he fell from a wall one night while sneaking into a house to see a woman (1552, 2:2r). After establishing himself in Cuba, his marriage with Catalina Juárez had been instrumental for him to coexist peacefully with Velázquez. But once Cortés became governor of New Spain, her timely death cleared the way for him to reach a higher position by arranging a better marriage. In fact, his success as a conquistador achieved social expression less in material compensation granted by the emperor for his services than in his marriage to *doña* Juana de Zúñiga, niece of the count of Aguilar. They became a transatlantic couple through the negotiations that *don* Álvaro de Zúñiga, duke of Béjar, and Martín Cortés, the conquistador's father, initiated as soon as the news of the death of his first wife, Catalina, arrived in Castile. This relationship brought Cortés to the pinnacle of his career, for Gómara stated that he "colmaua a nobleza, y antiguedad, de aquel linaje, e tuuo por bien casado, y emparentado" [attained nobility and antiquity from that lineage, and considered himself well married and connected in the family] (1552, 2:114r). This is an extraordinary outcome for Cortés, considering that whom a conquistador married often determined the degree of honor and success he would achieve.[23]

The conquistador is constructed as a function of his relative position with regard to other masculine figures of authority. In this sense, it is not gratuitous that Cortés's sexual agency would be a central aspect in Gómara's interpretation of his life. The chapter titled "Condicion de Cortes" (Cortés's nature), which concludes the *Conquista de México*, emphasizes his womanizing traits through various commentaries:

> Fue muy dado a mugeres, y diose sie[m]pre. . . . Gastaua liberalissimamente
> en la guerra, en mugeres, por amigos, y en antojos, mostrando escaseza en

algunas cosas. . . . Deleitauase de tener mucha casa, y familia. . . . Tratauase muy de señor. . . . Era celoso en su casa, siendo atreuido en las ajenas, condicion de putañeros (1552, 2:139v).

He was and remained very prone to women. . . . He spent most liberally on war, on women, on friends, and on whims, exhibiting meagerness in some things. . . . He delighted in having a large house and family. . . . He acted like a lord. . . . He was jealous in his house, while being daring in the houses of others, characteristic of womanizers.

It is meaningful that Gómara's *Conquista de México* should conclude with the image of Cortés as the patriarch presiding over a "casa poblada," according to the model of the noble household that "maintained a large establishment of relatives, retainers, and servants" (Lockhart and Schwartz 1983; see also Chocano Mena 2000, 105). Here his qualities as a womanizer also serve to stress his status as a male elite.[24]

Gómara extolled traits in Cortés that posed the greatest ethical difficulties during the conquest because they led to the injustices that discredited Spanish colonialism. The sexual offenses and plunder perpetrated by the conquistadors were associated with insatiable men who could not limit their appetites. Cortés's life allowed Gómara to construct an account where greed and violence were constrained by the rationalization of the conquest according to the Christian principles of the empire. His exaltation of the conquistador as a masculine figure of authority was based on a patriarchal notion of social order where the conquistador's seigniorial aspirations were channeled through economic, military, and sexual activities. Gómara argued that the Spaniards could use the native inhabitants as an instrument to achieve their individual interests and adequately satisfy the objectives of the colonizing project. He presented seigniorial ambition as the mobilizing force behind the conquest; thus he suggested that the Indies could not be colonized without making concessions to the impulses and appetites of those who maintained the stability of the social system.

THE PATRIARCHAL LIFE OF THE CONQUISTADOR

Gómara condoned the injustices of Spanish imperialism as matter of political pragmatism. The conquistadors' intervention in the New World limited the crown's ability to control the colonization process and uphold the rule of law in its dominions. When the emperor responded to the climate of disorder and mistreatment of the Indians in Peru by promulgating the New Laws of 1542, the general uproar they produced in the Indies posed a significant impediment to the reform effort. The Spanish residents howled when they were read, some were saddened, others swore, and everyone cursed Las Casas. Gómara's description emphasized their impact on all sectors of colonial society: "No comian los [h]ombres, llorauan las mugeres, y niños. Ensoberuecianse los indios que no poco temor era" [Men did not eat, women and children cried. The Indians became arrogant, which was no small fright] (1552, 1:82v). Gómara explained in some detail that many objected to the laws because they considered them unjust; they questioned the king's authority to promulgate them without the consent of his vassals, and regarded them as "instructions for friars." Particularly disturbing was his quotation of criticisms raised by *fray* Pedro Muñoz de la Merced, who "se desuergonço co[n]tra el virrei, y aun co[n]tra el rei" [was disrespectful to the viceroy and even the king] and said:

> [Q]uan mal pago daua su majestad, a los que tambien [sic] le [h]auian
> seruido. Y que olian mas aquellas leies a interese que a santidad, pues
> quitauan los esclauos que vendio, sin boluer los dineros. Y porque tomauan
> los pueblos para el rei, quita[n]dolos a monesterios, iglesias, hospitales, y
> conquistadores, que los [h]auia [sic] ganado. Y lo que peor era que
> imponian doblado pecho, y tributo, a los indios que assi quitauan, y ponian
> en cabeça del rei. Y aun los mesmos indios llorauan por esto (1552, 1:83v).

What a lousy reward his majesty gave those who had served him so
well, and that those laws smelled more of interest than of sanctity,
for they took away the slaves, which he sold without returning the
money, and because they transferred the Indian communities to the
king, taking them away from the monasteries, churches, hospitals,
and the conquistadors who had earned them. And what was worse,
they imposed double the burden and tribute on the Indians they
took away and put in the king's charge. And even the Indians
themselves cried about this.

Muñoz's accusation that the king had acted out of self-interest set a limit to the exercise of monarchical authority over the conquistador. This not only concerned those who had lent services to the monarch for which they expected to be compensated, the measures also affected previously established contracts. Muñoz also questioned their impact on the well-being of the Indians. He relied in part on an old argument that the colonists had used since the time of the Laws of Burgos. During the reign of the Catholic Monarchs, royal officials who were entrusted with the custody of the native communities had exploited the Indians to the fullest, knowing that in any moment they could lose control of them. It was argued that the Indians would be treated better if they were in the hands of the colonists interested in protecting them as part of their individual patrimony. The general idea that emerged in Gómara's account is that radical attempts at reform created the occasion for new injuries and abuses.

Gómara blamed Blasco Núñez de Vela for the 1544–1548 rebellion of Gonzalo Pizarro, the brother of Francisco Pizarro, the conquistador of the Peru. Núñez de Vela had been sent by the crown to supervise the implementation of the New Laws because people had advised the emperor to "embiasse [h]ombre de barua . . . al Peru. Por quanto [las leyes] eran rezias, y los Españoles de alli reboltosos" [send a "real man" . . . to Peru, for the laws were severe and the Spaniards there rebellious] (1552, 1:83r). Núñez de Vela tried to apply the laws in a rigid manner without taking into account the delicacy that the situation required. He confiscated the gold and silver that he suspected was acquired in the commerce of slaves or from Indian labor in mining, freed all the Indians whom he found, took away all of the Spaniards' Indian mistresses, proclaimed his intention of arresting the viceroy of Peru for illicit use of indigenous manual labor, and ignored all the warnings that he should act with moderation. Gómara presented his excess in the exercise of authority by his threat to hang those who "suplicauan de sus prouisiones, referdadas [*sic*] de vn su criado, que no era escriuano del rey" [requested their provisions, countersigned by a servant of theirs who was not a notary of the king], and added that "los vezinos de alli se escandalizauan mas de sus palabras, y aspereza que de las ordenanças" [the residents there were scandalized more by his words and surliness than by the ordinances] (1552, 1:83r). Moreover, his account suggests that the very implementation of the reforms polarized colonial society. Gómara asserted that these reforms delighted the Indians as much as they saddened the Spaniards, whose reaction against the viceroy suggests that they felt wronged: "Por lo qual le quitaua[n] la habla, y la comida, como a descomulgado. Y a la salida del lugar, le dieron grita las españolas. Y lo maldixeron como si lleuara consigo la yra de Dios" [Therefore they stopped speaking to and feeding him, like an excommunicant. And when leaving the place, the Spanish women yelled at him. And they cursed him as if he brought the wrath of God with him] (1552, 1:83r).

Gómara in part attributed the fury caused by the reforms to the fact that the crown had negotiated in 1539 with the Spanish settlers the right to retain their *encomiendas* by forcing them to abandon their Indian mistresses and get married (Ots y Capdequí 1982, 77). He explicitly said that some Spaniards

> *tenian dos cedulas del Emperador que les daua los repartimientos para si, y a sus hijos y mugeres, porque se casassen, manda[n]doles espressamente casar. Y otra que ninguno fuesse despajado [sic] de sus indios, y repartimientos sin primero ser oydo a justicia, y condenado (1552, 1:82v).*

had two *cédulas* from the emperor, one that gave them the *repartimientos* for themselves and their children and wives, so that they would marry, ordering them specifically to marry, and another that no one would be deprived of their Indians and *repartimientos* without first being heard by a justice and condemned.[25]

In this sense the reforms that Núñez de Vela attempted to implement not only violated the accords already established between the colonists and the king, but also constituted a threat to the patriarchal foundations upon which the households and estates of the conquistadors had been founded as domestic units of colonization. As news of the severe measures taken by Núñez de Vela spread through Peru, Gómara recorded the reaction of the colonists who denounced the situation:

> *Unos dezian que dexarian las mugeres. Y aun algunos las dexaran si les valiera. Ca se [h]auian casado muchos con sus amigas, mugeres de seguida, por mandamiento que les quitara[n] las haziendas si no lo hizieran. Otros dezian que les fuera mucho mejor no tener hijos, ni muger que mantener, si les [h]auian de quitar los esclauos, que los sustentaua[n] trabajando en minas, labrança, y otras granjerias. Otros pidian les pagasse los esclauos que les tomaua, pues los [h]auian comprado de los quintos del rei. Y tenia[n] su hierro, y señal. Otros daua[n] por mal empleados sus trabajos, y seruicios, si al cabo de su vejez no [h]auian de tener quien los siruiesse (1552, 1:83v).*

Some said that they would leave their wives. And some even would have if it made any difference. For many had married their mistresses right away, because of the order that they would lose their haciendas if they did not do so. Others said that it would be much better not to have children or a wife to maintain if they had to get rid of the slaves who supported them working in the mines, farming, and other enterprises. Others asked that he pay them for the slaves he took, for they had bought them from the king's fifth, and they had his brand and mark. Others considered their labors and services poorly employed, if ultimately in their old age they must not have anyone to serve them.

Gómara seemed to interpret the extraction of native labor as a basic condition to maintain the survival of the household and estate of the conquistador. If the conquistadors had married to retain their royal favors, then they had committed whole aspects of their life to the colonization project. They had first served the king, and then agreed to marry, in order to realize their aspirations to live as lords. Losing their slaves threatened their livelihood and well-being. It was an issue of social position, but it was formulated as an attack on the integrity of the patriarchal unit formed inside the conquistador's household.

Gómara's interpretation of the conquest and the *encomienda* involved the basic conditions for realizing self-sufficiency in Aristotelian political theory: reproduction and subsistence. The Greek philosopher had defined self-sufficiency as having everything and lacking nothing. Given that it is impossible for an individual to exist and reproduce on his or her own, society solves this problem by bringing together those who can complement each other for the sake of the common good. Individuals are organized into a family to enable reproduction and satisfy daily needs, families are incorporated into villages, and villages combine to form a state. The political community provides beyond daily needs, thus allowing a better way of life with a higher degree of sufficiency. The art of the administration of the household is the foundation of the life of the state, for the household is the basic unit of government and provides the things necessary for life and useful for the community. The things that a community cannot provide by itself are obtained through exchange. Exchange in Aristotle's *Politics* implies taking something that is plentiful or is found in excess in one place and bringing it to another place that lacks it. Exchange consists in providing only the things needed to live, therefore it has a limit. The art of the acquisition of wealth, on the other hand, has no limit because it is based on the human appetite for pleasure. Both commerce and slavery, according to Aristotle, are part of the art of administration of the household within the self-sufficient community because they serve the purpose of supplying the things necessary for life and nothing more (1995, 2:1994).

Gómara had portrayed the conquistador's appetite for gold and sex as the mobilizing force in the conquest. The drive to acquire wealth and power had brought destruction to the Indians while it remained unrestrained, but when guided by reason — as in the account of the conquest of Mexico — it worked as a form of exchange. The shift from acquisition to exchange becomes the key component in Gómara's understanding of colonial sufficiency. He raised the conquistadors' necessities to those of seigniorial life and lowered the Indians to the status of servants to justify the disparity in their relationship. He thus created the image of a colonial political community where the unlimited accumulation of gold makes it possible to fulfill the needs on both ends. The *encomienda* provided the framework to achieve sufficiency within the colonial political community by providing a means of life for the conquistadors and opening new forms of civil society, freedom, and life within native communities.

The traditional argument of the colonizers employed to justify extending the life of the *repartimientos* or *encomiendas* maintained that the Indians were incapable of living on their own. The *encomienda*, however, contradicted the decisions of the juridical commissions appointed by the Catholic Monarchs in 1494 and 1503, which declared that the Indians were free vassals of the crown. When Queen Isabel ordered the abolition of the *encomienda* in 1502, the Indians refused to work and abandoned the colonists, which resulted in a decrease in tribute, a shortage of manual labor, and stagnation in the process of evangelization. In 1503, Nicolás de Ovando recommended that the system of forced labor be restored, conditioning the Indians' freedom on their collaboration in the colonial order. Although freedom continued to be the basic principle of their legal status, their actual condition came to depend on their disposition toward serving and being integrated into the Christian community. The Clarification of the Laws of Burgos of 1513 (Las Casas 1988–1998, 5:1824–1826) intended to facilitate the gradual incorporation of the Indians into a wage-based labor system and their Christian conversion until they finally would became free of the *encomenderos'* tutelage. Therefore, when the colonizers claimed that the Indians were incapable of living on their own, they meant that they were not interested in being evangelized or providing the manual labor necessary to sustain the colonial economy.

This distinction between resistance and the incapacity of the Indians posed the problem of self-sufficiency, which Gómara would subsequently raise in his *Historia general*. The Indians' lack of interest for working in agriculture, mining, or the Spaniards' personal service was interpreted as an indication of their deficiency in adequate forms of civil life such as community. This is what Gómara is referring to in his dedication addressed to Charles V when he states that the Indians lacked the most important things for the "civility and livelihood of man." The modes of "sufficiency" in the indigenous world did not satisfy the levels of "necessity" that enabled the existence of a colonial economy. Gómara stated that when Cortés interrogated a Tabascan lord after defeating the Potonchanos, among other things, he "respondio q[ue] ellos no curauan mucho de viuir ricos, sino contentos, y a plazer. Y que por esso no sabia dezir que cosa era mina. Ny buscauan oro mas de lo que se hallauan" [responded that they did not much care to be rich, but rather to be content and to live as they pleased. And therefore he did not understand what a mine was. Nor did they look for more gold than what they found]. These different notions of sufficiency among the Indians and the Europeans are fundamental to understanding a key dynamic in colonial relationships that Gómara observed in the conquest: The Spaniards needed gold to enlarge their economy, but the Indians claimed not to need riches and scorned the greed of the conquistadors.

Indigenous communities in the *Historia general* had poorly exploited their resources, but the Spaniards had improved the Indies through the establishment of various economic activities. In his chapter "Las cosas de nuestra España, que hay agora en la Española" (The things from Spain that are now in Hispaniola), Gómara described the transformation of the island through the industry and commerce introduced by the Spaniards with wheat, sugarcane, livestock, and mining. The destruction of the indigenous population was not a setback, for he claimed that the few Indians left "viuen en libertad, y en descanso, q[ue] quiere[n], por merced del emperador, para q[ue] no se acabe la gente, y lenguaje de aq[ue]lla isla" [live in freedom and leisure, as they wish, by mercy of the emperor, so that the people and the language of that island are not destroyed] (1552, 1:19rv). This referred specifically to the provisions of the New Laws that decreed that "the surviving Indians in Española, Cuba, and Puerto Rico were to be exempted from all tribute and royal or personal service, so that they could rest and multiply" (Wagner 1967, 115). Throughout the *Historia general* Gómara argues that the conquest had helped to rectify the insufficient exploitation of resources in the Indies, creating communities better equipped for living.

Gómara felt that force was necessary to introduce these changes because he did not think that peaceful means could guarantee the consent of native communities. This led him to pose the equity of a society in which the indigenous population was subordinate to the conquistadors and to treat the harm caused by the conquest as a necessary evil. In the case of the missions of peaceful conversion he argued that "in this way they can hardly attract the Indians to our friendship." The ethical limitations of Gómara's perspective may be obvious to us, but it is important to note his interpretation of the dynamic of cultural interaction in colonial relationships. The political society of the empire resulted from the clash between forms of sufficiency based on different notions of need and thus what it meant to live as a human being. Aristotle's comparison between the family and the village sheds light on what Gómara may have had in mind. Both cases deal with addressing daily needs, but the village includes "something more." The point of contrast between indigenous and European notions of sufficiency lays precisely in this "something more," which implicitly juxtaposes the best way of life for human beings with the highest good to which society could aspire. Gómara stated in "Praise of Spaniards" that the conquest had made it possible to expose the Indians to "muchas buenas costu[m]bres, artes, y policia, para mejor passar la vida" [many good customs, arts, and behavior for living a better life] (1552, 1:121v).

The "something more" of the conquest would involve, as in the Clarification of the Laws of Burgos or in Sepúlveda's *Democrates secundus,* the gradual transformation of the Indians from a community of slaves to one of free men. Gómara's concept of slavery in the *Historia general* has gradations where a clear distinction is made between the Indian enslaved as punishment for obstinate resistance and the slave in the wider sense of someone whose work is instrumental to another person's benefit. In his chapter "De la libertad de los indios" (On the liberty of the Indians), Gómara said, "Libres dexaua[n] a los indios al principio los reyes catolicos. Aunque los soldados, y pobladores, se seruian dellos, como de catiuos, en las minas, labra[n]ça, cargas, y co[n]quistas" [At first the monarchs left the Indians free. Although soldiers and settlers were served by them, as captives, in the mines, agricultural fields, as carriers, and in the conquests] (1552, 1:117v). This service as captives was considered within the Indians' condition as free men, for Gómara distinguished it from *servidumbre* where their status was that of slaves. His account concerning the abolition of native slavery recognizes a violation of the Indian's personal dominion, implying that other forms of the indigenous population's employment in the Spaniards' service were acceptable. This was the case with the *encomienda* where Gómara referred to the Indians as vassals of a conquistador. It is within these gradations of slavery that Gómara suggested the possibility of realizing a common good in colonial relationships. This involved the adjustment of tribute in the *encomienda,* the possession of properties and enterprises among the Indians, the prohibition against employing them as carriers or in forced labor, and the organization of the work and government of the indigenous community under the authority of a *cacique.* Evidently this was not a situation that the Indians would have chosen to accept and for this reason Gómara considered the conquistadors' tutelage necessary to apply punishment and maintain control.

Gómara's reflection on the aspects of sufficiency in the indigenous communities allowed him to propose conditions that enabled the existence of a political community in the empire of the Indies. His discussion about questions of economy, labor, property, and liberty in colonial society refers to the fundamental problem of debating the forms of civil life that would result in the coordination of these factors. Gómara's account about the introduction of the mill to México precisely illustrates this point:

> *Quando en Mexico hizieron molino de agua, . . . vn Mexicano hizo mucha burla de tal ingenio, diziendo que haria holgazanes los [h]ombres, & iguales, pues no se sabria quien fuesse amo, ni quie[n] moço, y aun dixo que los necios nacian para seruir, y trabajar. Y los sabios para mandar, y holgar (1552, 2:137v).*

> When they set up a water mill in Mexico, . . . a Mexican made much fun of such a thing, saying that it would make men lazy and equal, for it would not be known who was the master or who was the servant, and he even said that fools were born to serve and work, and wise men to command and not to work.

The Mexican offers a theory of social order very similar to one espoused by Sepúlveda in his *Democrates secundus,* where Indians should be considered *natura servi* (slaves by nature) because they were inferior to Spaniards in the endowments of prudence or understanding. Gómara, however, situated the Mexican in the position of criticizing a techno-logical advance that would reduce the amount of labor involved in the production of flour. Although he restated Sepúlveda's notion of natural law where the superior ruled over the inferior, he did not recognize what Gómara understood as the "something else" that the conquest could bring to the Indians. Gómara observed that the mill had delighted Spaniards and Indians, especially native women who had the task of grinding maize to make tortillas. According to Aristotle, the barbarians are the ones who do not distinguish between women and slaves, for lacking natural rulers they are therefore a community of slaves. Gómara argued that before the conquest, indigenous communities lived under the tyranny of rulers who did not provide for the common good, but rather subordinated other communities in precarious living conditions under excessive burdens of tribute. These forms of indigenous social organization thus reduced the entire community to the condition of slaves.

Gómara's optimism with respect to the impact that the Spanish empire would have on the forms of civil life for the Indians is based on the reforms introduced with the New Laws of 1542, which assigned native tribute and eliminated Indian slavery, personal service, and employment as carriers. Gómara explained that the promulgation of the New Laws resulted from indignation over "la calidad de los indios, como el tratamiento, que se les hazia" [the condition of the Indians, such as the treatment they received] and, therefore, he considered them pertinent for "gouernar las indias buena, y christianamente" [governing the Indies well and in a Christian manner]. Nevertheless, Gómara objected to the rigid application of the ordinances and defended the *encomienda* as the appropriate method of recompensing the conquistadors for their services. Luis Millones (2001, 117–126), in his reading of Pedro de Cieza de León's *Crónica del Perú* (Chronicle of Peru), has pointed out that Pedro de la Gasca's *encomienda* reforms generated enthusiasm among the Spaniards. After narrating the civil wars of Peru and explaining how the abuses of the conquistadors had cut the native population in half, Gómara argued that the levy imposed by Gasca in Peru would make it possible to incorporate the indigenous population into the conquistadors' forms of civil life:

> [T]asaron los tributos mucho menos que los mesmos indios dezian que podria[n] buenamente pagar. Gasca lo mando assi. Y que cada pueblo

*pagase su pecho en aquello que su tierra produzia, si oro en oro, si
plata, en plata, si coca, en coca, si algodon, sal, y ganado en ello
mesmo. Aunque mando a muchos pagar en oro, y plata, no teniendo
minas. Por razon que se diessen al trabajo, y trato para [h]auer aquel
oro, criando aues, seda, cabras, puercos, y ouejas. Y lleuandolo a
vender a los pueblos, y mercados juntamente con leña, yerua, grano, y
tales cosas. Y porque se bezassen a ganar jornal trabajando, y siruiendo en
las casas y haziendas de los españoles. Y aprendiesen sus costu[m]bres,
y vida politicar [sic], christiana, perdiendo la idolatria, y borracherias
a que con la gran ociosidad mucho se dan[.] Publicose pues la tasa (1552,
1:103v).*

The tributes were adjusted more or less to what the Indians
themselves said that they could easily pay. Gasca thus ordered it.
And each community paid its tribute in what it produced in its
territory, if gold, in gold, if silver, in silver, if coca, in coca, if cotton,
salt, and livestock, thus in kind. But he ordered many to pay in gold
and silver that did not have mines. This was so they would be
forced to work and trade in order to get gold, raising birds, silk,
goats, pigs, and sheep, and bringing them to sell in the towns and
markets together with firewood, straw, grain, and the like. And
thereby they would get accustomed to working every day and
serving in the houses and estates of the Spaniards, and would learn
their Christian customs and ways of life, leaving behind the
idolatry, drunkenness, and great idleness, to which many are prone.
The rate then was made public.

Not only did Gómara state that the tribute the Indians paid was
much less under Spanish dominion, but the *tasa* forced them to work
and trade their products for gold. In other words, it served to integrate the indigenous communities into a system of colonial production,
while teaching them forms of civil life that the colonizers attempted to
implant in the New World. Gómara thought that the emperor had done
them a favor in "dexarlos casi francos, y señores de sus propias haziendas,
y granjerias" [leaving them nearly free and masters of their own estates and enterprises]. Wage labor and commerce would raise their
level of civility, while the tutelage of the *encomenderos* would serve to
prepare them for life in a Christian society.

In a similar manner, Gómara argued that the conquest of Mexico
had permitted the Indians to achieve an indispensable freedom within
the forms of their previous life:

Por la [h]istoria se puede sacar quan sujetos, y despechados, eran estos Indios. . . . Los villanos pechaua[n] de tres, que cogia[n], vno. Y aun les tassauan a muchos la comida. Si no pagauan la renta, y tributo, que deuian, quedaua[n] por esclauos hasta pagar. Y en fin los sacrificauan quando no se podian redemir. Tomauanles muchas vezes los hijos para sacrificios, y banquetes, que era lo tirano, y lo cruel. Seruianse dellos como de bestias en las cargas, caminos, y edificios. . . . Por manera que viuian muy trabajados, y como lo merecian, en la idolatria. . . . Agora son señores de lo que tienen con tanta libertad que les daña. Pagan tan pocos tributos, que viuen holgando. Ca el Emperador se los tassa (1552, 1:136v).

One may glean from the story how subjected and burdened these Indians were. . . . The peasants were taxed one-third of everything they got. And many were even taxed on food. If they did not pay the rent and tribute they owed, they were enslaved until they paid. And finally they were sacrificed when they were unable to redeem themselves. Many times their children were taken away for sacrifices and banquets, which was tyrannical and cruel. They used them like beasts for carrying loads and constructing roads and buildings. . . . In this way they lived very hard lives, as they deserved for their idolatry. . . . Now they are lords of what they have with so much freedom that it pains them. They pay such little tribute that they live in leisure because the emperor regulates it for them.

The freedom postulated by Gómara under the imperial dominion of Spain only has meaning as a product of his reflection upon the forms of sufficiency among the Indians. In Aristotle's *Politics,* relying on the necessities of life is the foundation that allows man to use his freedom to achieve excellence. The conquest and creation of the empire of the Indies would fulfill the plan of establishing a civil order in which the Indians would be able to accede to freedom through property, work, and commerce. In this way, Gómara could construct a theoretically coherent, narrative image of the formation of a colonial political community. Although history contradicts Gómara's sanitized image of colonial institutions, his propositions stand out for the way they articulate a project to reform colonial government. Gómara did not manage to resolve the ethical problems of the colonial project, but he clearly found a way to respond to criticism and formulate a civilizing mission for the Spanish empire in the Indies.

Within his narrative of colonization, Gómara presented the desire to acquire wealth as one of the driving forces for the Spanish conquest and used it to explain the injustices committed by the Spaniards. But he also considered that the Indians would not be adequately integrated within colonial society unless they were subdued by conquest and placed under the patriarchal authority of the conquerors. The *Historia general* sheds light on this paradox confronting Spanish imperialism. Colonization required economic incentives for conquest and settlement, but the pursuit of self-interest contradicted prevailing notions of dominion and legitimate rule and made it impossible to protect colonial subjects from abuse. Gómara's attempt to overcome these contradictions was doomed by internal dissent about the conquest and settlement of the New World and increasing international criticism of Spanish imperialism. His ideas about work and exchange suggest that a world of unlimited acquisition of wealth was colliding with another where limits were set by the basic necessities of life. Gómara distinguished two different kinds of sufficiency in order to show how interpretations of necessity and desire could articulate the dynamics of commerce and intercultural relations in Spanish colonialism.

The concepts of necessity and things necessary for life converge in the representation of exchange that Gómara proposed between Indians and Spaniards. Gómara tried to present the conquest and the *encomienda* as a necessity for civil life, trade relations, and evangelization. His supportive attitude toward the conquistadors' sexual and economic behavior viewed the detriment to native communities as an inevitable outcome and a defining factor of colonial life. His main question seems to have been whether any benefit from Spanish imperialism could be achieved when the fulfillment of seigniorial ambitions was the principal end of the conquistadors. He claimed to have found an answer in the conquest of Mexico but left many unanswered questions along the way. His willingness to accept the evils of colonialism placed him in a vulnerable position with many readers whose critical sensibility led them to conclusions quite different from what he had intended. In contrast, Las Casas had insisted on restitution, arguing that the conquistadors were obligated to return everything they had gained during the conquest to the native communities. The irony is that both Las Casas and Gómara would become sources for the criticism of Spanish colonialism. In his failure to come up with an effective response to the ethical problems besetting the empire, Gómara ended up revealing the profound human and moral costs involved in conquest and colonization. By acknowledging the impossibility of a dignified colonial experience in order to praise the conquest, the *Historia general* unwittingly took its place among the histories of infamy.

NOTES

1. Mexía cites Augustine's description of the dispute between Laelius and Philus on the necessity of injustice originally recounted by Cicero in *De re publica*; however, Lactantius's *Divinae institutiones* is the only extant source containing a full description of Carneades's statements.

2. For Mexía's position on the legitimacy of the conquest of the New World, see Chapter 1 of this book.

3. Although I am studying these disputes through printed sources, it is important to keep in mind that many of the core developments occurred in the form of public oratory. Best known is the debate of Las Casas and Sepúlveda held before a commission of Spanish theologians at Valladolid in 1550. The subject was Spain's claim of dominion over the Indians, and therefore involved the questions of whether the Spanish conquest had been legitimate and how they should be governed. Sebastián Trujillo published a summary of this controversy prepared by Domingo de Soto in 1552 (JCBL 1980, no. 552/9). Information about speeches taking place before the Valladolid debate is harder to come by but several have been documented. Some important instances include Antonio de Montesinos's sermon (Hispaniola, 1511), the debate of Las Casas and Juan de Quevedo before Charles V (Barcelona, 1519), the solemn speech of Cardinal Adrian of Utrecht before the Court Assembly (La Coruña, 1520), and the testimony of Tomás Ortiz before the Council of the Indies (1525). The main primary sources for these disputes are Las Casas (1988–1998, 5:1757–1765, 2402–2426, 2437–2440) and Martyr (1966, 223). See also Hanke (1974), Zavala (1977, 1988), Elliott (1989), Pagden (1990a, 1990b), Adorno (1992b), and Seed (1993a).

4. Montesinos's 1511 sermon condemned native exploitation at the hands of Spanish *encomenderos*. Las Casas gave a detailed account of this incident in his *Historia de las Indias* (1988–1998, 5:1757–1774). See also Seed (1993a).

5. Juan López de Palacios Rubios, *Libellus de insulis oceanis, quas vulgus Indias appellat* (Small book on the islands in the ocean, commonly called the Indies), and Matías de Paz, *De dominio regum Hispaniae super indos* (On the dominion of the monarchs of Spain over the Indians). Both Latin treatises have been translated into Spanish as *De las islas del mar océano* and *Del dominio de los reyes de España sobre los indios* and published together in a single volume by the Fondo de Cultura Económica (Mexico City) in 1954.

6. Aristotle stated that these principles of rule were based in nature as evidenced in living beings: "[T]he soul governs the body with despotic rule, whereas the intellect governs the appetites with a constitutional and royal

rule" (1995, 2:1990). From living beings he extrapolated the two kinds of rule, which he applied to the household to distinguish between the rule exerted by the father over his slaves and over his wife and children (1995, 2:1990–1992, 1998–2000). When applied to the state, this same distinction differentiates between government "with a view to the common interest" and government "with a view to the private interest" (1995, 2:2030–2031, 2047–2056). Monarchical and tyrannical rule had been codified in Spanish law since the thirteenth century according to Aristotle's definition. The *Siete partidas,* part 2, title 1, laws 5–10, composed under the auspices of Alfonso X (the Learned, 1221–1284), quote these distinctions from Aristotle's *Politics.*

7. The Black Legend grew out of a series of negative statements criticizing the morality and character of the Spaniards. The conquest was used as an example of the harm that Spanish imperialism could bring to Europe. See Carbia (1944), Gibson (1971), Maltby (1971), and Hillgarth (2000).

8. Aristotle (1995, 2:2113) defined "conditional action" as "the choice of a lesser evil" as opposed to "absolute action" as "the foundation and creation of good." The term "conditional" implies actions that "are good only because we cannot do without them," but "absolute" expresses "that which is good in itself."

9. On the universality of true law, Laelius added, "Nec erit alia lex Romae, alia Athenis, alia nunc, alia posthac, sed et omnes gentes et omni tempore una lex et sempiterna et immutabilis continebit, unusque erit communis quasi magister et imperator omnium deus" [And there will not be different laws at Rome and at Athens, or different laws now and in the future, but one eternal and unchangeable law will be valid for all nations and all times, and there will be one master and ruler, that is, God, over us all] (Cicero 1928, 210–211).

10. At this time, Charles V was attempting to subjugate Protestants within the Holy Roman Empire. After failing to organize a Christian council in 1545, he embarked on a war against Lutherans, which culminated in the Spanish victory at Mühlberg in 1547 (Merriman 1962, 352–359; Elliot 1990, 209). Thus Sepúlveda situated his debate about the justice of the conquest within the larger context of religious conflict in Europe.

11. The belief mentioned by Leopoldus is that all war is forbidden to Christians (Sepúlveda 1997, 43). Pagden (1990b, 18–24) shows that the arguments of Vitoria and other Spanish Thomists in favor of native dominion refuted the claim of some Protestant reformers that "no one can have civil dominion if he is in a state of mortal sin" (18). If Sepúlveda's questioning native dominion seems similar to the Lutheran position (Pagden 1990b, 30), he also made it clear that he was defending Spanish imperialism from a Catholic perspective.

12. Martyr says: "delapsi a praetorib[us] dista[n]tes, auri caeca raptati cupidi-tate, qui mitiores agnis hinc abeunt, applicati rapaces lupos co[n]muta[n]tur. Regiorum omniu[m] ma[n]datoru[m] immemores" [having crossed over, far

from the authorities, carried away by their blind greed for gold, those who leave from here as meek sheep, when they land are transformed into rapacious wolves, forgetting all the king's orders] (1966, 222).

13. Stephanie Wood also cautions us to consider that "[w]hile the cultural, social, political, and economic context may have been ripe for sexual violation in Spanish and Portuguese conquest expeditions, it remains to be explored whether it was a conscious tool" (1998, 25).

14. Las Casas presented this argument in his criticism of the Requirement because they were asked to subject themselves to a king whom they had never seen or heard "cuya gente y mensajeros son tan crueles, tan despiadados e tan horribles tiranos" [whose people and messengers are so cruel, so merciless, and such horrible tyrants] (1988–1998, 10:44). At the end of his *Brevísima relación* Las Casas also explained that "nunca en ninguna parte de ellas los indios hicieron mal a cristiano, sin que primero hobiesen rescebido males y robos y traiciones dellos" [in no place did the Indians ever harm a Christian unless they first had been mistreated, robbed, and betrayed by them] (1988–1998, 10:86).

15. On this topic see Mustapha (1979), Loesberg (1983), and Carman (1992).

16. On stressing gendered violence to conceal colonial desire in English narratives of discovery, see Montrose (1991).

17. Powers discusses some sixteenth-century accounts, including one example from Gómara, as well as contemporary historiographical discourse. She is mainly concerned with challenging "a historiography that continues to glorify male sexual domination and ascribes to women the constricted role of passive sexual objects" (2002, 7).

18. Asunción Lavrin (1994, 158–163) shows that the *palabra de casamiento* (promise of marriage) was frequently invoked by women who sought to restore their honor. She explains that from the canonical point of view, the promise initiated the process of marriage and had such legal force that it could lead a woman into premarital sexual intercourse.

19. According to Sedgwick homosocial desire is part of a gender arrangement based in male bonding through relations of "friendship, mentorship, rivalry, and hetero- and homosexuality" (1985, 1). This is the kind of bond that helps promote male interests, allows men to dominate women, and enhances men's power.

20. As Rubin explained, we must keep in mind that "[t]he 'exchange of women' is neither a definition of culture nor a system in and of itself. The concept is an acute, but condensed, apprehension of certain aspects of the social relations of sex and gender. A kinship system is an imposition of social ends upon a part of the natural world. It is therefore 'production' in the most general sense of the term: a molding, a transformation of objects (in this case, people) to and by a subjective purpose" (1975, 176).

21. Stephanie Wood (1998) has suggested that the practice of the leaders to distribute women among their soldiers could have served a strategic function as a mechanism of war. It would not be far fetched to assume a libidinal economy in the narration using this kind of event to attain a persuasive effect among male readers.

22. This character has become mainly known through the key role that Bernal Díaz del Castillo attributed to her in the conquest of Mexico. Contemporary scholars such as Sandra Messinger Cypess (1991), Sonia Rose-Fuggle (1991) and Frances Karttunen (1997) have shown how her symbolical polyvalence as a sexed subaltern subject has been exploited for rhetorical effect within narratives of the conquest. Georges Baudot (1993, 197), however, has attempted to reinterpret her participation in the conquest as an expression of a female discourse of vengeance. This discourse would manifest sexually through her *mestizo* offspring and politically through her collaboration with the Spaniards.

23. As Magdalena Chocano Mena (2000, 67–68, 106) explains, Cortés's story was not unique. Pedro de Alvarado, who was initially the lover of the Tlaxcalan princess *doña* Luisa Xicotencatl, would marry *doña* Francisca de la Cueva, a relative of *don* Francisco de los Cobos, Charles V's secretary. He used this marriage to get away with crimes against the natives, to recover goods that the crown had confiscated from him, and to have his grants of *encomienda* confirmed. *Doña* Francisca died just as she arrived to America, and ten years later Alvarado would marry her sister Beatriz de la Cueva, whose influences once again helped him get out of trouble.

24. Magdalena Chocano Mena (2000, 70–71) states that "[e]n el orden hispánico el honor pleno correspondía a los hombres de la elite y era un factor que regulaba las relaciones masculinas, de manera que sirvió a finalidades muy concretas de preservación del patrimonio dentro de un linaje" [in the Spanish order of things, honor pertained to men of the elite and was a factor that regulated masculine relations, so that it served the very concrete ends of preserving patrimony within a lineage].

25. Gómara is likely overstating the dimensions of the problem. Lesley Byrd Simpson (1982, 17 and note 3) has questioned the idea that the crown's attempts to promote interracial union met with any success in the Indies. For Hispaniola in 1514, he estimated the rate at 10 percent. In the case of Peru, James Lockhart (1994, 175) has said that *encomenderos* could avoid these ordinances and not marry. In fact, he states that in the early 1550s only two-thirds of the *encomenderos* in Cuzco were married at all. Moreover, their main incentive to comply would have been the hope of passing their grant of *encomienda* to an heir.

Bibliography and References Cited

Adorno, Rolena. 1988. "Discourses on Colonialism: Bernal Díaz, Las Casas, and the Twentieth-Century Reader." *Modern Languages Notes* 103, no. 2 (March): 239–258.

———. 1992a. "Censorship and its Evasion: Jerónimo Román and Bartolomé de las Casas." *Hispania* 75 (October): 812–827.

———. 1992b. "Los debates sobre la naturaleza del indio en el siglo XVI: Textos y contextos." *Revista de Estudios Hispánicos* (Río Piedras, Puerto Rico) 19: 47–66.

———. 1992c. "The Discursive Encounter of Spain and America: The Authority of Eyewitness Testimony in the Writing of History." *William and Mary Quarterly* 49, no. 2 (April): 210–228.

———. 1992d. *The Intellectual Life of Bartolomé de las Casas.* New Orleans, La.: Graduate School of Tulane University.

———. 1993. "Reconsidering Colonial Discourse for Sixteenth- and Seventeenth-Century Spanish America." *Latin American Research Review* 28, no. 3: 135–145.

———. 1994. "Peaceful Conquest and Law in the *Relación* (Account) of Alvar Núñez Cabeza de Vaca." In *Coded Encounters: Writing, Gender, and Ethnicity in Colonial Latin America,* edited by J. Cevallos-Candau, Nina M. Scott, and Nicomedes Suárez-Araúz, pp. 75–86. Amherst: University of Massachusetts Press.

Adorno, Rolena, and Patrick Pautz. 1999. *Álvar Núñez Cabeza de Vaca: His Account, His Life, and the Expedition of Pánfilo de Narváez.* Lincoln: University of Nebraska Press.

Alba, Ramón. 1989. "Introducción: Pedro Mártir de Anglería: Su vida y su obra." In Peter Martyr, *Décadas del Nuevo Mundo,* pp. iv–xliii. Madrid: Polifemo.

Amador de los Ríos, José. 1851. "Vida y escritos de Gonzalo Fernández de Oviedo y Valdés." In Gonzalo Fernández de Oviedo y Valdés, *Historia general y natural de las Indias, islas y Tierra-Firme del Mar Océano,* pp. ix–cvii. Madrid: Real Academia de la Historia.

Antonio, Nicolás. 1672. *Bibliotheca Hispana sive Hispanorum.* Rome: Nicolai Angeli Tinassi.

Aristotle. 1995. *The Complete Works of Aristotle.* Edited by J. Barnes. 2 vols. Princeton, N.J.: Princeton University Press.

Augustine. 1957–1995. *City of God.* 7 vols. Translated by William M. Green et al. The Loeb Classical Library. Cambridge, Mass.: Harvard University Press.

Ballesteros Gaibrois, Manuel. 1987. *La novedad indiana: Noticias, informaciones y testimonios del Nuevo Mundo.* Madrid: Alhambra.

Barnes, Harry Elmer. 1962. *A History of Historical Writing.* New York: Dover.

Barros, João de. 1932. *Asia de Joam de Barros: Dos feitos que os portugueses fizeram no descobrimento e conquista dos mares e terras do Oriente.* Edited by António Baião and Luís F. Lindley Cintra. Coimbra: Imprensa da Universidade.

———. 1988. *Ásia de João de Barros: Dos feitos que os portugueses fizeram no descobrimento e conquista dos mares e terras do Oriente.* Edited by António Baião, Luís F. Lindley Cintra, Hernâni Cidade, and Manuel Múrias, 2 vols. Lisbon: Imprensa Nacional–Casa da Moeda.

Bataillon, Marcel. 1953. "L'idée de la découverte de l'Amérique chez les espagnols du XVIe siècle (d'après un livre récent)." *Bulletin Hispanique* 55: 23–55.

———. 1954. "Historiografía oficial de Colón de Pedro Mártir a Oviedo y Gómara." *Imago Mundi* 1, no. 5 (September): 23–39.

———. 1956. "Hernán Cortés, autor prohibido." In *Libro jubilar de Alfonso Reyes,* pp. 77–82. Mexico City: Universidad Nacional Autónoma de México.

———. 1959. "Montaigne et les conquérants de l'or." *Studi Francesi* 3, no. 9 (September–December): 353–367.

Baudot, Georges. 1993. "Malintzin, imagen y discurso de mujer en el Primer México Virreinal." *Cuadernos Americanos,* nueva época, año 7, vol. 4, no. 40 (July–August): 181–207.

Benson, Robert L. 1976. "Medieval Canonistic Origins of the Debate on the Lawfulness of the Spanish Conquest." In *First Images of America: The Impact of the New World on the Old,* edited by Fredi Chiappelli, vol. 1, pp. 327–334. Berkeley: University of California Press.

Benzoni, Girolamo. 1969. *Historia del Mondo Nuovo*. Graz, Austria: Akademische Druck- und Verlagsanstalt.

———. 1989. *Historia del Nuevo Mundo*. Madrid: Alianza.

Bernáldez, Andrés. 1870. *Historia de los Reyes Católicos*. 2 vols. Seville: José María Geofrin.

Bethell, Leslie, ed. 1984. *The Cambridge History of Latin America*. Vol. 1. Cambridge: Cambridge University Press.

Bhabha, Homi K. 1994. *The Location of Culture*. New York: Routledge.

Binotti, Lucia. 1992. "Cultural Identity and the Ideologies of Translation in Sixteenth-Century Europe: Italian Prologues to Spanish Chronicles of the New World." *History of European Ideas* 14, no. 6 (November): 769–788.

Blake, Jon Vincent. 1975. "Fernández de Oviedo ante López de Gómara." *Romance Notes* 16, no. 2 (winter): 536–542.

Boemus, Joannes. 1542. *Omnium gentium mores, leges, & ritus*. Antwerp: Jan Steels.

Breisach, Ernst. 1994. *Historiography: Ancient, Medieval, and Modern*. Chicago: University of Chicago Press.

Bunes Ibarra, Miguel Ángel de. 1987. "Cortés y los hermanos barbarrojas, vidas paralelas en los escritos de Francisco López de Gómara." *Revista de Indias* 47, no. 181 (September–December): 901–906.

Burkett, Elinor C. 1978. "Indian Women and White Society: The Case of Sixteenth-Century Peru." In *Latin American Women: Historical Perspectives*, edited by Asunción Lavrin, pp. 101–128. Westport, Ct.: Greenwood Press.

Carbia, Rómulo D. 1934. *La crónica oficial de las Indias Occidentales*. Buenos Aires: López.

———. 1944. *Historia de la leyenda negra hispano-americana*. Madrid: Consejo de la Hispanidad.

Carman, Glen. 1992. "The Voices of the Conqueror in López de Gómara's Historia de la conquista de México." *Journal of Hispanic Philology* 16, no. 2 (winter): 223–236.

———. 1993. "Cortés, Gómara, and the Rhetoric of Empire." Ph.D. dissertation, Cornell University.

Carrasco, Davíd. 2000. "When Strangers Come to Town: The Return of Quetzalcoatl and Millennial Discourse." In *Quetzalcoatl and the Irony of Empire: Myths and Prophecies in the Aztec Tradition*, pp. 205–240. Revised edition. Boulder: University Press of Colorado.

Carrasco, Pedro. 1997. "Indian-Spanish Marriages." In *Indian Women of Early Mexico*, edited by Susan Schroeder, Stephanie Wood, and Robert Haskett, pp. 87–103. Norman: University of Oklahoma Press.

CDIA. 1864–1884. *Colección de documentos inéditos relativos al descubrimiento, conquista y organización de las antiguas posesiones españolas de América y Oceanía*. Madrid: Manuel G. Hernández.

CDIU. 1885–1932. *Colección de documentos inéditos relativos al descubrimiento, conquista y organización de las antiguas posesiones españolas de ultramar*. Madrid: Tipografía de la "Revista de Archivos, Bibliotecas y Museos."

Certeau, Michel de. 1986. *Heterologies: Discourse on the Other.* Minneapolis: University of Minnesota Press.

Chiappelli, Fredi, ed. 1976. *First Images of America: The Impact of the New World on the Old.* 2 vols. Berkeley: University of California Press.

Chocano Mena, Magdalena. 2000. *La América colonial, 1492–1763: Cultura y vida cotidiana.* Madrid: Síntesis.

Church, Elihu Dwight. 1951. *A Catalogue of Books Relating to the Discovery and Early History of North and South America Forming a Part of The Library of E. D. Church (1482–1590).* Compiled and annotated by George Watson Cole. New York: Peter Smith.

Cicero, Marcus Tullius. 1928. *De re publica. De legibus.* Translated by Clinton Walker Keyes. The Loeb Classical Library. Cambridge, Mass.: Harvard University Press.

———. 1959–1960. *De Oratore.* 2 vols. Edited and translated by Edward W. Sutton and Harris Rackham. The Loeb Classical Library. Cambridge, Mass.: Harvard University Press.

Colás Latorre, Gregorio, Jesús Criado Mainar, and Isidoro de Miguel García. 1998. *Don Hernando de Aragón.* Zaragoza: Caja de Ahorros de la Inmaculada de Aragón.

Colón, Fernando. 1985. *Historia del Almirante.* Madrid: Historia 16.

Columbus, Christopher [Cristoforo Colombo, Cristóbal Colón]. 1983. *La carta de Colón sobre el descubrimiento.* Granada: Excma. Diputación Provincial de Granada.

———, ed. 1996. *The Book of Privileges Issued to Christopher Columbus by King Fernando and Queen Isabel, 1492–1502.* Edited and translated by Helen Nader. Berkeley: University of California Press.

Conley, Tom. 1989. "Montaigne and the Indies: Cartographies of the New World in the *Essais*, 1580–88." In *1492–1992: Re/Discovering Colonial Writing*, edited by René Jara and Nicholas Spadaccini, pp. 225–262. Minneapolis, Minn.: Prisma Institute, 1989.

———. *The Graphic Unconscious in Early Modern French Writing.* New York: Cambridge University Press, 1992.

Cortés, Hernán [Fernando Cortés]. 1524. *Praeclara Ferdina[n]di Cortesii de Noua maris Oceani Hyspania Narratio Sacratissimo, ac Inuictissimo Carolo Romanoru[m] Imperatori semper Augusto, Hyspaniaru[m] & c[hristianorum].* Translated by Pietro Savorgnano. Nuremberg: Friedrich Peypus.

———. 1993. *Cartas de relación.* Madrid: Castalia.

Cypess, Sandra Messinger. 1991. *La Malinche in Mexican Literature: From History to Myth.* Austin: University of Texas Press.

Dannenfeldt, Karl H. 1954. "The Italian Renaissance." In *The Development of Historiography*, edited by Matthew A. Fitzsimons, Alfred G. Pundt, and Charles E. Nowell, pp. 91–103. Harrisburg, Pa.: Stackpole.

Díaz del Castillo, Bernal. 1982. *Historia verdadera de la conquista de la Nueva España.* Edited by C. Saenz de Santa María. Madrid: Instituto "Gonzalo Fernández de Oviedo," Consejo Superior de Investigaciones Científicas.

————. 1992. *Historia verdadera de la conquista de la Nueva España.* Madrid: Espasa Calpe.

Diccionario de autoridades. 1726–1739. *Diccionario de la lengua castellana.* 6 vols. Madrid: Real Academia Española.

Durand, José. 1952. "López de Gómara: Encrucijada." *Historia Mexicana* 2: 210–222.

Eberenz Greoles, Rolf. 1979. "Literariedad y estructura textual en la historiografía de Indias: Análisis de fragmentos paralelos de H. Cortés, B. Díaz del Castillo y F. López de Gómara." *Travaux de Linguistique et de Littérature* 17, no. 1: 295–318.

Elliott, John H. 1976. "Renaissance Europe and America: A Blunted Impact?" In *First Images of America: The Impact of the New World on the Old*, edited by Fredi Chiappelli, vol. 1, pp. 11–23. Berkeley: University of California Press.

————. 1984a. "The Spanish Conquest and Settlement of America." In *The Cambridge History of Latin America*, edited by Leslie Bethell, vol. 1, pp. 149–206. Cambridge: Cambridge University Press.

————. 1984b. "Spain and America in the Sixteenth and Seventeenth Centuries. In *The Cambridge History of Latin America*, edited by Leslie Bethell, vol. 1, pp. 287–339. Cambridge: Cambridge University Press.

————. 1989. *Spain and Its World, 1500–1700: Selected Essays.* New Haven, Ct.: Yale University Press.

————. 1990. *Imperial Spain, 1469–1716.* 1963. Harmondsworth: Penguin.

————. 1992. *The Old World and the New, 1492–1650.* New York: Cambridge University Press.

————. 1995. "Final Reflections: The Old World and the New Revisited." In *America in European Consciousness*, edited by Karen Ordahl Kupperman. Chapel Hill: University of North Carolina Press.

Enciso, Martín Fernández de. 1519. *Suma de geographia q[ue] trata de todas las partidas & prouincias del mundo, en especial de las Indias, [y] trata largame[n]te del arte del marear, juntame[n]te con la espera en roma[n]ce, con el regimie[n]to del sol [y] del norte, nueuamente hecha.* Seville: Juan Cromberger.

Esteve Barba, Francisco. 1964. *Historiografía indiana.* Madrid: Gredos.

Ficino, Marsilio, ed. and trans. 1546. *Omnia divini Platonis opera tralatione Marsilii Ficini, emendatione et ad Graecvm codicem collatione Simonis Grynaei, summa diligentia repurgata, quibus subiectus est index quam copiossimus*, by Plato. Basel: Officina Frobeniana.

Foresti, Jacobo Filippo, da Bergamo. 1503. *Supplementum supplementi cronicarum.* Venice: Albertinum de Lissona Vercellemsem.

————. 1513. *Supplementum supplementi chronicarum.* Venice: Georgius de Rusconibus.

Foucault, Michel. 1972. *The Archaeology of Knowledge.* Translated by A. M. Sheridan Smith. New York: Pantheon.

Garcés, María Antonia. 1992. "Coaches, Litters, and Chariots of War: Montaigne and Atahualpa." *Journal of Hispanic Philology* 16, no. 2 (winter): 155–183.

Gaunt, David. 2001. "Kinship: Thin Red Lines or Thick Blue Blood." In *Family Life in Early Modern Times 1500–1789,* edited by David I. Kertzer and Marzio Barbagli, pp. 257–287. New Haven, Ct.: Yale University Press.

Gibson, Charles. 1964. *The Aztecs Under Spanish Rule.* Stanford, Calif.: Stanford University Press.

———. 1966. *Spain in America.* New York: Harper & Row.

———, ed. 1971. *The Black Legend: Anti-Spanish Attitudes in the Old World and the New.* New York: Knopf.

Gilbert, Felix. 1965. *Machiavelli and Guicciardini: Politics and History in Sixteenth-Century Florence.* Princeton, N.J.: Princeton University Press.

Giovio, Paolo. 1550. *Historiarvm svi temporis tomus primus.* Florence: Lorenzo Torrentino.

Gómara, Francisco López de. 1552. *La* [*h*]*istoria de las Indias, y conquista de Mexico.* 2 vols. Zaragoza: Agustín Millán.

———. 1553a. *Primera y segunda parte dela historia general de las Indias con todo el descubrimiento y cosas notables que han acaecido dende que se ganaron ata el año de 1551: Con la co*[*n*]*quista de Mexico y de la Nueua España.* 2 vols. Zaragoza: Agustín Millán for Miguel Capila.

———. 1553b. *Primera y segunda parte dela historia general de las Indias con todo el descubrimiento y cosas notables que han acaecido dende que se ganaron ata el año de 1551: Con la conquista de Mexico y dela Nueua España.* Medina del Campo: Guillermo de Millis.

———. 1554a. *La historia general de las Indias y Nueuo Mundo, con mas la Conquista del Peru y de Mexico, agora nueuamente añadida y emendada.* Zaragoza: Pedro Bernuz.

———. 1554b. *La historia general de las Indias, con todos los descubrimientos, y cosas notables que han acaescido en ellas, dende que se ganaron hasta agora.* Antwerp: Jan Steels.

———. 1554c. *Historia de Mexico, con el descvbrimiento de la Nueua España, conquistada por el muy illustre y valeroso principe don Fernando Cortes, Marques del Valle.* Antwerp: Jan Steels.

———. 1554d. *La historia general de las Indias, y todo lo acaescido en ellas dende que se ganaron hasta agora y la Conquista de Mexico, y de la Nueua España.* Antwerp: Martin Nuyts.

———. 1554e. *La segunda parte de la Historia general de las Indias que contiene la Conquista de Mexico, y de la Nueua España.* Antwerp: Martin Nuyts.

———. 1554f. *La historia general de las Indias, con todos los descubrimientos, y cosas notables que han acaescido en ellas, dende que se ganaron hasta agora.* Antwerp: Hans de Laet.

———. 1554g. *Historia de Mexico, con el descubrimiento de la Nueua España general de las Indias y Nueuo Mundo, conquistada por el muy illustre y valeroso principe don Fernando Cortes, Marques del Valle.* Antwerp: Hans de Laet.

———. 1555. *La historia general de las Indias y Nueuo Mundo, con mas la Conquista del Peru y de Mexico, agora nueuamente añadida y emendada.* Zaragoza: Agustín Millán.

———. 1578. *Histoire generalle des Indes Occidentales et Terres Nevves, qui iusques à present ont esté descouuertes.* Translated by Fumée Sieur de Marly le Chastel. Paris: Michel Sonnius.

———. 1588. *Voyages et conquestes du capitaine Ferdinand Courtois, és Indes Occidentales.* Translated by Guillaume Le Breton. Paris: Abel l'Angelier.

———. 1749. *Historia de las Indias.* In *Historiadores primitivos de las Indias Occidentales,* vol. 2, edited by Andrés González de Barcía Carballido y Zúñiga. Madrid.

———. 1853. *Crónica de los Barbarrojas.* In *Memorial histórico español: Colección de documentos, opúsculos y antigüedades,* vol. 6, *Real Academia de la Historia,* pp. 327–439. Madrid: Real Academia de la Historia.

———. 1912. *Annals of the Emperor Charles V.* Edited by Roger Bigelow Merriman. Cambridge, Mass.: Harvard University Press.

Grafton, Anthony, with April Shelford and Nancy Siraisi. 1995. *New Worlds, Ancient Texts: The Power of Tradition and the Shock of Discovery.* Cambridge, Mass.: Harvard University Press.

Greenblatt, Stephen J. 1991. *Marvelous Possessions: The Wonder of the New World.* Chicago: University of Chicago Press.

Gurría Lacroix, Jorge. 1979. "Prólogo." In Francisco López de Gómara, *Historia general de las Indias y vida de Hernán Cortés,* vol. 1, ix–xxxi. Caracas: Ayacucho.

Gutiérrez, Ramón. 1984. "From Honor to Love: Transformations of the Meaning of Sexuality in Colonial New Mexico." In *Kinship Ideology and Practice in Latin America,* edited by Raymond T. Smith, pp. 237–263. Chapel Hill: University of North Carolina Press.

———. 1994. "A Gendered History of the Conquest of America: A View from New Mexico." In *Gender Rhetorics: Postures of Dominance and Submission in History,* edited by Richard C. Trexler, pp. 47–63. Binghamton, N.Y.: Medieval & Renaissance Texts & Studies.

Hanke, Lewis. 1959. *Aristotle and the American Indians: A Study in Race Prejudice in the Modern World.* London: Hollis & Carter.

———. 1970. *All the Peoples of the World Are Men.* Minneapolis: Associates of the James Ford Bell Library, University of Minnesota.

———. 1974. *All Mankind Is One.* DeKalb: Northern Illinois University Press.

Haring, Clarence H. 1947. *The Spanish Empire in America.* New York: Oxford University Press.

———. 1964. *Trade and Navigation between Spain and the Indies in the Time of the Hapsburgs.* Gloucester, Mass.: Peter Smith.

Harrisse, Henry. 1866. *Bibliotheca Americana Vetustissima: A Description of Works Relating to America Published between the Years 1492 and 1551.* New York: G. P. Philes.

Hay, Denys. 1968. *Europe: The Emergence of an Idea.* Edinburgh: Edinburgh University Press.

———. 1977. *Annalists and Historians: Western Historiography from the Eighth to the Eighteenth Centuries.* London: Methuen.

Heers, Jacques. 1986. "Le projet de Christophe Colomb." In *Columbeis,* vol. 1, pp. 7–26. Genoa: Università di Genova, Facoltà di Lettere, Istituto di Filologia Classica e Medievale.

Hillgarth, Jocelyn N. 2000. *The Mirror of Spain, 1500–1700: The Formation of a Myth.* Ann Arbor: University of Michigan Press.

Hirsch, Elisabeth Feist. 1965. "The Discoveries and the Humanists." In *Merchants and Scholars: Essays in the History of Exploration and Trade,* edited by John Parker, pp. 33–46. Minneapolis: University of Minnesota Press.

Histoire de la Terre Nevve du Perù, L'. 1545. *L'histoire de la Terre Nevve du Perù en l'Inde Occidentale, qui est la principale mine d'or du monde, nagueres descouuerte, & conquise, & nommée la nouuelle Castille.* Paris: Pierre Gaultier, for Iehan Barbé & Vincent Sertenas.

Hodgen, Margaret T. 1971. *Early Anthropology in the Sixteenth and Seventeenth Centuries.* Philadelphia: University of Pennsylvania Press.

Hoffmann, George. 2002. "Anatomy of the Mass: Montaigne's 'Cannibals.' " *Publications of the Modern Language Association of America* 117, no. 2 (March): 207–221.

Hulme, Peter. 1986. *Colonial Encounters: Europe and the Native Caribbean, 1492–1797.* London: Methuen.

———. 1994. "Tales of Distinction: European Ethnography and the Caribbean." In *Implicit Understandings: Observing, Reporting, and Reflecting on the Encounters Between Europeans and Other Peoples in the Early Modern Era,* edited by Stuart B. Schwartz, pp. 157–197. Cambridge: Cambridge University Press.

Iglesia, Ramón. 1940. "Two Articles on the Same Topic: Bernal Díaz del Castillo and Popularism in Spanish Historiography and Bernal Díaz del Castillo's Criticism of the History of the Conquest of Mexico, by Francisco López de Gómara." *Hispanic American Historical Review* 20, no. 4 (November): 517–550.

———. 1942. *Cronistas e historiadores de la conquista de México: El ciclo de Hernán Cortés.* Mexico City: Colegio de México.

———. 1944. *El hombre Colón y otros ensayos.* Mexico City: Colegio de México.

———. 1969. *Columbus, Cortés, and Other Essays.* Berkeley: University of California Press.

JCBL [John Carter Brown Library]. 1980. *European Americana: A Chronological Guide to Works Printed in Europe Relating to the Americas 1493–1776.* Edited by J. Alden. New York: Readex Books.

Jos, Emiliano. 1927. "El cronista de Indias F. L. de Gómara: Apuntes biográficos." *Revista de Occidente* (Madrid), año 5, vol. 18, no. 53 (November): 274–278.

Karttunen, Frances. 1997. "Rethinking Malinche." In *Indian Women of Early Mexico*, edited by Susan Schroeder, Stephanie Wood, and Robert Haskett, pp. 291–312. Norman: University of Oklahoma Press.

Keniston, Hayward. 1958. *Francisco de los Cobos, Secretary of the Emperor Charles V.* Pittsburgh: University of Pittsburgh Press.

Klor de Alva, J. Jorge. 1995. "The Postcolonization of the (Latin) American Experience: A Reconsideration of 'Colonialism,' 'Postcolonialism,' and 'Mestizaje.'" In *After Colonialism*, edited by Gyan Prakash, pp. 241–275. Princeton, N.J.: Princeton University Press.

Lactantius, Lucius Caelus Firmianus. 1994. *The Divine Institutes.* Translated by William Fletcher. In *The Ante-Nicene Fathers: Translations of the Writings of the Fathers Down to AD 325*, edited by Alexander Roberts and James Donaldson, vol. 7. Grand Rapids, Mich.: W. B. Eerdmanns.

Las Casas, Bartolomé de. 1988–1998. *Obras completas.* 14 vols. Madrid: Alianza.

Lavrin, Asunción. 1994. "*Lo Femenino*: Women in Colonial Historical Sources." In *Coded Encounters: Writing, Gender, and Ethnicity in Colonial Latin America*, edited by Javier Cevallos-Candau, Nina M. Scott, and Nicomedes Suárez-Araúz, pp. 153–176. Amherst: University of Massachusetts Press.

León Pinelo, Antonio de. 1629. *Epitome de la biblioteca oriental i occidental, nautica i geografica.* Madrid: Juan González.

Leonard, Irving A. 1992. *Books of the Brave: Being an Account of Books and of Men in the Spanish Conquest and Settlement of the Sixteenth-Century New World.* Berkeley: University of California Press.

Lewis, Robert E. 1983. "The Humanistic Historiography of Francisco López de Gómara, 1511–1559." Ph.D. dissertation, University of Texas at Austin.

———. 1984. "El testamento de Francisco López de Gómara y otros documentos tocantes a su vida y obra." *Revista de Indias* 44, no. 173 (January–June): 61–79.

———. 1986. "Retórica y verdad: Los cargos de Bernal Díaz a López de Gómara." In *De la crónica a la nueva narrativa mexicana: Coloquio sobre literatura mexicana*, edited by Merlín H. Forster and Julio Ortega, pp. 37–47. Oaxaca: Oasis.

Lockhart, James. 1994. *Spanish Peru, 1532–1560: A Social History.* Madison: University of Wisconsin Press.

Lockhart, James, and Stuart B. Schwartz. 1983. *Early Latin America: A History of Colonial Spanish America and Brazil.* New York: Cambridge University Press.

Loesberg, Jonathan. 1983. "Narratives of Authority: Cortés, Gómara, Díaz." *Prose Studies* 6, no. 3: 239–263.

MacCormack, Sabine G. 1988. "Atahualpa y el libro." *Revista de Indias* 48, no. 184 (September–December): 693–714.

MacLeod, Murdo. 1984. "Spain and America: The Atlantic Trade 1492–1720." In *The Cambridge History of Latin America*, edited by Leslie Bethell, vol. 1, pp. 341–388. Cambridge: Cambridge University Press.

Madariaga, Salvador de. 1986. *Hernán Cortés.* Madrid: Espasa Calpe.

Maltby, William. 1971. *The Black Legend in England: The Development of Anti-Spanish Sentiment, 1558–1660*. Durham: Duke University Press.

Marineo Sículo, Lucio. 1539. *Obra*. Alcalá de Henares: Juan de Brocar.

Martínez, José Luis. 1981. "Una muestra de la elaboración de la *Historia verdadera*, de Bernal Díaz del Castillo." *Revista de Indias* 41, nos. 165–166 (July–December): 723–732.

Martyr, Peter [Pietro Martire d'Anghiera]. 1964–1965. *Décadas del Nuevo Mundo*. Edited by Edmundo O'Gorman. 2 vols. Mexico City: Porrúa.

———. 1966. *Opera. Legatio babylonica. De orbe novo decades octo. Opus epistolarum*. Graz, Austria: Akademische Druck- und Verlagsanstalt.

———. 1989. *Décadas del Nuevo Mundo*. Madrid: Polifemo.

———. 1990. *Cartas sobre el Nuevo Mundo*. Madrid: Polifemo.

Mauss, Marcel. 1990. *The Gift: The Form and Reason for Exchange in Archaic Societies*. New York: Routledge.

Maximilianus, Transylvanus. 1523. *De Moluccis Insulis, itemque aliis pluribus mirandis, quæ nouissima Castellanorum nauigatio*. Cologne: Cervicornus.

———. 1524. *Maximiliani Transyluani Caesaris a secretis epistola, de admirabili & nouissima Hispanoru in Orientem nauigatione, qua uariæ, & nulli prius accessae regiones inuetae sunt*. Rome: Calvo.

Maximilianus, Transylvanus, Antonio Pigafetta, and Antonio Francini. 1536. *Il viaggio fatto da gli spagnivoli a torno a'l mondo*. Venice: Luca-Antonio Giunta.

Medina, José Toribio. 1958. *Biblioteca americana*. Vol. 1. Santiago de Chile: Fondo Histórico y Bibliográfico José Toribio Medina.

Menéndez Pidal, Ramón. 1963. *Idea imperial de Carlos V*. Madrid: Espasa Calpe.

———. 1966. "Un imperio de paz cristiana." In *Historia de España*, vol. 18, pp. xi–lxxii. Madrid: Espasa Calpe.

Menéndez y Pelayo, Marcelino. 1942. "De los historiadores de Colón." In *Estudios y discursos de crítica histórica y literaria*, vol. 7, pp. 69–122. Santander: Consejo Superior de Investigaciones Científicas.

Merriman, Roger Bigelow. 1912. "Introduction." In Francisco López de Gómara, *The Annals of the Emperor Charles V*, pp. ix–lv. Cambridge, Mass.: Harvard University Press.

———. 1962. *The Rise of the Spanish Empire in the Old World and in the New*. New York: Cooper Square Publishers.

Mexía, Pedro. 1945. *Historia del Emperador Carlos V*. Madrid: Espasa Calpe.

———. 1947. *Coloquios*. Seville: Hispalense.

Mignolo, Walter D. 1982. "Cartas, crónicas y relaciones del descubrimiento y la conquista." In *Historia de la literatura hispanoamericana*, edited by Luis Íñigo Madrigal, vol. 1, pp. 57–116. Madrid: Cátedra.

———. 1995. *The Darker Side of the Renaissance: Literacy, Territoriality, and Colonization*. Ann Arbor: University of Michigan Press.

Millones Figueroa, Luis. 2001. *Pedro de Cieza de León y su crónica de Indias: La entrada de los incas en la historia universal*. Lima: Pontificia Universidad Católica del Perú, Instituto Francés de Estudios Andinos.

Momigliano, Arnaldo. 1963. "Pagan and Christian Historiography in the Fourth Century AD." In *The Conflict Between Paganism and Christianity in the Fourth Century*, pp. 79–99. London: Oxford University Press.

Montaigne, Michel de. 1998. *Essais*. 3 vols. Paris: Imprimerie Nationale Éditions.

Montrose, Louis. 1991. "The Work of Gender in the Discourse of Discovery." *Representations* 33 (winter): 1–41.

Moreno y Moreno, Miguel. 1972. "López de Gómara, historiador." In *Conozca sus estatuas: Radiografía de Soria*, pp. 42–46. Soria: Diputación Provincial.

Motolinía, Toribio de Benavente. 1985. *Historia de los indios de la Nueva España*. Edited by Claudio Esteva Fabregat. Madrid: Historia 16.

Muldoon, James. 1979. *Popes, Lawyers, and Infidels*. Philadelphia: University of Pennsylvania Press.

———. 1999. *Empire and Order. The Concept of Empire, 800–1800*. New York: St. Martin's.

Muro Orejón, Antonio. 1967. *Pleitos colombinos*. Vol. 1. *Proceso hasta la sentencia de Sevilla, 1511*. Seville: Escuela de Estudios Hispanoamericanos.

Muro Orejón, Antonio, Florentino Pérez-Embid, and Francisco Morales Padrón. 1967. "Introducción." In Antonio Muro Orejón, *Pleitos colombinos*, vol. 1, *Proceso hasta la sentencia de Sevilla, 1511*, pp. xiii–xxvi. Seville: Escuela de Estudios Hispanoamericanos.

Mustapha, Monique. 1979. "Géographie et humanisme: Note sur la structure de la Historia general de las Indias de Francisco López de Gómara." In *Les Cultures ibériques en devenir: Essais publiés en hommage à la mémoire de Marcel Bataillon, 1895–1977*, pp. 431–442. Paris: Fondation Singer-Polignac.

———. 1994. "Le Statut de l'épisode colombien dans la Historia General de las Indias de Francisco López de Gómara." In *Christophe Colomb et la découverte de l'Amérique: Réalités, imaginaire et réinterprétations*, edited by José Guidi and Monique Mustapha, 201–209. Aix-en-Provence: Publications de l'Université de Provence.

Navarra, Pedro de. 1565. *Dialogos de la preparacion de la mverte*. Toulouse: Jacques Colomer.

O'Gorman, Edmundo. 1951. *La idea del descubrimiento de América*. Mexico City: Centro de Estudios Filosóficos.

———. 1964. "Pedro Mártir y el proceso de América." In Peter Martyr, *Décadas del Nuevo Mundo*, vol. 1, pp. 9–37. Mexico City: Porrúa.

———. 1977. *La invención de América*. Mexico City: Fondo de Cultura Económica.

Ots y Capdequí, José María. 1982. *El estado español en las Indias*. México: Fondo de Cultura Económica.

Oviedo y Valdés, Gonzalo Fernández de. 1535. *La historia general de las Indias con priuilegio imperial*. Seville: Jacobo Cromberger.

———. 1992. *Historia general y natural de las Indias*. Edited by J. Pérez de Tudela y Bueso. 4 vols. Biblioteca de autores españoles, vols. 117–121. Madrid: Atlas.

Padrón, Ricardo. 2002. "Charting Empire, Charting Difference: Gómara's *Historia general de las Indias* and Spanish Maritime Cartography." *Colonial Latin American Review* 11, no. 1 (September): 47-69.

Pagden, Anthony. 1990a. *The Fall of Natural Man: The American Indian and the Origins of Comparative Ethnology.* Cambridge: Cambridge University Press.

———. 1990b. *Spanish Imperialism and the Political Imagination, 1513-1830.* New Haven, Ct.: Yale University Press.

———. 1991. "*Ius et factum*: Text and Experience in the Writings of Bartolomé de las Casas." *Representations* 33 (winter): 147-162.

Palacios Rubios, Juan López de. 1954. *De las islas del mar océano.* Mexico City: Fondo de Cultura Económica.

Palencia-Roth, Michael. 1993. "The Cannibal Law of 1503." In *Early Images of the Americas,* edited by Jerry M. Williams and Robert E. Lewis, pp. 21-63. Tucson: University of Arizona Press.

Parry, John H. 1940. *The Spanish Theory of Empire in the Sixteenth Century.* Cambridge: Cambridge University Press.

———. 1971. *The Spanish Seaborne Empire.* New York: Alfred A. Knopf.

———. 1981. *The Age of Reconnaissance.* Berkeley: University of California Press.

Paz, Matías de. 1954. *Del dominio de los reyes de España sobre los indios.* Mexico City: Fondo de Cultura Económica.

Pennington, Kenneth J. 1970. "Bartolomé de las Casas and the Tradition of Medieval Law." *Church History* 39, no. 2 (June): 149-161.

Penrose, Boies. 1952. *Travel and Discovery in the Renaissance, 1420-1620.* Cambridge, Mass.: Harvard University Press.

Pérez de Oliva, Fernán. 1991. *Historia de la invención de las Indias.* Edited by José Juan Arrom Estudio. Mexico City: Siglo Veintiuno.

Pérez Pastor, Cristóbal. 1895. *La imprenta en Medina del Campo.* Madrid: Rivadeneyra.

Pigafetta, Antonio. 1525. *Le Voyage et nauigation faict par les espaignolz es Isles de Mollucques des Isles quilz ont trouue audict voyage des Roys dicelles de leur gouuernement & maniere de vivre avec plusieurs autres choses.* Paris: Simon de Colines.

Pinilla, José. 1951. "López de Gómara en el Archivo de Protocolos de Madrid." *Celtiberia* (Soria) 1, no. 2 (July–December): 390-392.

Porras Barrenechea, Raúl. 1941. "Los cronistas y la conquista: Molina, Oviedo, Gómara y Las Casas." *Revista de la Universidad Católica del Perú* 9, nos. 4-5: 235-252.

Powers, Karen Vieira. 2002. "Conquering Discourses of 'Sexual Conquest': Of Women, Language and *Mestizaje*." *Colonial Latin American Review* 11, no. 1 (September): 7-32.

R. Commissione Colombiana. 1892-1896. *Raccolta di documenti e studi pubblicati dalla R. Commissione Colombiana, pel quarto centenario dalla scoperta dell'America.* 6 parts. Rome: Ministero della Pubblica Istruzione.

Rabasa, José. 1993. *Inventing America: Spanish Historiography and the Formation of Eurocentrism.* Norman: University of Oklahoma Press.

———. 2000. *Writing Violence on the Northern Frontier.* Durham, N.C.: Duke University Press.

Ramírez Cabañas, Joaquín. 1943. "Introducción." In Francisco López de Gómara, *Historia de la conquista de México,* pp. 9–34. Mexico City: Pedro Robredo.

Ramos Pérez, Demetrio. 1972. *Ximénez de Quesada en su relación con los cronistas y el Epítome de la conquista del Nuevo Reino de Granada.* Seville: Escuela de Estudios Hispanoamericanos de Sevilla.

———. 1981. *Las variaciones ideológicas en torno al descubrimiento de América: Pedro Mártir de Anglería y su mentalidad.* Valladolid: Museo de Colón and Seminario Americanista de la Universidad de Valladolid.

Ramusio, Giovanni Battista. 1550. *Primo volume delle navigationi et viaggi nel qual si contiene la descrittione dell' Africa, et del paese del Prete Ianni, con uarii uiaggi, dal mar Rosso à Calicut, & insin all' isole Molucche, doue nascono le spetierie, et la nauigatione attorno il mondo.* Venice: The Heirs of Luca-Antonio Giunta.

Remensis, Robertus, and Christopher Columbus. 1533. *Bellum Christianorum principum, praecipue Gallorum, contra Saracenos.* Basel: Henricus Petrus.

Roa-de-la-Carrera, Cristián. 1998. "La historiografía del descubrimiento en la *Historia* de Francisco López de Gómara," Ph.D. dissertation, Princeton University.

———. 2001. "La historia de las Indias y los límites del consenso: Gómara en la cultura del imperio." *Colonial Latin American Review* 10, no. 1 (September): 69–86.

Roche, Paul. 1994. "Historiographie et politique: l'image de Christophe Colomb dans les *De Orbe Novo Decades* de Pierre Martyr D'Anghiera." In *Christophe Colomb et la découverte de l'Amérique: Réalités, imaginaire et réinterprétations,* edited by José Guidi and Monique Mustapha, pp. 191–200. Aix-en-Provence: Publications de l'Université de Provence.

Rodríguez Garrido, José Antonio. 1993. "Las citas de los cronistas españoles como recurso argumentativo en la segunda parte de los *Comentarios reales.*" *Lexis* 17, no. 1 (July): 93–114.

Rose-Fuggle, Sonia. 1991. "Bernal Díaz del Castillo frente al otro: Doña Marina, espejo de princesas y damas." In *Les représentations de l'Autre dans l'espace ibérique et ibéro-américain,* vol. 1, pp. 77–87. Paris: Presses de la Sorbonne Nouvelle.

Rubin, Gayle. 1975. "The Traffic in Women: Notes Toward a Political Economy of Sex." In *Toward an Anthropology of Women,* edited by Rayna R. Reiter, pp. 157–210. New York: Monthly Review Press.

Ryan, Michael T. 1981. "Assimilating New Worlds in the Sixteenth and Seventeenth Centuries." *Comparative Studies in Society and History* 23, no. 4 (October): 519–538.

Sabellico, Marco Antonio. 1498–1504. *Enneades Marci Antonii Sabellici ab orbe condito ad inclinationem Romani Imperii.* 2 vols. Venice: Bernardinum Vercellensem.

Sabin, Joseph. 1868–1936. *Bibliotheca Americana: A Dictionary of Books Relating to America, from Its Discovery to the Present Time.* 29 vols. New York: Bibliography Society of America.

Sahagún, Bernardino de. 1986. *Coloquios y doctrina cristiana.* Edited by Miguel León-Portilla. Mexico City: Universidad Nacional Autónoma de México.

Said, Edward W. 1979. *Orientalism.* New York: Vintage Books.

———. 1994. *Culture and Imperialism.* New York: Vintage Books.

Sánchez Alonso, Benito. 1941–1950. *Historia de la historiografía española: Ensayo de un examen de conjunto.* 3 vols. Madrid: Consejo Superior de Investigaciones Científicas.

Santa Cruz, Alonso de. 1920. *Crónica del emperador Carlos V.* Madrid: Imprenta del Patronato de Huérfanos de Intendencia é Intervención Militares.

Sanz, Carlos. 1960. *Bibliotheca americana vetustissima: Últimas adiciones.* 2 vols. Madrid: Librería General Victoriano Suárez.

Scaglione, Aldo. 1976. "A Note on Montaigne's 'Des Cannibales' and the Humanist Tradition." In *First Images of America: The Impact of the New World on the Old,* edited by Fredi Chiappelli, vol. 1, pp. 63–70. Berkeley: University of California Press.

Schäfer, Ernst. 1935. *El Consejo Real y Supremo de las Indias, su historia, organización y labor administrativa hasta la terminación de la casa de Austria.* Vol. 1. Seville: Escuela de Estudios Hispano-Americanos, Consejo Superior de Investigaciones Científicas.

Schedel, Hartmann.1493. *Liber chronicarum.* Nuremberg: Anton Koberger.

Schwartz, Stuart B., ed. 1994. *Implicit Understandings: Observing, Reporting, and Reflecting on the Encounters Between Europeans and Other Peoples in the Early Modern Era.* Cambridge: Cambridge University Press.

Sedgwick, Eve Kosofsky. 1985. *Between Men: English Literature and Male Homosocial Desire.* New York: Columbia University Press.

Seed, Patricia. 1992. "Taking Possession and Reading Texts: Establishing the Authority of Overseas Empire." *William and Mary Quarterly* 49, no. 2 (April): 183–209.

———. 1993a. "'Are These Not Also Men?': The Indians' Humanity and Capacity for Spanish Civilisation." *Journal of Latin American Studies* 25, no. 3 (October): 629–652.

———. 1993b. "More Colonial and Postcolonial Discourses." *Latin American Research Review* 28, no. 3: 146–152.

———. 1993c. "Taking Possession and Reading Texts: Establishing the Authority of Overseas Empire." In *Early Images of the Americas,* edited by Jerry M. Williams and Robert E. Lewis, 111–147. Tucson: University of Arizona Press.

———. 1995. *Ceremonies of Possession in Europe's Conquest of the New World, 1492–1640.* New York: Cambridge University Press.

————. 2001. *American Pentimento: The Invention of Indians and the Pursuit of Riches*. Minneapolis: University of Minnesota Press.

Sehm, Gunter G. 1991. "The First European Bison Illustration and the First Central European Exhibit of a Living Bison, with a Table of the Sixteenth-Century Editions of Francisco López de Gómara." *Archives of Natural History* 18, no. 3 (October): 323–332.

Sepúlveda, Juan Ginés de. 1987. *Historia del Nuevo Mundo*. Edited and translated by Antonio Ramírez de Verger. Madrid: Alianza.

————. 1997. *Demócrates segundo*. Edited and translated by Alejandro Coroleu Lletget. In *Obras completas*, vol. 3. Pozoblanco, Spain: Excmo. Ayuntamiento de Pozoblanco.

Silvio Piccolomini, Eneas [Pope Pius II]. 1992. *Descripción de Asia*. Madrid: Alianza.

Simpson, Lesley Byrd. 1982. *The Encomienda in New Spain*. Berkeley: University of California Press.

Thacher, John Boyd. 1903. *Christopher Columbus: His Life, His Work, His Remains as Revealed by Original Printed and Manuscript Records Together with an Essay on Peter Martyr and Bartolomé de las Casas, the First Historians of America*. 3 vols. New York and London: G. P. Putnam's Sons.

Todorov, Tzvetan. 1984. *The Conquest of America: The Problem of the Other*. Translated by Richard Howard. New York: Harper & Row.

Tudela Bueso, Juan Pérez de. 1992. "Vida y escritos de Gonzalo Fernández de Oviedo." In Gonzalo Fernández de Oviedo y Valdés, *Historia general y natural de las Indias*, vol. 1, pp. vii–clxxv. Biblioteca de autores españoles, 117. Madrid: Atlas.

Valcárcel Martínez, Simón. 1989. "Una aproximación a Francisco López de Gómara." *Caravelle* 53: 7–24.

Vedia, Enrique de, ed. 1852. "Preliminares." In *Historiadores primitivos de Indias*, vol. 1, pp. v–xv. Biblioteca de autores españoles, 22. Madrid: Rivadeneyra.

Vega, Inca Garcilaso de la. 1944. *Historia general del Perú: Segunda parte de los Comentarios reales de los Incas*. Edited by Ángel Rosenblat, introduction by José de la Riva Agüero. 3 vols. Buenos Aires: Emecé.

Verardo, Carlos, and Christopher Columbus. 1494. *De insulis nuper inuentis epistola Christoferi Colom*. Basel: J. Bergmann.

Verdesio, Gustavo. 1999. "Hacia la descolonización de la mirada geográfica: Las prácticas territoriales indígenas en la 'prehistoria' de la ribera norte del Río de la Plata." *Revista Iberoamericana* 65, no. 186 (January–March): 59–80.

Vespucci, Amerigo. 1503. *Alberic[us] Ve[s]pucci[us] Lauretio Petri Franci[s]ci de Medicis salutem plurimã dicit*. Paris: Félix Baligault and Jean Lambert.

Vitoria, Francisco de. 1967. *Relectio de Indis, o Libertad de los indios*. Edited by Luciano Pereña and J. M. Pérez Prendes. Madrid: Consejo Superior de Investigaciones Científicas.

Vulgate. 1994. *Biblia sacra: Iuxta Vulgatam versionem.* Edited by Bonifatius Fischer and Robert Weber. Stuttgart: Deutsche Bibelgelsellschaft.

Wagner, Henry Raup. 1924. *Francisco López de Gómara, La Historia de las Indias y Conquista de México.* Berkeley.

———. 1949. "Francisco López and His Works." *Proceedings of the American Antiquarian Society,* new series, 58: 263–282.

Wagner, Henry Raup, with Helen Rand Parish. 1967. *The Life and Writings of Bartolomé de las Casas.* Albuquerque: University of New Mexico Press.

Wallerstein, Immanuel M. 1974. *The Modern World-System: Studies in Social Discontinuity.* New York: Academic Press.

Wood, Stephanie. 1998. "Sexual Violation in the Conquest of the Americas." In *Sex and Sexuality in Early America,* edited by Merril D. Smith, pp. 9–34. New York: New York University Press.

Zamora, Margarita. 1993. *Reading Columbus.* Berkeley: University of California Press.

Zavala, Iris M. 1989. "Representing the Colonial Subject." In *1492–1992: Re/Discovering Colonial Writing,* edited by René Jara and Nicholas Spadaccini, pp. 323–348. Minneapolis, Minn.: Prisma Institute.

Zavala, Silvio A. 1954. "Las doctrinas de Palacios Rubios y Matías de Paz ante la conquista de América." In Juan López de Palacios Rubios, *De las islas del mar océano,* pp. ix–cxxx. Mexico City: Fondo de Cultura Económica.

———. 1977. *Filosofía de la conquista.* Mexico City: Fondo de Cultura Económica.

———. 1988. *Las instituciones jurídicas en la conquista de América.* Mexico City: Porrúa.

≈ Index ≈

Index